INSIDE HAMILTON'S MUSEUMS

INSIDE HAMILTON'S MUSEUMS

JOHN GODDARD

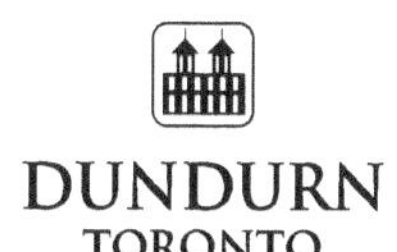

DUNDURN
TORONTO

Project Editor: Allison Hirst
Editor: Michael Carroll
Design: Courtney Horner
Cover Design: Laura Boyle
Cover Image: Courtesy of Philip Curwen
Printer: Webcom

Library and Archives Canada Cataloguing in Publication

Goddard, John, 1950-, author
Inside Hamilton's museums / John Goddard.

Includes bibliographical references and index.
Issued in print and electronic formats.
ISBN 978-1-4597-3354-1 (paperback).--ISBN 978-1-4597-3355-8 (pdf).--
ISBN 978-1-4597-3356-5 (epub)

1. Hamilton (Ont.)--History--Anecdotes. 2. Hamilton (Ont.)--Biography--Anecdotes. 3. Historic sites--Ontario--Hamilton. 4. Museums--Ontario--Hamilton. 5. Cultural property--Ontario--Hamilton. I. Title.

FC3098.4.G63 2016 971.3'52 C2015-908785-6
C2015-908786-4

1 2 3 4 5 20 19 18 17 16

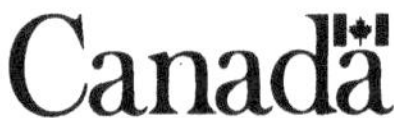

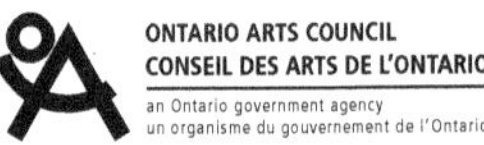

We acknowledge the support of the **Canada Council for the Arts** and the **Ontario Arts Council** for our publishing program. We also acknowledge the financial support of the **Government of Canada** through the **Canada Book Fund** and **Livres Canada Books**, and the **Government of Ontario** through the **Ontario Book Publishing Tax Credit** and the **Ontario Media Development Corporation**.

Visit us at

Dundurn.com | @dundurnpress | Facebook.com/dundurnpress | Pinterest.com/dundurnpress

Dundurn
3 Church Street, Suite 500
Toronto, Ontario, Canada
M5E 1M2

CONTENTS

PREFACE AND ACKNOWLEDGEMENTS

A medical test found a small growth a few years ago in my intestines. Cancer could not be ruled out. Surgery was recommended. "Do you want to do it in Toronto or do you want the best?" asked the specialist in Toronto, where I live, and when I said, "the best," he referred me to Dr. Mehran Anvari at St. Joseph's Hospital in Hamilton.

Dr. Anvari found no cancer and the incision healed well, forever placing Hamilton high in my affections. Sometimes fondness for a city comes from a happy childhood experience in the place, or a love affair with somebody who is from there. For me, emotional closeness to Hamilton came from being wheeled down the corridors of the Sister Mary Grace Wing at St. Joseph's Hospital, through a set of wide, automatic doors, and into a bright operating theatre smelling of fresh laundry where Dr. Anvari, with businesslike cheerfulness, wished me, "Good morning."

On one of my pre-op trips to Hamilton, I visited a heritage-house museum two blocks from the downtown GO Centre. The museum is called Whitehern Historic House and Garden, built in about 1852. I was writing a book at the time on Toronto's heritage museums, since published as *Inside the Museums: Toronto's Heritage Sites and Their Most Prized Objects*. I like these museums because of the family stories they tell and because of the rare objects they often display. I also like them for the way they deepen a connection to a city. I can hardly walk through my own neighbourhood now, in what was once the Town of York, without feeling the haughty presence of Bishop John Strachan or the irascible spirit of William Lyon Mackenzie.

I visited other Hamilton museums. The one I most tell friends about is the one I most resisted seeing at first — the Hamilton Museum of Steam and Technology. I didn't want a science lecture. The place turned out to be one of the best little museums in the country, a gem, and the perfect introduction to Hamilton's heritage-museum network. The "Steam and Tech" is an old waterworks originally powered by two giant steam engines to pump fresh drinking water from Lake Ontario into people's homes and shops as running water. Walk through its doors and you instantly step into 1859. All the antique machinery, wooden floorboards, and polished balustrades are still there, and one of the engines still turns, powered now by an electric motor to re-create the exact motion the pistons and pumps traced more than 150 years ago.

There were other surprises. Toronto has Casa Loma, an architectural horror built by a disagreeable man whose name goes largely forgotten. I excluded Casa Loma from my Toronto book and approached Dundurn Castle with skepticism. I need not have worried. Dundurn endures as a tasteful and captivating mansion, built by Sir Allan Napier MacNab, whose rags-to-riches story is inseparable from Hamilton's. I liked his exuberance and ambition, and his daughter left behind one of the era's most endearing artifacts. When she was thirteen years old, as her mother lay slowly dying of a lung disease, Sophia MacNab wrote a tender diary that illuminates daily life at Dundurn in mid-nineteenth-century Upper Canada.

Battlefield House I knew I would like, especially its annual re-enactment of the Battle of Stoney Creek, which stopped the American army from overrunning the colony in the War of 1812. Griffin House, the Joseph Brant Museum, and the Erland Lee Museum, all in their different ways, told me stories of the city that would be difficult to access any other way. I discovered teenager Billy Green, the accidental spy who helped the British against the Americans. I saw the eighteen-carat gold ring that Mohawk leader Joseph Brant bought to identify his body if he were killed. I came to admire the resourcefulness of refugee slaves Enerals Griffin and Sophia Pooley, and the curious drive of homemaking champion Adelaide Hoodless.

The one complaint I had was the same as I had had in Toronto. After visiting a museum, I wanted something to take away, something to read. At Whitehern, the interpreter/guide led me upstairs to the upper hallway and offered me a chair in front of a wall display of family photos. The guide then delivered a brilliant introduction. With the photos as a reference, she steered me through three generations of McQuestens and their various accomplishments and misadventures. It was a riveting story but a lot to take in. I wanted a way to digest the material afterward. Biographer Mary Anderson has written a couple of books on the McQuestens, which I have since enjoyed, and I found John C. Best's biography of Thomas McQuesten informative. But I also wanted something simpler and more immediate.

I have written the book that I wanted to read. It comes at a time when Torontonians are curious about Hamilton. The Toronto media

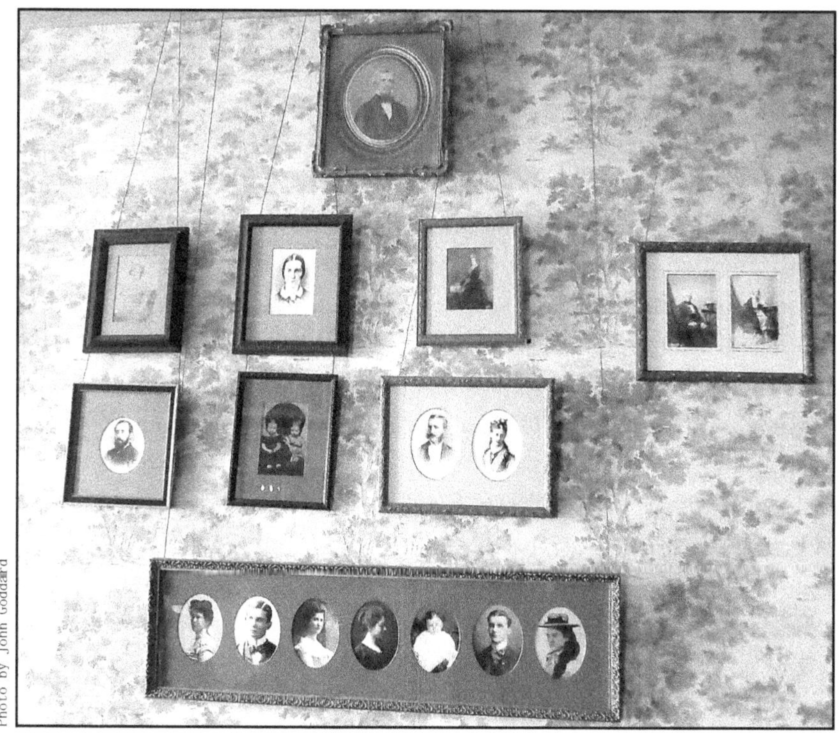

Photo by John Goddard

Photographs hang in an upstairs hallway like a McQuesten family tree. Historic interpreters tell a riveting story of three generations of accomplishments and misadventures.

keep running stories about how up-and-coming the city is, how cheap the real estate can be, and how appealing it has proved to independent artists colonizing the city's north end. The reports tell of the monthly Art Crawl of gallery openings and the annual James Street Supercrawl music festival. They tell of a city in transition from a robust industrial past to a knowledge-based economy with an expanding cultural infrastructure. In my research I also discovered the city to be bicycle-friendly, with a network of lanes and routes, and teeming with natural attractions — from the Royal Botanical Gardens, which includes the Cootes Paradise Nature Reserve, to the many conservation areas and waterfalls.

I have written not only for outsiders and newcomers but also for old-stock Hamiltonians. I suspect that most have not visited all of their local heritage museums. I encourage them to do so. Entry fees are cheap. The Hamilton Public Library also offers free passes that can be borrowed for two weeks to visit Dundurn, Whitehern, the Waterworks, Battlefield House, and Griffin House.

I have focused on heritage-house museums, most of them owned and operated by the City of Hamilton. One exception is the Erland Lee Museum, owned by the Federated Women's Institutes of Ontario. The other is the Joseph Brant Museum, on Hamilton's border in Burlington. Hamilton also operates the Children's Museum, which I left out. It is less a museum than an activity centre, or what it calls "a place where learning happens through play." Other omissions include the Canadian Warplane Heritage Museum, the Canadian Football Hall of Fame, and the HMCS *Haida* Naval Museum, none of which fit my heritage-house theme.

Sometimes I stopped for coffee at the first Tim Hortons, at Ottawa Street North and Dunsmure Road in Hamilton's east end. Instead of a low-slung 1964 coffee hut, I found a sleek two-storey building with much glass and an upstairs memorabilia section that does not live up to its billing as a "museum." A future edition of this book might include the Dundas Museum & Archives built in 1956 with money from the industrialist Bertram family. The museum recently underwent a major renovation and expansion, and its main permanent local-history exhibition is undergoing redevelopment. A future edition might also include the

Workers Arts and Heritage Centre housed in the 1860 Hamilton Custom House. Although not yet a full-fledged museum with regular hours, the centre holds special events and stages exhibitions dedicated to workers, their unions, and other labour-related interests.

This book covers four bigger heritage museums and three smaller ones. The chapters are weighted accordingly. Each begins with a statement answering the question "Why go?" Museum websites always list addresses, opening hours, admission prices, and special events, but rarely say why anybody might want to visit the place. This book does.

For each museum I also give directions by public transit. I do not own a car but live near Toronto's Union Station GO Transit terminal. I almost always travel to Hamilton on a GO bus, sometimes mounting my bicycle on the front rack. The local Hamilton bus system still goes by the charming name of "Hamilton Street Railway" and in addition to keeping a helpful website issues a printed route map.

Most chapters first tell about the people associated with the house, or waterworks, or battlefield. Anybody like me wanting to keep the Whitehern characters straight now has a handy guide. Most chapters

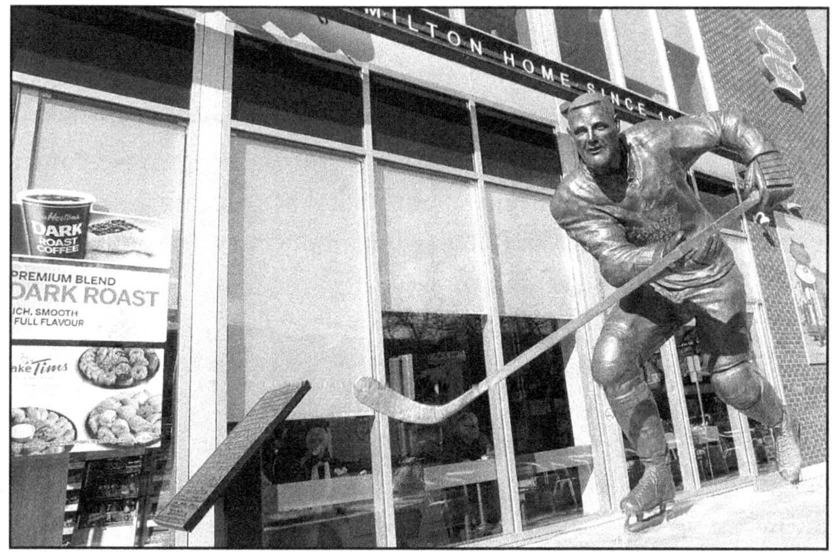

Photo by John Goddard

A statue outside the original 1964 Tim Hortons, in Hamilton's east end, shows Toronto Maple Leafs defenceman Tim Horton in full stride. An upstairs memorabilia section displays period uniforms and models of vintage doughnuts.

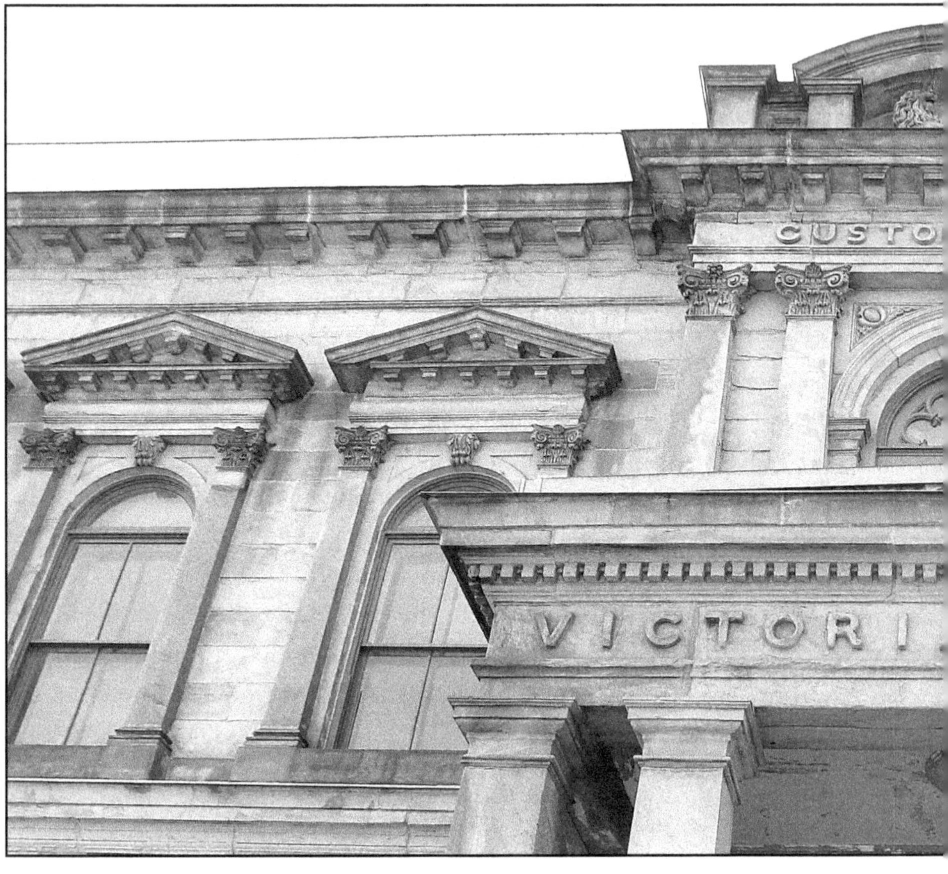

also give what I call a "walk-through," a section taking the reader mentally through the museum and pointing out the highlights. This section is best read before visiting the museum, or afterward, or both. Other sections address various other angles.

Five of the seven museums covered are designated National Historic Sites: Dundurn Castle, Whitehern, the Waterworks, Battlefield Park, and the Erland Lee Museum.

The book's title comes from my favourite Bob Dylan song, "Visions of Johanna," and the line that begins "Inside the museums." Some of the museum experts who helped me are acknowledged in the text but many are not, or deserve to be again. I thank Ken Heaman, Tom Minnes, Elizabeth Tessier, Debra Seabrook, Susan Ramsay, Kimberly Watson, Anne Jarvis, Daryl Mactavish, Alyssa Gomori, and Joanna Rickert-Hall.

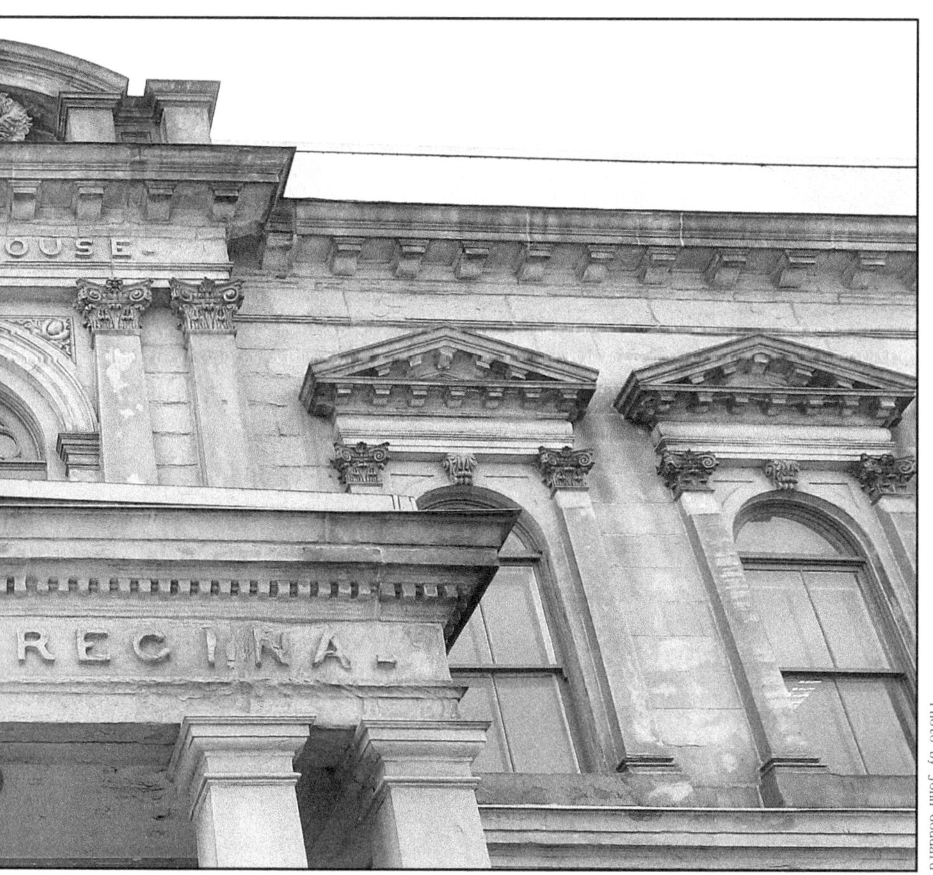

Photo by John Goddard

The 1860 Custom House, on Stuart Street near the port and railway yards, houses the Workers Arts and Heritage Centre. A fledgling museum, it holds special events and stages labour-oriented exhibitions.

Special guidance came from Ian Kerr-Wilson and Christopher Redford. I have already mentioned my esteem for Dr. Mehran Anvari. For friendship and other support I am grateful to October Browne, Anne Finlay, Michael Green, Carol Green, Fabienne Heim, Rolf Heim, Suzanne Jaeger, Lucrezia LaRusso, and Marie Royer. At Dundurn Press special thanks goes to president and publisher Kirk Howard, who named his company after Dundurn Castle and gave this project his blessing. I hold particular regard for Margaret Bryant, who brought me to the publishing house. Thank you also to editorial director Carrie Gleason, publicist Jaclyn Hodsdon, and to my editor on this book, Michael Carroll.

Why Go?

Dundurn Castle once stood as the biggest house in British North America. It reflects the outsized personality of its builder, Sir Allan Napier MacNab, a man of wealth, taste, and what he liked to call "devilish cunning." In his day he stood as one of the colony's best-known citizens, and far and away Hamilton's leading mover and shaker. Little girls tend to fall in love with his daughter, Sophia MacNab, whose portrait hangs in the drawing room, showing her at the age of four wearing a coral necklace. Of Hamilton's museums, Dundurn Castle ranks as the biggest and most famous. Camilla, Duchess of Cornwall, serves as its royal patron. Admission includes entry to the Hamilton Military Museum, occupying MacNab's former gatehouse and specializing in the War of 1812.

Address

610 York Boulevard.

Getting There by Public Transit

The GO bus from Toronto will stop on request at Main Street West and Dundurn Street South. From there, walk straight north for about fifteen minutes to Dundurn Castle. You can also take the bus to the Hamilton GO Centre and catch a No. 8 York bus to York Boulevard at Strathcona Avenue North at the edge of the Dundurn property.

DUNDURN NATIONAL HISTORIC SITE

(AND HAMILTON MILITARY MUSEUM)

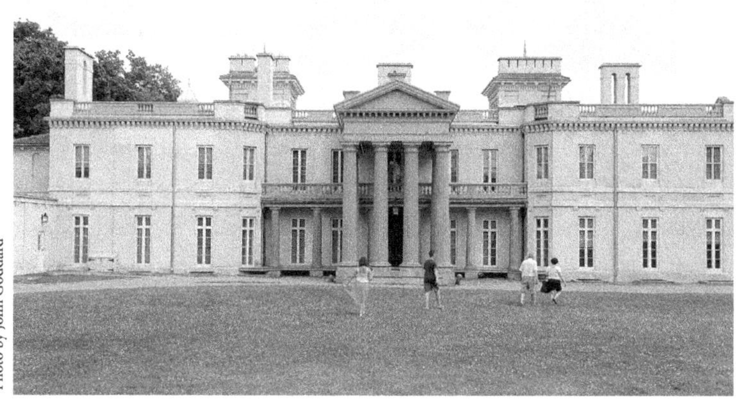

Photo by John Goddard

To express his outsized personality, Allan MacNab built an Italianate villa modelled after the sprawling farmhouses of Tuscany. "Hamilton's House," senior curator Ken Heaman calls it.

SIR ALLAN OF DUNDURN, THE MAN HERO

Allan MacNab arrived in Hamilton with almost nothing more to lose. His life had hit a low point. He had three small children, three adult sisters lived with him as dependents, his assets totalled $8, and his wife was dying. Less severe circumstances might have defeated an ordinary man, but MacNab could never be called ordinary. At twenty-eight years old, he possessed a buoyant enthusiasm for life. He was energetic and handsome. He stood taller than average, with a large chest tapering to the waist, and he possessed a rare physical courage, distinguishing himself at fifteen as the "Boy Hero" of the War of 1812. He was outgoing and convivial. He liked people and people liked him. In almost everything he tackled he showed dynamism and talent, although his biographers say he could be more of a doer than a thinker. "Surprisingly little capacity for quiet reflection," writes Donald R. Beer in *Sir Allan Napier MacNab*. "Not much given to the processes of abstract thought," writes Marion MacRae in *MacNab of Dundurn*. He could also be underhanded and devious. "I am devilish cunning," he once boasted, "and it is seldom I am caught." Most of all he possessed a burning ambition. He fancied himself a descendant of the chiefs of Scotland's Clan MacNab, destined to play the role of landed aristocrat in the New World, with all the responsibilities that came with such a station, and all the rewards and entitlements. Within a decade of arriving nearly penniless in Hamilton, MacNab would emerge as a central figure in the town's social and economic life and build the largest house in British North America.

"He had dreamed of it, hoped for it, perhaps at times despaired of achieving it," biographer MacRae says of the mansion, Dundurn, meaning "Fort on the Hill." For him, she says, the house was "not so much an economic symbol as an extension of personality."

Allan Napier MacNab was born in 1798 at Niagara-on-the-Lake, then called Newark, capital of the British colony of Upper Canada. His father was a former aide-de-camp to John Graves Simcoe, a British military commander appointed as the colony's first lieutenant governor. Simcoe moved the capital to Toronto, which he called York. The MacNabs soon followed, and young Allan grew up there with three sisters and a brother, and he attended the village's first pioneer school. In 1813, when he was fifteen, an American naval fleet landed at York as part of an attempt to conquer British North America in the War of 1812. Young MacNab rushed to the capital's defence. "I volunteered," he later recalled, "[and] accompanied the grenadier company of the Eighth Regiment to prevent the landing of the Americans."

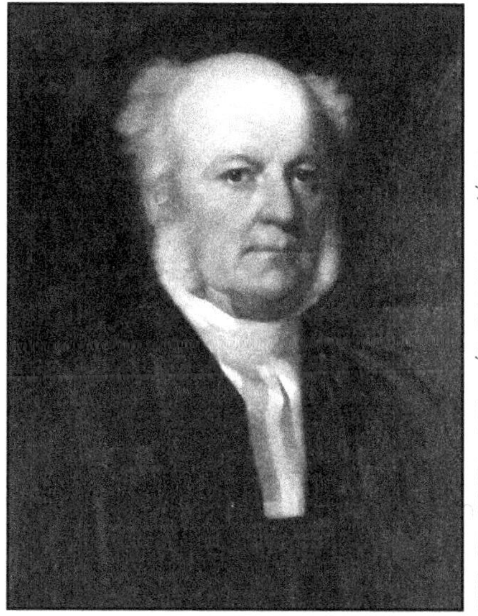

Photo by John Goddard courtesy of Dundurn National Historic Site

Sir Allan Napier MacNab sports furry mutton chops and a high lawyer's collar in an undated portrait hanging in the front entrance hall of Dundurn Castle. He possessed a buoyant enthusiasm for life and a rare physical courage.

Despite the regiment's best efforts, the invaders overran York and set fire to the British barracks, naval docks, and Parliament Buildings. The British Army fled and MacNab went with them. At Kingston, British naval commander James Yeo hired him as a midshipman for an attack on the American base across the lake at Sackets Harbor, New York, and when the attack failed, MacNab returned to his Niagara birthplace to join the 100th Regiment under Lieutenant-Colonel John Murray.

In those days, troops generally restricted their fighting to the battlefields. By late 1813, however, the war had turned nasty. As the American militia retreated over the border, they burned Newark to the ground. It was December. The weather was cold. Ninety-eight houses, barns, and stables went up in flames, as did all the public buildings, including the jail, courthouse, and library. Four hundred people were left homeless in the snow, the majority of them women and children. Most of the men were either serving in the Canadian militia or sitting imprisoned across the border in upper New York State.

One week later, at around midnight, Colonel Murray led a stealth revenge attack. A force of 562 men, including MacNab, overran Fort

Niagara. The British killed sixty-five American soldiers and sustained six dead of their own. The retaliation did not end there. Over the next ten days a separate British force set fire to Lewiston, Youngstown, and Manchester, now called Niagara Falls, New York. The rampage opened the road to the villages of Black Rock and Buffalo, and MacNab fought with the British force that laid waste to both. In Buffalo the British left only three structures standing, including the jail and blacksmith shop, both fireproof.

Through it all MacNab showed exceptional valour. He displayed "great bravery and zeal" at Fort Niagara, Colonel Murray wrote, praising the boy as being "amongst the foremost during the attack of the picquets [forward line] and the assault of the works." Murray recommended a commission, and MacNab sewed a gold epaulette onto his shoulder to mark his rank as ensign with the 49th Regiment stationed in Montreal. In 1814, shortly after his sixteenth birthday, he commanded an advance guard at the Saranac Bridge as part of a British march on Plattsburgh, New York. The British aborted the attack, but MacNab had more than proven himself. Later that year he returned to York nicknamed "the Boy Hero."

The next several years proved restless ones for MacNab. He tried a variety of jobs. He worked as a carpenter, a miller, a pedlar, a distiller, and an actor. In 1821 he got married. He and Elizabeth Brooke began their life together in rented rooms on downtown King Street and had two children, Robert and Anne Jane. Seeking to advance himself, MacNab undertook to study law, a profession that promised an entrée into the colony's highest echelons.

In Upper Canada the British colonial government encouraged the development of a type of local aristocracy, a governing class of gentlemen, who with their ladies also occupied the top social circles. The government promoted a class system and suppressed American-style democracy. Power in Upper Canada rested with the lieutenant governor, who represented the British Crown. He took advice from two bodies: an appointed executive council of permanent members and an appointed legislative council whose members sat for fixed terms. An elected assembly also existed, but the lieutenant governor could ignore its debates and legislation, and, by extension, the wishes of the people.

Such a system encouraged favouritism and nepotism. Blood ties and marriage counted for everything among the oligarchy, later nicknamed the "Family Compact," and MacNab sought to develop the right connections. He worked briefly as a land agent with Henry John Boulton, who was to become attorney general, and acquired a patron in Henry John's father, D'Arcy Boulton, a former attorney general and a first-generation member of the Family Compact. Boulton Senior accepted MacNab as a law student, and although the protégé took twice as long as usual to complete his legal studies, complete them he did, and in 1826 MacNab departed for Hamilton and his fresh start.

Hamilton at the time amounted to a settlement of barely forty buildings. Neighbouring Dundas and Ancaster were bigger and more important. MacNab had almost no money. Some accounts say that his wife, Elizabeth, died while giving birth to their second child, Anne Jane, in 1825, but biographer Donald R. Beer cites primary sources to show that

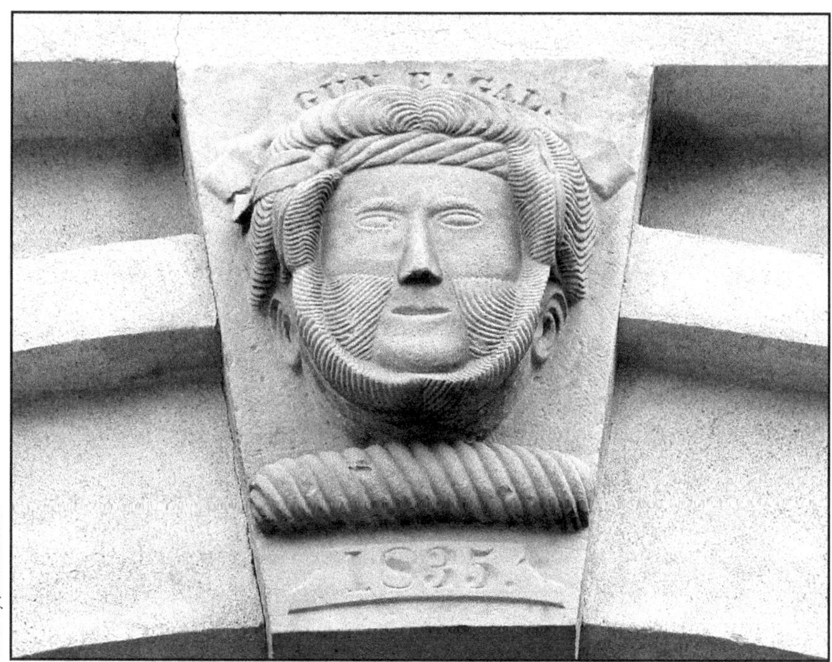

Photo by John Goddard

The MacNab family crest carved into the exterior of the pigeon house features the head of an ancestral enemy and the date of Dundurn's construction, 1835. The words "Gun Eagal" come from a phrase meaning "fear not."

in 1826 the couple had a third child, Elizabeth. The baby died after ten months in 1827 and MacNab's wife died a few months later the same year, meaning that when MacNab first took up residence in a wooden building on Hamilton's downtown James Street he did so with three children, three unmarried sisters, and an ailing wife.

He opened a law practice in Hamilton but built his fortune by speculating in land. The town might have been small but it was growing. Money could be made by acquiring land cheaply, subdividing it into lots, and selling the lots to newcomers. Sometimes MacNab developed the lots before selling them. In 1831, a year when land prices in Hamilton tripled, he built twelve stores with residences and sold thirty-eight lots at auction. The following year he advertised the sale of more than forty lots of undeveloped land in the Gore, Home, Niagara, and London districts, along with a two-hundred-acre farm in Woolwich and another one hundred acres of half-cleared land on the Grand River near Galt. Profits could be substantial. "On a single transaction involving an outlay of £2,500," Beer writes of one instance, "MacNab expected to clear between £10,000 and £15,000."

By then the lawyer and land speculator had also become a politician. Upper Canada's elected assembly might have lacked genuine political clout, but membership brought social standing and recognition. An assembly seat conferred a sense of importance. In 1830, MacNab ran successfully in Wentworth, which included Hamilton, and for the next twenty-seven years pursued a political career that was to culminate in his achieving the highest elected position in the land. In 1854, Upper Canada was to join Lower Canada to form the united Province of Canada, and MacNab was to become premier, or "prime minister."

That distinction lay in the future, but MacNab continued to open himself to opportunities. On trips to York, he wooed Mary Stuart and in 1831 married her. He was thirty-three, she nineteen and powerfully connected. MacNab might have been friends with Henry John Boulton, but Mary knew him as her uncle married to her mother's sister.

By 1832, MacNab was ready to build his dream home. He chose a prime spot. For years when approaching Hamilton from York, either by boat or by carriage, he could see perched on Burlington Heights the handsome brick residence of militia Lieutenant-Colonel Richard Beasley, a former fur trader and one of the area's first settlers. Beasley enjoyed a commanding site with a stellar view. "More fit for the reception of Inhabitants than any part of the Province I have seen," Elizabeth Simcoe, wife of the first lieutenant governor, wrote on a visit in 1796. MacNab bought Beasley's house, his outbuildings, and surrounding lands on Burlington Heights and began drawing plans for a house.

He wanted to go big — bigger than anything in York, let alone Hamilton. In 1817, D'Arcy Boulton, Jr., erected "The Grange," a solid red-brick Georgian mansion on York's western fringes and now part of the Art Gallery of Ontario. In 1818, the powerful cleric John Strachan built "The Palace," a particularly opulent Georgian edifice, since demolished, at the northwest corner of Front Street West and University Avenue. In 1822, William Campbell, later Sir William, chief justice of Upper Canada, similarly built a brick Georgian home in Old York, since relocated to Queen Street West and University Avenue as the Campbell House Museum. Other Family Compact luminaries erected grand homes with similar materials in a similarly conservative style, gradually replacing the wooden structures of York's early days.

MacNab resolved to outdo them all. He wished to announce that he had arrived by establishing a country seat as a gentleman of the Upper Canada aristocracy. First, he tossed out the Georgian architectural format, which emphasized the symmetry of door and window alignments in houses standing upright and dominant against the landscape. MacNab favoured a more elegant approach. He had taste. In his later years, writes biographer Marion MacRae in *MacNab of Dundurn*, he clearly revealed a visual orientation. "Form, proportion and colour must always have been important to him," she says.

In Hamilton, MacNab found an architect newly arrived from England named Robert Wetherell, who was familiar with the more fluid and fashionable Regency Italianate style. Together, client and architect sketched drawings for a stately villa modelled after the sprawling farmhouses of Tuscany. "Dundurn was designed as a commodious country house," MacRae says, "which could accommodate formal ceremonial occasions with graceful ease when the need arose, and would, at the same time, allow a young family to grow up in comfortable, undemanding surroundings."

Throughout his life, at periods of his greatest triumphs, MacNab also suffered his greatest losses. When he moved to Hamilton and launched his law practice, his wife and infant daughter died within months of each other. The very day that he signed papers to purchase Burlington Heights from Beasley, a fire destroyed the finest part of downtown Hamilton, including two of MacNab's stores, two of his offices, and his nearly completed three-storey tavern.

Now, as he was digging the foundations for the great house that history mostly remembers him for, his eldest child and only son and heir, eleven-year-old Robert, went hunting with a friend and was accidentally shot and killed. Workers digging the house excavations turned to digging a family cemetery. "Inchbuie," MacNab called it, after the family's ancestral burial site in Scotland. On Dundurn's grounds he laid Robert to rest, had the body of his late wife, Elizabeth, transferred from a grave in York, and similarly reinterred his parents.

In 1835, the house was ready. MacNab moved in with his family of females, including his three sisters, his daughter Anne Jane, his second wife, Mary, and two young daughters from his second marriage, three-year-old Sophia and one-year-old Minnie. In 1836, another daughter was born but lived only briefly. In business and politics MacNab remained as active as ever. He led the push to establish the Gore Bank in Hamilton. He served as president of the Desjardins Canal Company, which built a shipping canal from Burlington Bay to Dundas. He operated a steamship line running between Hamilton and New York State, and owned a dock on Burlington Bay. He served as president of the newly formed Hamilton and Port Dover Rail Road Company, and as a director of the Great Western Railway. He continued to speculate in land. He built, sold, and rented houses and stores, and owned a tavern, and increased his social prominence by becoming president of Hamilton's newly formed St. Andrew's Society. In the legislative assembly he was elected speaker.

Almost everything that happened in Hamilton, MacNab seemed to be part of, and the more he prospered the more he had to lose. A threat emerged in the form of William Lyon Mackenzie, a journalist and publisher turned opposition politician. He opposed almost everything MacNab stood for. MacNab believed in a British type of graded social order governed by a privileged oligarchy bound by education, wealth, and family ties. Mackenzie believed in democracy. He believed in equality and the innate intelligence of the common man. A diminutive, agitated character, he devoted his restless energy and barbed wit to exposing waste, hypocrisy, cronyism, and corruption. In 1834, when York incorporated to become the City of Toronto, Mackenzie served as its first mayor, but after one year resumed his campaign against the Family Compact, pushing for democratic government and what he called Radical Reform.

In late 1837, Mackenzie went further. He turned his reform campaign into a dissident movement that gained widespread support throughout the countryside. Then he launched an open rebellion. He gathered hundreds of men at Montgomery's Tavern in Toronto, just above where Eglinton Avenue now crosses Yonge Street, and led a sneak nighttime march to seize Government House, the Bank of Upper Canada, and other strategic targets. His goal was to establish an independent republic, and he might have succeeded. The British had emptied Fort York of regular troops to help suppress the Lower Canada Rebellion, leaving Toronto vulnerable, but word of the planned attack got out and Mackenzie lost the element of surprise. In the Gore District, which included Hamilton, MacNab rounded up sixty volunteer militiamen, ominously dubbed "The Men of Gore," and, as he had in 1813, set out valiantly to defend the capital. Mackenzie, his political rival, was now his enemy in battle. Acting under the general command of Colonel James FitzGibbon, MacNab led a column north to Montgomery's Tavern to help crush the rebels. He might have killed Mackenzie, but the rebel leader escaped into exile across the U.S. border.

Most capsule accounts of the Upper Canada Rebellion end with Mackenzie's defeat, but the uprising continued sporadically for another two years. In the next phase, sometimes called the Western Rising, MacNab played a starring role. He led six hundred of his Men of Gore — militiamen and First Nations fighters — against rebels of the London district led by Charles Duncombe, a doctor who had opened the colony's first medical school.

In the face of MacNab's army, Duncombe's followers dispersed. MacNab proceeded to Niagara. He arrived at Chippewa to head off a renewed threat from Mackenzie, who had installed himself on British-owned Navy Island, in the Niagara River, and declared a mini-republic. The rebels were being supplied by the steamer *Caroline*, which could be seen sailing back and forth between the island and the U.S. mainland. MacNab ordered a nighttime attack on the ship. A party of seven boats, with nine men each, crossed to the New York side and overran the crew. The Canadians then set the ship ablaze. American authorities protested the violation of U.S. sovereignty, but in mid-January 1838 the rebels abandoned the island and the crisis passed.

With the victory over the rebels, the former Boy Hero emerged as the Man Hero. In March 1838, for his role in suppressing the Upper Canada Rebellion, Queen Victoria awarded him a knighthood. At forty years old he became Sir Allan and his wife Lady Mary. Three years later, four hundred Men of Gore, including First Nations chiefs, arrived at Dundurn in sixty-two sleighs to present their former commander with a ceremonial sword. "Among the richest prizes of my life," MacNab called the honour. The sword symbolized, he said, "all those thrilling associations touchingly clear to a Soldiers feelings."

Following the hostilities, MacNab returned to his business affairs and the speaker's chair. As the colony entered the railway age, so did he. At various times after 1845 he served as president of three railways, chairman of one, and director of at least two others. In 1846, Lady Mary died of a lung disease, possibly tuberculosis, and he was often ill himself with gout and rheumatoid arthritis. He kept getting elected, however, leading to perhaps his highest honour of all.

In 1841, Upper Canada and Lower Canada had been renamed Canada West and Canada East, and had united to become the Province of Canada. In 1854, MacNab found himself the compromise choice to become co-leader of a coalition government. He was given the title "premier," while his Canada East counterpart took the title "deputy." Within two years he would be manoeuvred out of the job by John A. Macdonald and others, but from September 1854 until May 1856 — twenty months — Sir Allan held the top elected political office in the united Canadas. On a plaque at Dundurn the Ontario Archaeological and Historic Sites Board grandly calls him, "Prime Minister of Canada 1854–56."

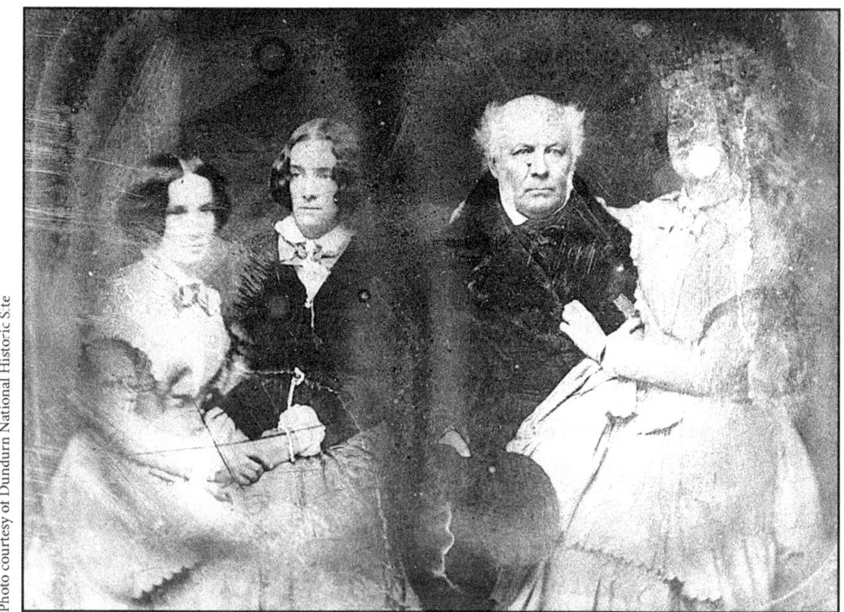

Photo courtesy of Dundurn National Historic Site

A damaged family photo from the 1850s shows Sir Allan with his two daughters, Sophia (far left) and Minnie (right), and his late wife's younger sister, Sophia, or "Aunt Sophia" to the daughters. She moved in permanently after Lady Mary's death.

MacNab resigned from politics in 1856. Six years later, in 1862, he died at Dundurn following a particularly severe attack of gout. By then failed business dealings had caught up to him. He died penniless. All his belongings were auctioned to pay debts, and the house was repurposed as a school for the deaf.

"We are not dealing with a Great Canadian," biographer MacRae says in summary, "but with a loveable, hateable man who built a great house and who served his country and his community to the best of his ability."

MacNab is also partly remembered for one last hurrah. In 1855, when he was "prime minister," he ordered renovations to Dundurn, including the addition of the portico with its huge columns that stands now as perhaps the building's most identifying feature. At around the same time, biographer MacRae says, he had the city assessor list the house as "Dundurn Castle." The refurbishing and rebranding set the stage for what by all accounts shone as the social event of the year. At Dundurn Castle on November 15, 1855, MacNab threw a sumptuous wedding for the first child of his second marriage, his bright and fashionable daughter, Sophia.

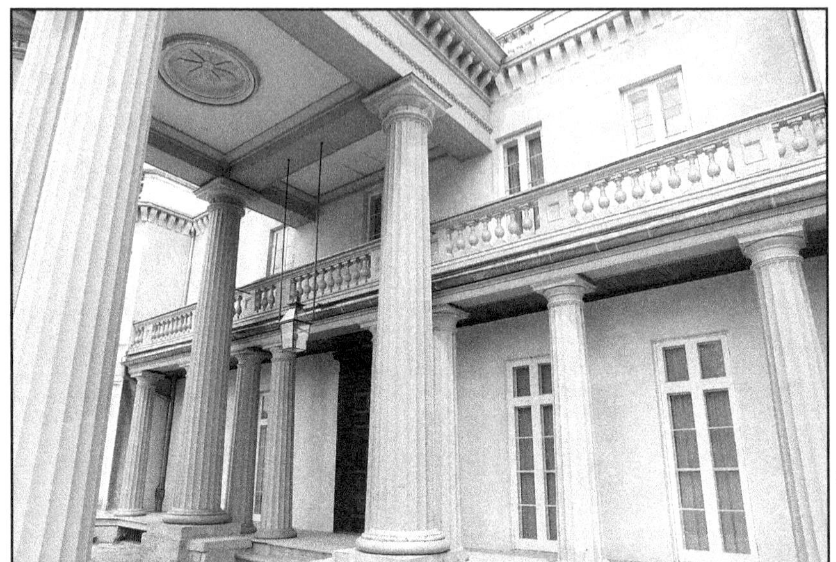

Photo by John Goddard

Partly to prepare for Sophia's wedding, partly to signal his status as "prime minister" of the Province of Canada, Sir Allan built a grand front entrance in 1855. It stands now as perhaps the building's most identifying feature.

The main ceremony took place in Dundurn's most formal room, the large drawing room, with more than a hundred guests, mostly top business and political leaders, including Governor General Sir Edmund Head and his wife, Lady Head. Bishop John Strachan, long one of Upper Canada's most powerful figures, officiated.

"A splendour unequalled in those times," Beer calls the occasion.

"The bride," the *Hamilton Mirror* reported, "was attired in white [glazed] silk, trimmed with Honiton lace, and wreaths of orange blossoms, and veil.... Her extreme beauty was the theme of every tongue."

Afterward, Sophia moved with her husband to county Norfolk, England, where they had ten children. Prominent among her descendants is Camilla Parker Bowles, the Duchess of Cornwall. She now serves as Dundurn Castle's royal patron, and in 2009 visited her ancestral home with her husband, Prince Charles, heir to the British throne. Camilla's great-great-great-grandfather is Sir Allan Napier MacNab.

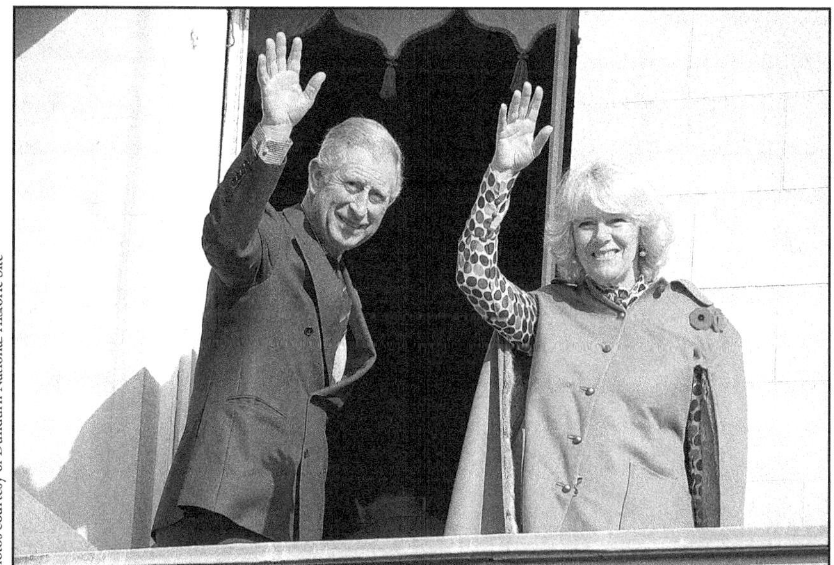

Photos courtesy of Dundurn National Historic Site

↗ *Charles, Prince of Wales, and Camilla, Duchess of Cornwall, wave from the front balcony of Dundurn Castle during their 2009 visit to Camilla's ancestral home. Sir Allan is her great-great-great-grandfather.*

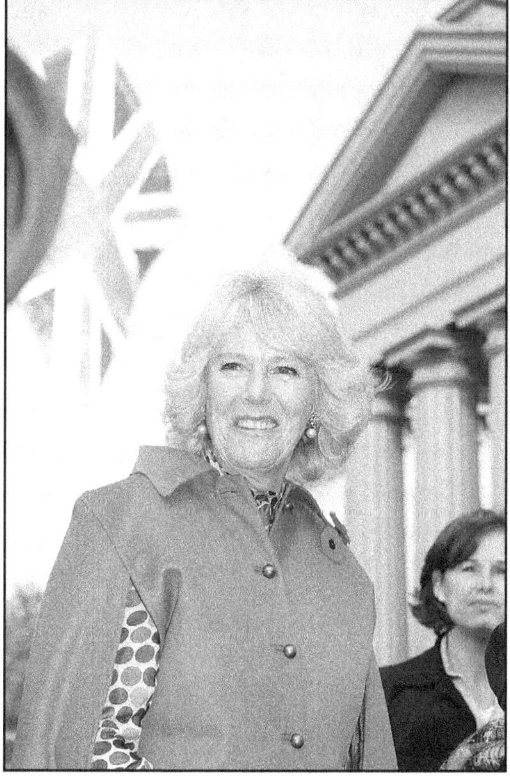

→ *Camilla, Duchess of Cornwall, departs Dundurn Castle under the British flag during her 2009 visit. Her great-great-great-grandfather, Sir Allan, invited her husband's great-great-grandfather, Prince Albert Edward, to lunch at Dundurn in 1860.*

MY MOTHER'S DEATH: THE DIARY OF SOPHIA MACNAB

Sophia MacNab has received a diary, perhaps as a Christmas gift, but does not know how to begin. She is thirteen years old. "Mamma told me to note down what we were all about on the 4th of January 1846," she finally writes on January 20. "We were all standing round dear Mammas bed talking to her about her being so sick."

Her mother, Lady Mary MacNab, is dying of an unspecified lung disease, possibly tuberculosis. The next day she tells Sophia how it feels to be near death, and the girl writes everything down. She uses a quill pen and writes quickly so as not to blot the page.

"I went up stairs to get something for my lessons and I found that dear Mamma was very ill indeed," the girl writes. "She complained of Giddness and a sort of light headed feeling as if the back of her head was off. She said she knew us all and understood perfectly what we were saying to her, but she said she felt as if she had little or no mind, and she wondered if it could be death. She said that she was always told it would come like a thief in the night when we least expected it and that those who were in health always thought O when death comes plenty time will be allowed me to prepare my self but O when we are stretched on the bed of death and feel that we must go alone into the other world, and no body to excuse us."

For the next four months, Sophia (pronounced *So-FIE-ah*) maintains her excruciating deathwatch and continues writing for another two months beyond her mother's sad demise at the age of thirty-four. In the process the girl opens a window into daily life at Dundurn. Almost all other documents connected to Sir Allan have been lost. Four fires in six years destroyed almost all of his records in the legislative archives, which included manuscripts of prepared speeches and ministerial letter books containing manuscript copies of all outgoing correspondence. At some unknown date MacNab's personal papers also somehow disappeared from the Wentworth County archives, and when MacNab tried to import his ancestral family papers from Scotland, he was shipwrecked in the Gulf of St. Lawrence and lost those, too.

"The only major document to survive him was Dundurn," biographer Marion MacRae writes, meaning that the house itself speaks volumes about the man's ambition, taste, and outsized personality. His daughter's diary and a few surviving political and business papers, MacRae also says, mean that "the opening months of 1846 are the most thoroughly documented of Sir Allan's life."

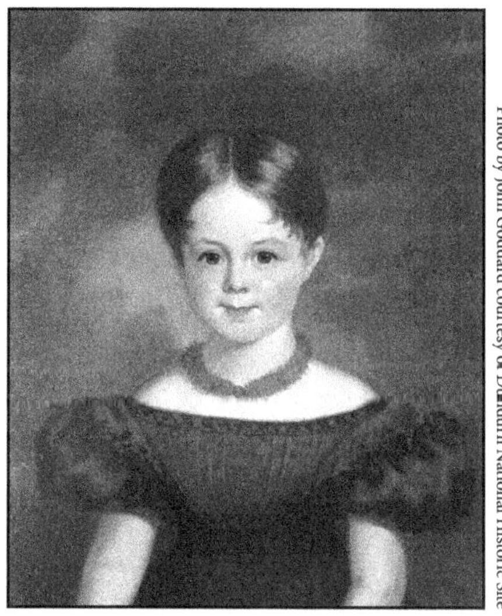

Photo by John Goddard courtesy of Dundurn National Historic Site

A portrait hanging in the large drawing room shows Sophia MacNab with rosy cheeks at the age of four, wearing a coral necklace that was said to ward off evil spirits. Little girls who visit tend to fall in love with her.

In her journal young Sophia follows her mother's uneven decline — the rallies and relapses. Touchingly, she often refers to her mother as "Dear Mamma," "Dearest Mamma," and "Dear, Dear Mamma." Sometimes she leaves exact dates unclear.

> January 23: "Dearest Mamma said she felt that Giddy feeling returning."
>
> January [27?]: "She complained of a very uncomfortable sensation shortness of breath."
>
> February 8: "She has had no fever for the last two days."
>
> February [21?]: "She has her shortness of breath and feels very weak."
>
> March 11: "We are all delighted for dearest Mamma seems so much better this morning, and Aunt Sophia [Lady Mary's younger sister] says that although it is such a disagreeable day without we care not for we have our sunshine within."

The household functions in a kind of limbo. Lady Mary never leaves her suite. Sir Allan continues his duties as a businessman and as speaker of the legislature for the united Province of Canada, but life for the family cannot truly move forward.

A routine develops. Sophia takes instruction from tutors, sits with her mother, sews, attends church on Sundays, makes almost daily trips downtown in a horse and sleigh, and sometimes visits her father's sister, Aunt Maria, and Maria's three-year-old son, Allan. Doctors, clerics, and other relatives come and go, including Sir Allan's sisters Hannah and Lucy, and Lady Mary's Aunt Eliza, with her husband, Uncle Henry John Boulton. For a young teenage girl the days could seem deadly dull.

"I can think of nothing more to put in today's journal," Sophia writes on March 30. "It is the same old routine every day. I think it would almost do as well to write one day and copy all the rest down from it, there is so little variety."

She and her younger sister, Minnie, eleven, attend lessons at Dundurn with a Mr. Thompson on such subjects as reading, writing, arithmetic, and botany. They also take music lessons from Charles Ambrose, the organist and choirmaster at Christ Church, Anglican. Sophia sometimes has trouble concentrating. "Mr. Ambrose came," she writes in mid-February. "I took my lesson & he said I was more attentive and better than the last day he was here."

Lady Mary likes to have company. "I sat with Mamma and read her prayers to her," Sophia writes on February 13. "We have decided upon my sitting with Mamma every night during tea."

The girl keeps track of what her mother eats:

> January 25: "Nine oysters and half a tumbler of beer."
>
> January [28?]: "Mamma had a Quail which she relished very much."
>
> January 31: "I had a sweet bread cooked for her."

> February 5: "I made some cakes for Mamma's breakfast."
>
> February 22: "She got her dinner which consisted of a Pygion [pigeon] (this is Mamma's usual diet at one oclock every day) and a tumbler of beer."
>
> March 7: "She ate two eggs [for breakfast] as usual and a piece of Johnny cake."

Sophia's half-sister, Anne Jane, twenty at the time, and their Aunt Sophia, Lady Mary's younger sister, serve as the main caregivers. "Aunt Sophia returned and made some cushions for dear Mamma's ears which were very sore," reads one entry. Another reads: "Dear Anne Jane made a very good nurse as usual. She bathed Mamma's head with cold water and Camphor and gave her a drink of cold water which relieved her very much."

All through February and March, everybody around Sophia seems to fall ill. With her mother dying, perhaps the girl is especially attuned to sickness, but she is also living at a time when medications are ineffective and causes of disease little understood. People rarely wash their hands. Sir Allan suffers much of the time from gout, an arthritic condition mainly affecting the feet, and others come down with an assortment of other ailments.

"Papa was not very well but Aunt Sophia administered a little remedy to him," Sophia writes with underlining. Other entries strike a similar note:

"Minnie has a very bad cold."

"Aunt Sophia has not been well all day."

"Nanny … was suffering a great deal of pain in her head."

"Aunt Lucy had rush of blood to the Head last evening."

"The poor old Vicar says he has been very sick since Sunday."

"Both [cousin] Allan and [his father] Captain Stuart are very sick."

"We went to see Old Anne [the cook] and found her sick in bed with the ague."

"After breakfast I remained with Anne Jane until about ten oclock when Dr. King cut out a small lump that was behind her ear. It gave her a great deal of pain but she bore it very well."

In another glimpse into nineteenth-century Upper Canada life, Sophia reveals how unstable a horse and sleigh can be. "We had one upset & were very near having another," she writes of one ride into town with Anne Jane. That Sunday she says, "on our road to Church we got an up set & we all spilt out." Such spills could be awkward, as when Anne Jane drives the vicar home. She "upset the poor old Vicar & laid on him for some time without being able to move," Sophia says. "At last she managed to clime over the side of the sleigh & Donald assisted the poor old gentleman out of the snow." Once, her younger sister made a game of the sleigh's precariousness: "We went over in the wood sleigh & Minnie was very busy in trying to upset it by pulling the rack first to one side & then to the other."

In the diary, Sir Allan comes off as the more endearing of Sophia's parents. At one point he travels to Kingston to preside over the elected assembly and thinks of his young daughters cooped up in their melancholy home. How could he offer them distraction and amusement? "My dear Long Legs," he writes affectionately to Sophia, informing her that he has bought two white poodles, one each for her and Minnie. "I washed my dog and brushed him," Sophia says when the poodles arrive. "Anne Jane made him a very pretty blue collar and then I took him over to Aunt Maria's. Little Allan was delighted with him and the way he showed his affection was by squeezing him with all his might."

By contrast, in the final weeks of her life, Lady Mary comes across as severe and unaffectionate. At her funeral local women would come out in droves to acknowledge her visits to the poor and the sick, but when her thirteen-year-old daughter is in most need of warmth and love, Lady Mary cannot give it. One evening Lady Mary speaks of the virtue of modesty, but her words come across as almost scolding. Sophia records the conversation this way:

> Sophia if you were in School and learning to paint and were doing a most beautiful picture but the School mistress and scholars helped you and did even more than

> you yourself and on returning home you showed the picture to Strangers who praised it very much and said it was beautifully executed would you not immediately say "O you are praising me more than I deserve the mistress and scholars did nearly all of it for me" and I said yes dear Mamma I should.

In the same vein, in mid-March, Sophia records this: "Mamma told me to write down in my journal that it is her wish that we should never waltz & I am sure I never shall."

Did Lady Mary ever tell her daughter that she loved her? The diary gives no hint of it. On May 7, the day before her mother's death, Sophia writes:

> Anne Jane came to the schoolroom crying and beconed [beckoned] to Minnie and I to come out. She told us that dear Mamma was very ill indeed and that Dearest Mamma herself thought she was dying. We were dreadfully alarmed. Anne Jane asked Mr Thompson to excuse us and we went into Mamma's room. Papa was sitting by her and had his hand in hers. Aunt Sophia was standing at the head of her Couch. Dear Mamma was very ill indeed, her fingers turned almost black down to the first joint. Dearest Mamma could not get her breath for two hours at least it was as short as possible. She spoke very little merely for what she wanted. Once she said to Papa "Allan will you take [care] of them all but then she said I need not ask you to do that for you have ever done it." Dear dear Mamma kissed us all and said to me "Will you be a good girl and never forget your Mother."

The next night, before going to bed, the girls go to their mother's room to say good night. Sophia leaves the room first and waits in the upper hall for Minnie, who comes out and says, "Mama's gone."

She is mistaken but not by much.

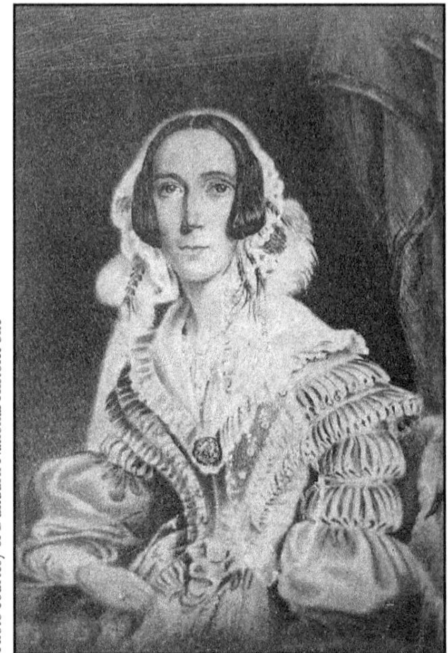

Photo courtesy of Dundurn National Historic Site

A drawing from the early 1940s shows Lady Mary in apparent good health and dressed to suit her lofty station in life. Sir Allan might have been friends with Family Compact luminaries, but Lady Mary grew up in the oligarchy.

"I rushed into [Mother's] room and soon perceived the awful change which was about to take place," Sophia writes. "This was about ½ past eight and by nine poor dear dear dear Mamma was no more. She did struggle [no] longer than ten minutes but just died as if she were going to sleep."

Fortunately, the diary does not end there. One evening in late June or early July 1846 — about two months after Lady Mary died — Sophia and her father take visitors to the orchard west of the house to pick cherries. The irrepressible Sir Allan starts to play.

"Uncle Jonas said to Papa 'Come' 'MacNab' get up this tree and get us some Cherries,'" the girl writes with awkward punctuation. "And Papa not wishing to be out done immediately got the steps and got up into the tree, he through [threw] us down lots of Cherries and also met with a great many adventures, he stained his shirt sleeve with Cherries, he tore his coat sleeve nearly half out and got some Cherries juice on his coat, and as a finale he sat down on a lot of Cherries."

In the bounty of Dundurn's orchard, among the ripening cherry trees, Sir Allan and his young daughter find hilarity, and a cathartic release from their grieving.

WALK-THROUGH: "QUITE A LITTLE PARADISE IN ITSELF"

Dundurn Castle is a castle in the way Hamilton Mountain is a mountain. It is the biggest of its kind around, helping to define the city and stir the affections of its people. Any motorist arriving over the High Level Bridge immediately spots Dundurn's grand edifice and enormous portico of four giant pillars, along with its surrounding parklands, walkways, outbuildings, gates, and panoramic view of Burlington Bay.

"Hamilton's House," Dundurn's senior curator Ken Heaman calls it. For more than forty years he has worked in historic homes and has visited thousands of them in travels through many parts of the world. Rarely, he says, has he seen people respond to a home the way Hamiltonians respond to Dundurn.

"A father and his daughter used to come to Dundurn Castle every Christmas," Heaman says, giving one example. "The parents were divorced and this was the father's custodial time with his daughter. They would come to Dundurn Castle, see a Christmas tree, see a dining room with the thought of a turkey dinner, and take part in all these aspects of celebrating Christmas together. They didn't go to church, they came to Dundurn Castle, and I think their spiritual and emotional needs were met by way of simply taking an hour-long tour. It became their personal tradition."

The location alone inspires visitors. Elizabeth Simcoe enthused about it during a trip on June 11, 1795, with her husband, John Graves Simcoe, the first lieutenant governor of Upper Canada. They were calling on the fur trader and militia officer Richard Beasley, who had built a brick house at what was then called Head-of-the-Lake, on a rise of land known as Burlington Heights.

"We landed at it & walked up the hill from whence is a beautiful view of the Lake," Mrs. Simcoe wrote in her diary. "The country appears more fitt for the reception of Inhabitants than any part of the Province I have seen."

During the War of 1812, the British commandeered Beasley's property as a military camp. By 1813 the war was going badly for the British. The Americans had taken the Niagara Region, forcing the British Army to retreat. At Burlington Heights they dug in. They fortified their position with earthworks, and on June 6, 1813, they launched a victorious nighttime attack against their sleeping American pursuers a few kilometres away at Stoney Creek.

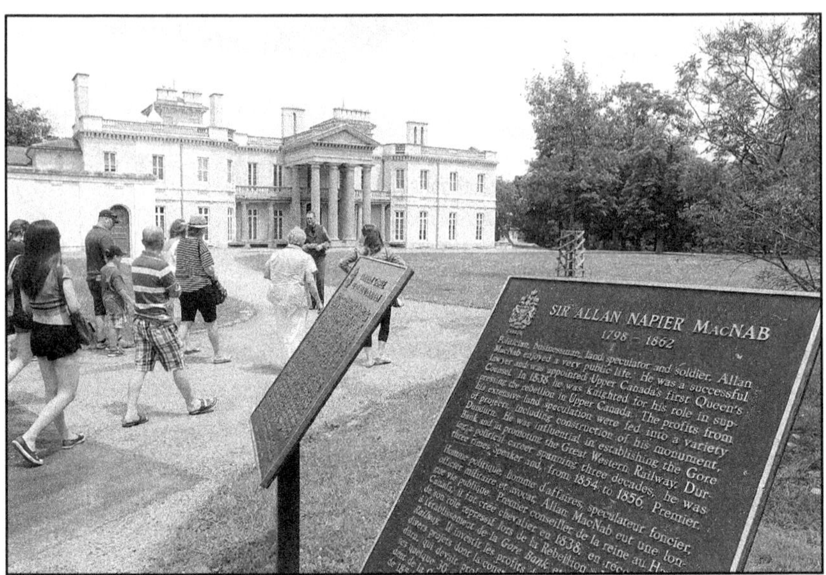

Photo by John Goddard

A tour begins by rounding a corner to view the full length of Dundurn Castle, partly characterized by long French casement windows on the ground floor and balcony. Sir Allan died at the home penniless and in debt in 1862.

Later that year, in November, militiamen in the western part of the colony captured a number of settlers accused of working for the American side. In the spring of 1814, nineteen suspects went on trial in Ancaster, at the Union Hotel on Wilson Street where the Coach & Lantern Pub now stands. The trial became known as the Bloody Assize, an assize being a temporary court. Fifteen of the nineteen were found guilty of treason. The court sentenced eight to death. As an example to others, they were brought to specially built scaffolds on Burlington Heights where they were hanged. One of them died not by hanging but by blunt-force trauma when a gallows beam fell on him after the noose was attached. Archaeologists have not yet determined the exact spot, but the executions are believed to have taken place near present-day Inchbury Street at the eastern end of the Dundurn property.

In 1832, Allan MacNab bought the heights. He bought Beasley's house and grounds, and began to plan his masterpiece. Principal construction took place in 1834 and 1835. When the MacNabs moved in, the building stood as the largest home in British North America. It had forty rooms. (References to seventy-two are incorrect.)

"The garden looking beautiful, the Cherries are ripe enough to eat and the roses are in full bloom," thirteen-year-old Sophia MacNab wrote of returning home from a trip to Quebec in 1846 after her mother died, "the hay has just been mown and smells so sweet and altogether Dundurn is quite a little paradise in itself."

In 1899, the City of Hamilton bought the estate, and to mark Canada's centennial in 1967 renovated it as a historic-house museum. People refer to it as "Dundurn Castle," even though they know it was not really a castle, and in 2014 a *Hamilton Spectator* columnist reported that the Queen was unhappy.

"The Queen would prefer that Hamilton stop calling Dundurn a castle," Paul Wilson wrote as though citing an inside source. The Queen, he said, presides as honorary chair of the Royal Society of Castle Standards, dedicated to ensuring that "true castles of the world are not cheapened and devalued." Maybe the name could be changed to Dundurn Abbey, Wilson suggested. The Queen would be mollified and the revision would capitalize on the popularity of the BBC show *Downton Abbey*. Wilson gave himself away, however, by referring to Dundurn's curator not as Ken Heaman but as "Avril Blague." He was writing on April 1, and his entire column was an April Fool's joke.

When touring the museum — or any historic-house museum — it is worth keeping in mind that curators constantly re-evaluate their interpretations. Some room designations might be solidly grounded on research, others might be educated guesses. New information can come to light, motivating curators to move things around.

Main Floor: Front Entrance Hall

The solid black-walnut front door under Dundurn's columned portico remains shut for conservation reasons, meaning that modern-day visitors enter by the servants' corridor beside a rough courtyard. Once inside the front hallway, however, a visitor can easily imagine a stunning first impression. High plaster walls have been painstakingly hand-painted to resemble hefty blocks of yellow marble. To the right rises the celebrated "flying staircase," built free of the walls and originally fastened only at the top and bottom. In her diary of 1846, thirteen-year-old Sophia MacNab calls it the "walnut staircase," because it is also made of black walnut.

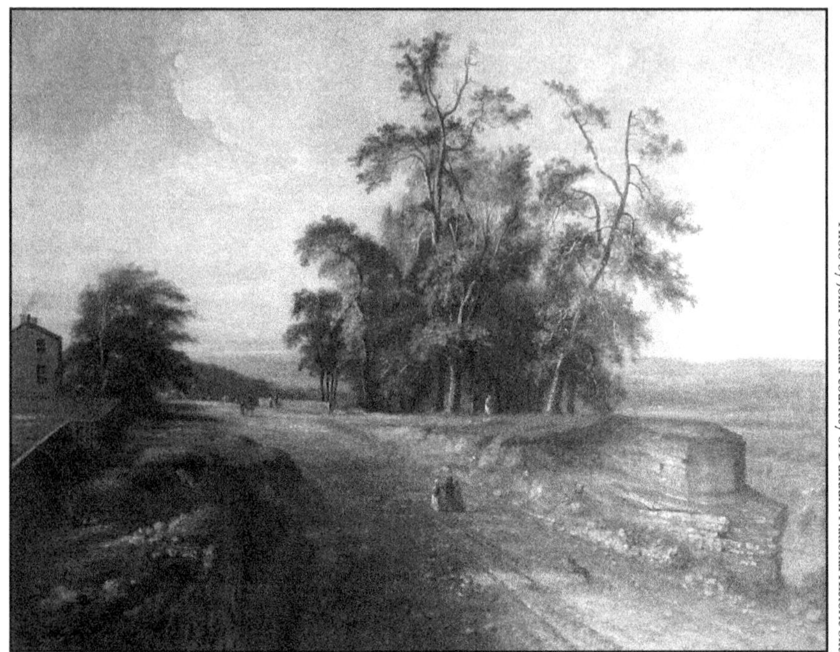

Photo by John Goddard courtesy of Dundurn National Historic Site

English-born artist Robert Whale painted a scene on Hamilton Mountain that includes the house built for lawyer James Chisholm. "It is the oldest house on Claremont Drive and the house I used to live in," says Dundurn's senior curator, Ken Heaman.

Three paintings on the front wall catch the eye. In the middle, Sir Allan appears in furry mutton chops and a high lawyer's collar. Nobody knows who painted the portrait or when. On either side hang two landscapes by English-born artist Robert Whale, whose works can also be found at the Art Gallery of Hamilton, the Royal Ontario Museum, and the National Gallery of Canada. Both landscapes depict Hamilton from the escarpment in the 1850s. The left-hand one shows the city spread out below, with Dundurn as a cluster of small white dots at the top left. In the right-hand one, Whale has turned his gaze westward along the escarpment edge. A house stands at the left. It was built for James Chisholm, law partner with Isaac McQuesten of Whitehern and later mentor to Isaac's son, Thomas McQuesten. "It is the oldest house on Claremont Drive and the house I used to live in," says senior curator Heaman, also a former Whitehern curator. In 1998, he bought and restored the Chisholm house for himself and his family and lived in it for twelve years.

Main Floor: Drawing Room

After a meal, guests would withdraw to the drawing room, the most formal room in the house. Designers of 1967 restored the room as mauve, although more recent evidence shows that in MacNab's day the colour scheme was an amber-bronze. In about 1850, Dundurn became one of the first homes in the Canadas with gas lighting produced from coal.

A few features are original to the home. The marble fireplace mantel, part of mid-1850s renovations, bears the MacNab family crest. The white crank on the wall to the left of the fireplace is called a bell pull, used to ring one of eleven bells in the cellar, each with its distinct ring, to summon a servant. Where the high walls meet the ceiling, original plaster-and-horsehair moulding swirls in elaborate floral patterns. To the left of the entrance the pronounced curvature of the large black walnut door fits the curve of the room.

The portrait on the left wall shows MacNab's second daughter, Sophia, at the age of four, with wide eyes, rosy red cheeks, and hair parted in the middle. Around her neck she wears a coral necklace of the type often worn by girls at the time in the belief that it would ward off evil spirits.

"We have had grandmothers ask if we can find a pattern for a dress that looks just like Sophia's in the portrait," curator Heaman says. "They want to make the dress because their granddaughter fell in love with Sophia."

In 1854, when she was twenty-two, Sophia moved to Montreal with her father when he took his job as premier, sometimes referred to as "prime minister," of the united Province of Canada. That same year an English baron of the same age named William Coutts Keppel, the future 7th Earl of Albemarle and otherwise known as Viscount Bury, rented lodgings next door as the new superintendent of Indian Affairs. Sophia and William fell in love. The following year, on November 15, 1855, they got married in Hamilton twice. The first ceremony took place with a small number of guests at St. Mary of the Immaculate Conception Church (since demolished) because Sophia was raised as a Catholic, like her mother. A second, Anglican, ceremony took place in the drawing room with more than a hundred guests because her father and Viscount Bury's family were Anglican. Bishop John Strachan, one of Upper Canada's most powerful figures, performed the ceremony. Guests included Governor General Sir Edmund Head and his wife, Lady Head.

"The bride was attired in white [glazed] silk, trimmed with Honiton lace, and wreaths of orange blossoms, and veil," the *Hamilton Spectator* reported. "Her extreme beauty was the theme of every tongue."

Afterward, Sophia moved with her husband to county Norfolk, England, where they had ten children. Sophia's great-great-granddaughter is Camilla, Duchess of Cornwall, the former Camilla Parker Bowles.

Main Floor: Library

Through the curved door a short hallway leads to MacNab's library and study, a distinctly masculine room of dark colours and window curtains of Scottish MacNab tartan. The portrait above the fireplace depicts a kilted Archibald MacNab, Sir Allan's cousin and thirteenth chief of the Clan MacNab. Just before he died, Archibald conferred the chieftainship on Sir Allan, who sailed overseas to retrieve the family papers. On the return voyage, however, he was shipwrecked in the Gulf of St. Lawrence, lost the official documents, and was never able to claim the title. Near the fireplace a straight-backed chair bears the MacNab family crest on its backrest. Bookcases line the available walls. Records from MacNab's bankruptcy auction indicate that he kept a library of more than 1,500 books on everything from law and gardening to Sir Walter Scott and Thomas Jefferson. Notice how the shelves are not nailed in place. They slide into grooves and can be adjusted up and down.

Main Floor: Smoking Room

As a post-dinner ritual, men could either remain at table, or if the group was small, gather in the cozy smoking room for a cigar. Only men smoked, not women, and gentlemen smoked cigars, not cigarettes or pipes. Cigarettes had not yet become common and lower-class men smoked pipes. Caps and jackets were provided to cover the hair and clothes, reducing tobacco smells otherwise carried afterward into the drawing room where the ladies were gathered.

Main Floor: Dining Room

This is the largest room in the house. Three floor-to-ceiling windows also open as doors onto the back lawn leading to the lip of Burlington Heights. In 1860, Queen Victoria's eldest son, Prince Albert Edward, dined here with Governor General Edmund Walker Head and the Duke of Newcastle, Henry Pelham-Clinton, Britain's secretary of state for the colonies. Among other duties, the nineteen-year-old prince was in town to open the Hamilton Waterworks, now the Museum of Steam and Technology.

One hundred and forty-nine years later, in 2009, Prince Charles and his wife, Camilla, Duchess of Cornwall, entered the room. Senior curator Heaman guided them to the full-length windows. He pointed to a pillar immediately outside, then at a photo in his hand showing the 1860 lunch guests standing next to the same pillar. Speaking to Charles, he said, "Your great-great-grandfather [Prince Albert Edward] is here," and speaking to Camilla, he said, "Your great-great-great-grandfather is here." Addressing them both, he said, "Your ancestors met in this room in 1860 — yours was a match made in Hamilton."

An 1861 inventory of Dundurn's contents included the notation, "dinner set double," meaning a double dinner set of twenty-four place settings. Accordingly, curators have installed a table that can be extended with leaves to twenty-four place settings. Formal dinners at

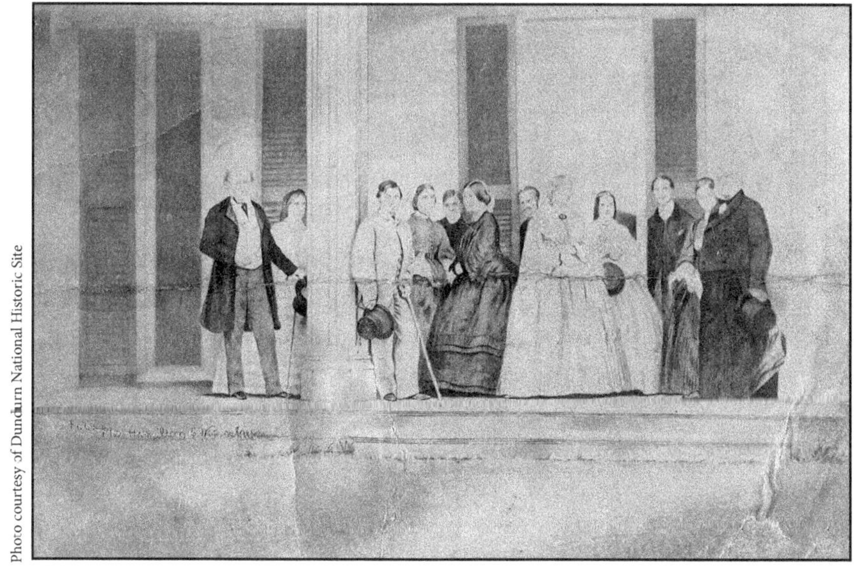

Photo courtesy of Dundurn National Historic Site

Nineteen-year-old Prince Albert Edward, Queen Victoria's eldest son, stands cane and hat in hand next to a pillar outside Dundurn Castle's dining room during a lunch visit in 1860. His host, Sir Allan, stands at the far right.

Dundurn could run as long as five to six hours, with three to four courses of three to four dishes each.

The centrepiece silver candelabra, or epergne, features three female figures representing Justice, Peace, and Truth. Anthony Adamson, who oversaw Dundurn's 1967 restoration, discovered it in a Toronto antique shop. Although the original inscriptions are missing, he recognized it as almost certainly the gift that the Mechanics Institute of Hamilton presented to MacNab in 1855 as part of a twenty-two-piece dinner service on his silver anniversary as their parliamentarian. Adamson said its provenance can never be known for sure. "Presented to Colonel the Honourable Sir Allan Napier MacNab, Prime Minister of Canada," the original inscription read, "as an acknowledgement of his valuable services ... [and] for the important aid which he has rendered in the construction of the Great Western Railway, which has conferred the most important and lasting benefits — moral, physical and political — upon Hamilton and upon Canada, 1855." The figure "Peace" held a palm leaf inscribed "G.W.R.," meaning "Great Western Railway."

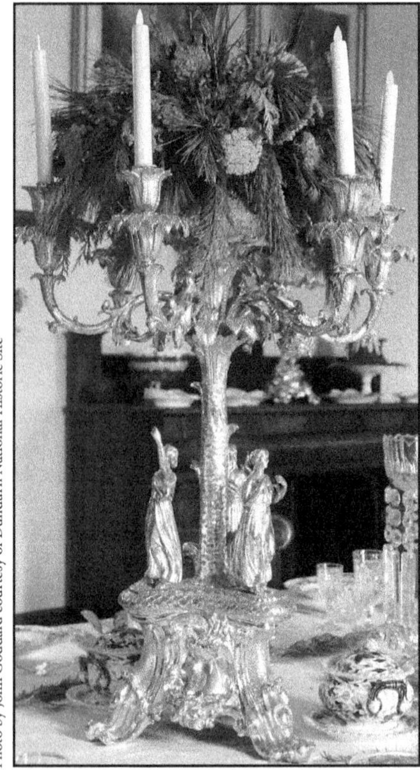

Photo by John Goddard courtesy of Dundurn National Historic Site

The centrepiece silver candelabra, or epergne, features three female figures representing Justice, Peace, and Truth. It is almost certainly the gift from the Mechanics Institute of Hamilton on MacNab's silver anniversary as their parliamentarian in 1855.

At either end of the room built-in sideboards original to the home would have displayed desserts during dinner. A third, free-standing sideboard bears the MacNab family crest reading, "Dreadnought Gun Eagal," roughly translated as "No Fear." The piece is believed to have belonged to Sir Allan's cousin and clan chieftain, Archibald MacNab.

Three family portraits grace the walls. One shows Sir Allan's mother-in-law, Sophia Stuart, the mother of his second wife, Mary, fashionably wreathed in a lace headdress and looking stern. Nobody smiled for portraits then. She lived in Toronto, a seven-and-half-hour carriage ride away, and died at Dundurn on March 30, 1837. The portrait opposite is of Lady Mary MacNab, appearing bemused but delicate. She died of a lung disease in 1846 when her two daughters, Sophia and Minnie, were thirteen and eleven respectively. "A firm and competent manager of the household," one obituary said of her, "a generous and devoted worker among the poor of the town, and an astute adviser on political questions." On the same wall a young Sir Allan is portrayed looking handsome and successful, but with a slightly quizzical expression that conveys none of his burning ambition.

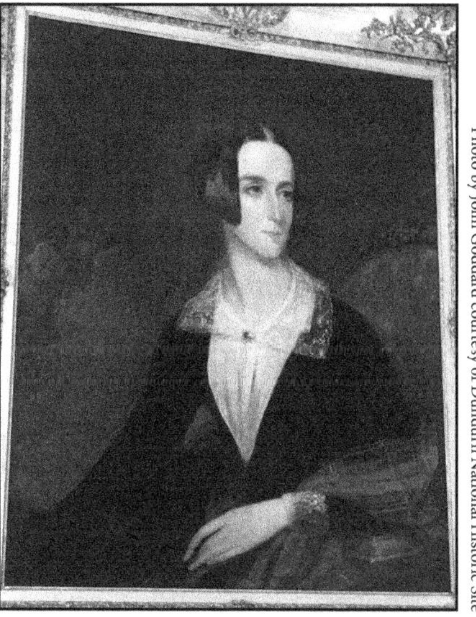

Photo by John Goddard courtesy of Dundurn National Historic Site

"A generous and devoted worker among the poor of the town," an obituary writer said of Lady Mary MacNab, who died at thirty-four in 1846. Her portrait in the large dining room depicts her as bemused but delicate.

Main Floor: Butler's Bedroom

As the highest-ranking member of the household staff, Sir Allan's long-time butler, Wellington, was thought to have his own quarters on the main floor. Curators have assigned him this room, with a view of the bay. Wellington managed the other servants, ensured the security of the home, brewed the beer, took charge of serving and presenting meals, and assisted Sir Allan in getting dressed. Notice the wide, painted, wooden floorboards, hallmark of a servant's area as opposed to a family area. The stove displayed here, made by "D. Moore & Co. Hamilton, C.W.," used coal, which burned hotter than wood and lasted longer.

Main Floor: Butler's Pantry

Wellington used this room off the dining room as his staging area for meals. The wooden cabinet houses a dumb waiter to the basement. At formal dinners he would transfer food to fine china, garnish the dishes, and bring them to the table. Afterward he would wash the china and store it on the shelves lining the walls, although at one time the room included cupboards for the dishes, not just shelves. High on the far wall, two bells connect to a pull at the front door and to a cook's pull to signal that the dumb waiter was heading up with food. The decorative ceramic container with the spigot is an 1830 water purifier from Manchester, England, a reminder of the poor quality of the colony's well water. Privies would pollute the groundwater, which would then transmit diseases such as cholera and typhoid fever. Layers of minerals, charcoal, and ceramic in the container could filter debris and other impurities but usually proved no match for micro-organisms.

Second Floor: Nursery

At this point of the tour the interpreter usually leads visitors up the servants' stairs, also used by the MacNab children. The first stop is the former nursery with two adjoining children's bedrooms. In 1835, when the family moved into Dundurn, Sophia was three, Minnie one. They were raised by a nanny. They likely ate in this room and were likely visited here by their parents. When they got older, they shared the space as a sitting room. The house is presented as it was in 1855 when Sophia was twenty-three and Minnie was twenty-one.

Second Floor: Guest Bedroom

A small corridor leads to a bedroom possibly once used by Anne Jane, Sir Allan's eldest daughter and only surviving child from his first marriage. By 1855, she had married and moved with her husband to the West Indies.

Second Floor: School Room

This tiny room at the back of the house served as a study where tutors taught Sophia and Minnie as children. The girls had two instructors. A Mr. Thompson taught such subjects as reading, writing, arithmetic, and botany. He lived on-site at Battery Lodge, now the Military Museum. Charles Ambrose, the organist at Christ's (Anglican) Church where Sir Allan worshipped, taught piano.

Second Floor: Aunt Sophia's Three-Room Suite

Sophia MacNab figures prominently in the Dundurn story. She was twice Sir Allan's sister-in-law, being Lady Mary's younger sister as well as the widow of Sir Allan's younger brother, David. Two brothers married two sisters. Sir Allan and Lady Mary wed in 1831, Sophia and David in 1838. When David died in 1840, Sophia moved into Dundurn permanently. She cared for Lady Mary until her death in 1846 and afterward helped Sir Allan run his household and escorted him to social events.

For twenty-two years, until Sir Allan's death in 1862, Sophia — aunt to Sir Allan's two youngest girls — lived at Dundurn. The question is: which rooms were hers? For a long time the museum designated two main-floor rooms as her sitting room and bedroom. In 2015, however, new evidence led curators to restore three rooms above the dining room as her sitting room, bedroom, and washroom/dressing room.

In the bedroom, curators have placed a portrait of Jesus above a prayer bench or prie-dieu, alluding to Aunt Sophia's strict Roman Catholicism. Sir Allan and Lady Mary agreed to raise their daughters as Catholic and sons as Anglican, although they had no sons. Sir Allan's first wife, Elizabeth, was mother to their son Robert, who died at eleven in a hunting accident.

Second Floor: Sick Room

Lady Mary is thought to have shared Sir Allan's bedroom, but in the 1840s she fell mortally ill with a lung disease. In a Victorian home such a patient would take a sick room, usually facing north to avoid the hot afternoon sun, as this room does. The metal container with the long wooden handle leaning against the fireplace is a bed warmer. Hot embers from the fireplace would be transferred to the container, and a servant would rub the bed vigorously between the sheets to warm it. On the table sits a medicine chest that typically contained remedies laced with such narcotics as cocaine, laudanum, and opium. A particularly well-crafted version of today's hospital tray allowed a patient to eat in bed, drink tea, and read comfortably. Lady

Mary's doctors recommended a diet of pigeon, oysters, egg yolks, and beer. Two doctors attended her. Dr. John King of Toronto was married to a cousin. The local doctor, James Hamilton, was married to one of her nieces. "Dr. Hamilton came, and just saw Mamma," Sophia writes in her journal, "but said he would stay all night, so that he could see Mamma in the morning."

Second Floor: Boudoir

Off the sick room, with a view of Burlington Bay, Lady Mary had the use of a second room in which to read, write, and — she was a practising Roman Catholic — pray. "Dear Mama took the last sacrament," daughter Sophia writes in her entry of May 7, 1846. "During the whole ceremony poor dear Mama did not seem the least agitated. But you could see her lips moving repeating the prayers after the vicar." She died the next day.

Second Floor: Sir Allan's Master Bedroom and Dressing Room

Three steps at one end of the upper hall lead to Sir Allan's chambers, including a room that he used for shaving and dressing. His bedroom is the home's largest, with windows on three sides looking out to Battery Lodge, the kitchen garden, and Burlington Bay. On the wall hangs a portrait of Sir Allan's father, also named Allan. The portrait by the door shows Sir Allan's daughter Sophia in adulthood, sketched by her husband, Viscount Bury.

Outside Sir Allan's bedroom door in the hallway, curators have hung two works by the Bavaria-born artist Benjamin Zobel (1762–1831), who decorated dinner tables at Windsor Castle for King George III. Working in coloured sand, marble dust, powdered glass, and bread crumbs, Zobel created elaborate designs on the royal tablecloths for formal dinners, and in his spare time composed artworks with sand instead of paints. He depicted battle scenes and landscapes and particularly liked farm animals such as these contented-looking pigs.

Second Floor: Upper Hall

Directly above the front entrance hall, with walls also finished in faux marble, the upper hall served as an informal family area for card games and piano playing. "[Mother] asked me to go & play on the Piano for her," Sophia writes in her journal, "as she said 'don't you know music soothes.'"

The rosewood piano on display was made in Hamilton by C.L. Thomas and Co., which operated from 1856 to 1893. At one end of the room hangs a portrait believed to be of Sir Allan as a young man. The French windows open as doors to a long, narrow balcony from which Prince Charles and Camilla, Duchess of Cornwall, waved to spectators during their 2009 visit.

Grand Staircase

Now is the chance to descend to the front entrance hall using what curators call the "flying" or "floating" staircase of black walnut, one of Dundurn's signature features and pictured on the cover of this book. Stylishly fastened only at the top and bottom, it proved structurally sound, although a supporting pole has since been added.

Main Floor: Small Drawing Room and Small Dining Room

A furniture inventory from 1861 refers to a "small drawing room" and "small dining room" to distinguish them from the main drawing room and main dining room. For years the museum presented these two main-floor rooms as Aunt Sophia's sitting room and bedroom. In 2016, her sitting room was restored as the informal family drawing room. Plans also exist to re-create the small dining room. In her diary, daughter Sophia writes of sewing and doing her homework in the dining room, likely meaning the smaller one. "I then sat in Mamma's room sewing until bed time except just between light & dark when they had no candles," she writes in March 1846, "so I came down to the dining [room] and got a candle and sewed there until tea was ready."

Main Floor: Bathroom and Water Closet

In 1847, Sir Allan installed a technologically advanced bathroom for himself with gaslights, cold running water from cisterns on the roof, and a particularly beautiful china sink for hand washing and shaving. Heated water could be added. To drain the tub Sir Allan would simply pull a plug. The "Bramah Valve flushing water closet" next door, named after the English inventor of the flush toilet, features a bench seat and a decorated blue china bowl. Pulling a handle up causes water from a tank in the attic to flush the bowl into a drainage system. MacNab's indoor toilet would have been one of the first in Upper Canada.

Cellar

With a few exceptions, such as the butler, Wellington, house servants generally worked below stairs. Sir Allan would have employed at least ten servants to wash laundry, polish boots, pump water, and prepare meals. Dundurn's working conditions were considered relatively good for the time. Running water, gas lighting, and drains could be found even in the cellar. A dumb waiter ran from the kitchen to the butler's pantry, saving servants from running up and down stairs. Windows let in abundant natural light.

Cellar: Ice Pit and Dairy

Sir Allan incorporated a few pre-existing features on the property into Dundurn, among them a brick-lined pit four metres deep that the original owner, Richard Beasley, had dug for storing ice. In midwinter, men with sleds and horses cut blocks of ice from the bay and lowered them — insulated by sawdust — into the pit. The ice lasted all summer. The ice also kept the room next door cool enough to be used as a refrigeration space for cheese, milk, cream, and meat that had not yet been cured.

Cellar: Tunnel and Laundry Room

The British Army, which used the Dundurn site as its main Upper Canada base in 1813, built an arched, brick-lined tunnel to its underground gunpowder magazine. Sir Allan incorporated the structure into his cellar. Off it is a spacious laundry with a boiler, scrub sinks, and a wringer. A large table served as an ironing board. Try lifting the largest flatiron. It weighs twenty-four pounds, or more than ten kilograms. Irons displayed on the upper shelves took care of ribbons, collars, and cuffs.

Cellar: Scullery

The scullery maid, who assisted the kitchen maid and cook, ranked as the youngest and poorest-paid female servant of the house. She could be as young as twelve and would rise before dawn to light fires throughout the house. In this room she washed dishes, pots, and pans. The scullery is well equipped. It has its own hand pump for dishwater, a fireplace, a high ceiling, a window, and a wooden floor instead of a brick one, which could be hard on the back.

Cellar: Brewery

Off the scullery a small room served as a brewery where Wellington brewed ale for the household. Ale of higher alcohol content went to the family and guests. That of lower alcohol content, or "small beer," made from reused mash, went to the servants. The brewing process killed bacteria, making beer a safer and healthier drink than water. "On returning we found Mamma much better than we left her," Sophia writes in her diary on January 25, 1846, "and busily employed eating her lunch which consisted of nine Oysters and half a tumbler of beer."

Cellar: Workroom

A central corridor leads past a series of small rooms: a wine cellar; a room for maintaining candles and lamps; a wet larder for pickles and preserves; and a trunk room for storing travelling trunks, chests, and cases. Victorians did not pack lightly. At the end of the hall is an all-purpose workroom where servants could pluck chickens, wash vegetables, or heat water for bathing. A vaulted fireproof chamber off the room served as a locked storage area for valuable documents such as land deeds, receipts, and legal briefs. Only Sir Allan and the butler had keys. Sir Allan's Dundurn never had a fire.

Cellar: Servants' Hall

Directly under the drawing room, servants enjoyed a kind of hand-me-down luxury in their own dining hall. It had big windows, gas lighting, a painted pine floor, and wallpaper on the walls. Here the staff ate three times a day, usually root vegetables, inexpensive cuts of meat, and other locally available products. Meals were served in courses, with diners expected to observe proper table manners and etiquette, reflecting the refinement of the household above. Female servants, other than the cook, shared the two bedrooms off the kitchen. Men and boys slept in the coach house.

Cellar: Kitchen and Cook's Bedroom

A bright, narrow hallway leads past a dry larder used for storing such expensive imported items as tea, coffee, spices, and tall, distinctive cones of sugar — grown on plantations in India or the Caribbean and refined in England. The cook kept the room locked and maintained a logbook tracking quantities of each item. The MacNabs used expensive white sugar as a sweetener; the servants settled for honey and maple syrup.

Farther along comes the cook's bedroom. Male cooks tended to work at hotels and inns, females in domestic service. In her diary, Sophia refers to the cook as "Old Anne" and as "Brolanac." She would have been the top-ranked female servant, with her own bedroom off the warm kitchen. She oversaw the preparation of seven meals a day, four for the MacNabs, including afternoon tea, and three for the servants. She could read and write. She ordered supplies, planned dinner parties, trained new servants, and oversaw pickling and preserving.

Dundurn Castle tours usually conclude in the kitchen, a large, bright room, usually with treats for visitors such as shortbread, pickles, and juices. Visitors are also invited to try the hand pump. The cooking range dates to 1869, a relatively modern piece of equipment that uses the entire stove surface. Meat was still cooked rotisserie style at the open hearth. High on one wall runs a line of service bells, activated in different parts of the house by a "bell pull," actually a crank, which tugged on a wire connected to the bell. Each has a different sound, which servants memorized to know which room to attend. Gas lighting meant that the Dundurn kitchen was better lit at night than most dining rooms in the homes of Hamilton's doctors and lawyers, who in 1855 were just beginning to afford the technology.

Grounds and Walkways

Dundurn was more than a house. It was a country estate with outbuildings, walking paths, orchards, and a vegetable garden called a "kitchen garden." To the west of the house, used now as a visitor centre and gift shop, stand the former coach house and stables, handsomely built of rough stone in 1873 by a later owner, Senator Donald McInnes. The structure opposite with the tall roof is called a dovecote, or pigeon house, with forty-eight dormered flight holes to accommodate the birds for their eggs, meat, and fertilizing guano.

To the east of the house at the cliff edge stands the two-storey octagonal Cockpit. Sir Allan is said to have enjoyed cockfighting, but whether he actually held cockfights in the building cannot be verified. It is used now

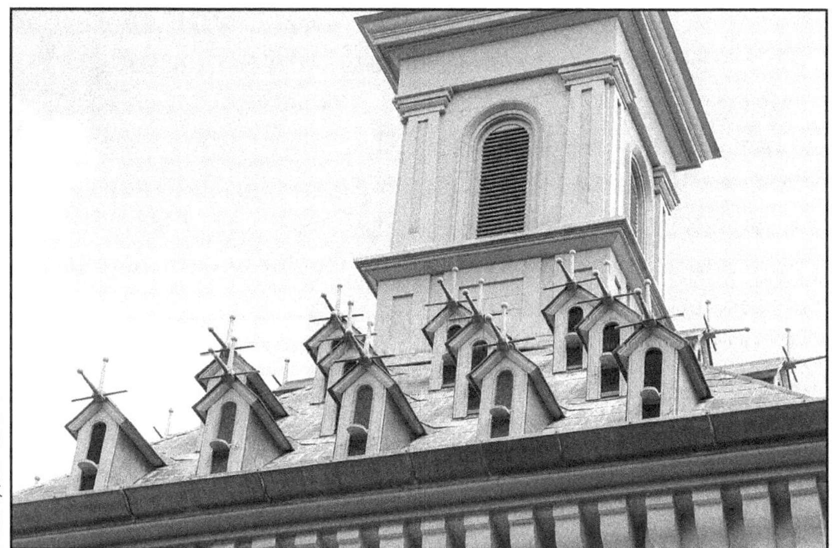

Photo by John Goddard

Sir Allan raised pigeons opposite the stables in a pigeon house, or dovecote. In her diary, daughter Sophia spells pigeon as Pygion. *"She got her dinner which consisted of a Pygion (this is Mamma's usual diet at one oclock every day) and a tumbler of beer."*

as a wedding chapel. The patch of land once used as the family graveyard, "Inchbuie," was sold in the late 1800s and the bodies reinterred separately. Sir Allan was reburied at Holy Sepulchre Cemetery in Burlington.

Kitchen Garden

The kitchen garden east of the house grew vegetables for the MacNab household. The current version replicates Sir Allan's original. It covers almost one hectare, including a potting shed as well as a tiny pond that allows water pumped from the cold ground to warm before going to the plants. Museum staff members in period costume and using period hand tools grow what Sir Allan's gardener, William Reid, and his staff grew in the mid-1800s. They tend rows of potatoes, tomatoes, eggplants, and sweet peppers. They water lettuce and beans. They nurture such root vegetables as carrots, turnips, onions, radishes, and leeks, and raise rhubarb and Swiss chard. The gardeners employ the same nineteenth-century techniques as Reed did to extend the growing season, using brick boxes and windows in early May to create a type of greenhouse environment.

Such technology was not the latest even in MacNab's time, as Sophia discovered in the summer of 1846. After her mother died, the family took a trip to Quebec City. One day they visited Spencer Wood, the estate of wood merchant Henry Atkinson, who with his gardener, Peter Lowe, had turned the grounds into one of the best-known showcase gardens in North America. The house has since burned down, but the grounds endure as Parc du Bois-de-Coulonge, just south of the Plains of Abraham.

"The great beauty of Spencer Wood consists in the Garden Hot House Green House Conservatory," Sophia writes in her diary on June 13, 1846. "The hot beds are on an improved plan not like our common hot beds but heated with tanks of hot water. There is a little fig tree which bears fruit. The gardener said they would be ripe in three weeks."

Produce from Dundurn's garden goes to the museum kitchen where cooks make jams, pickles, and other types of preserves and serve them to visitors year-round. The surplus goes to people visiting the garden itself and to local charities. During the summer, free guided tours are offered on Sundays.

Hamilton Military Museum (Battery Lodge)

Up the hill from Dundurn Castle, near York Boulevard, stands Battery Lodge, originally Sir Allan's gatehouse. In her diary, Sophia says that her father invited her teacher, Mr. Thompson, to live there. "Papa asked him if he would like to live in the Lodge," the girl writes in 1846. "We went up after lessons to show it to him. He was very much pleased with it. There is just himself and a girl who is a distant relative of his wife who lives with him."

The building functions now as the Hamilton Military Museum, dedicated mostly to the War of 1812, but also the 1899–1902 Boer War and the First World War. From 1813 to 1815, Dundurn's grounds, known as Burlington Heights, served as the main British garrison for Upper Canada, home to men, women, and children connected to the British Army and its First Nations allies. Entry to the museum is included with admission to Dundurn Castle, and a separate ticket is issued for use anytime.

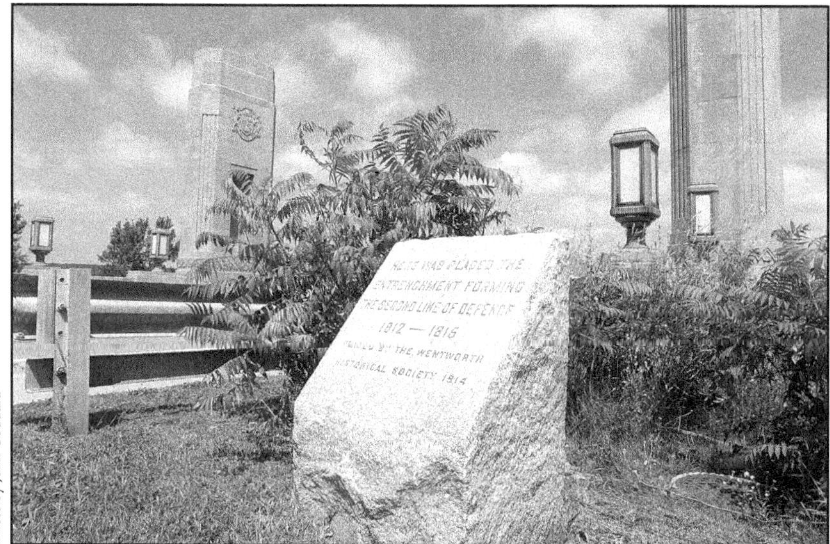

Photo by John Goddard

A stone marker delineates the limit of War of 1812 defensive earthworks that the British Army built at the western end of Burlington Heights next to today's High Level Bridge. The British commandeered the land in 1813 as their army headquarters.

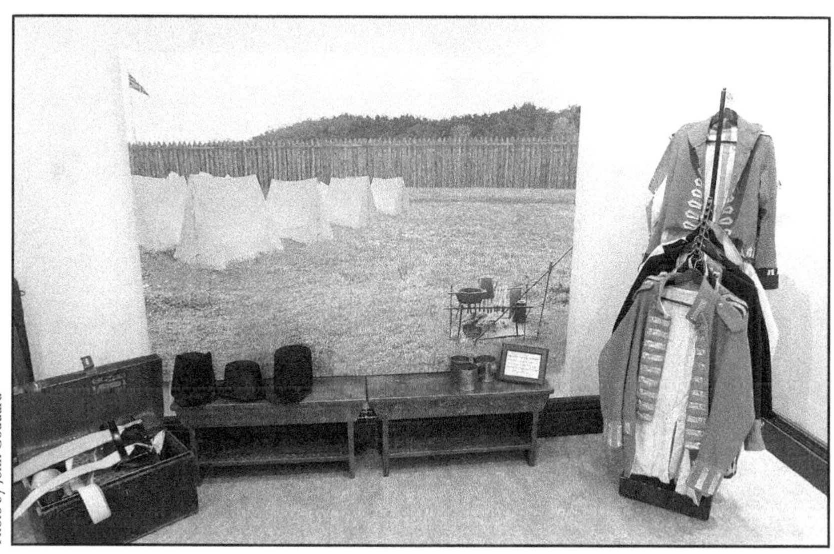

Photo by John Goddard

Exhibitions at the Military Museum typically include interactive portions. In the 2015 show Blood Ties to a Gentle Landscape*, visitors could dress up as British War of 1812 officers.*

Why Go?

Whitehern, rare for museums, came to the City of Hamilton complete with three generations' worth of family possessions — everything from antique furniture bought new in New York and Boston to paintings, photographs, diaries, letters, nail scissors, bobby pins, and the legs of broken toys. In life the family remained discreet, hiding their secrets. In death they reveal all. Three main characters stand out. First-generation patriarch Dr. Calvin McQuesten made a fortune with the first iron foundry in what was to become "Steel City." Second-generation matriarch Mary McQuesten endured financial ruin to raise six children and restore the family to social respectability. Third-generation prodigy Tom McQuesten ascended to high political office to create lasting highway infrastructure and beautification works for Hamilton and Ontario.

Address

41 Jackson Street West, behind the old courthouse and next to the back of City Hall.

Getting There by Public Transit

Getting to Whitehern could not be easier. It stands two blocks west of the Hamilton GO Centre and three blocks from the city's main King-and-James intersection.

WHITEHERN HISTORIC HOUSE AND GARDEN

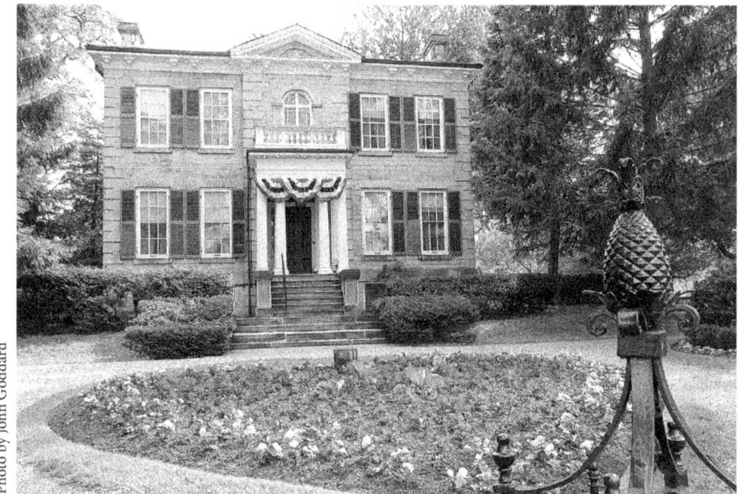

Photo by John Goddard

An iron gate and a formal heart-shaped flowerbed welcome the visitor to the front door of the Whitehern urban estate. Dr. Calvin McQuesten grew rich on a par with Sir Allan MacNab of Dundurn, but lived far more modestly.

DAYS OF OUR LIVES: THE MCQUESTENS OF WHITEHERN

Only one family ever lived at Whitehern. Their name was McQuesten, a family of Scottish origin by way of the United States. For 116 years — from 1852 to 1968 — three generations successively occupied the house until the last elderly family member bequeathed it to the city as a museum. The old gentleman also left the family furniture, much of it dating to the mid-1800s, as well as three generations' worth of books, clothes, artwork, dishes, carpets, toiletries, gardening tools, sports equipment, and more than ten thousand pages of assiduously preserved family letters dating as far back as 1819.

The McQuestens contributed to Hamilton in ways that make their story inseparable from the city's. Family patriarch Dr. Calvin McQuesten thrived as one of the region's wealthiest manufacturers. He helped establish the first iron foundry in what was to become "Steel City," one of Canada's foremost industrial centres. His grandson Thomas rose to become one of Ontario's most powerful politicians. He helped to beautify and economically improve the entire Golden Horseshoe of western Lake Ontario and helped transform Hamilton from a factory town into a city with a university, a renowned botanical garden, and more parks and recreational spaces at the time than any other city in Canada.

The McQuestens were also exceptionally neurotic. Their lives unfolded like a soap opera. A hateful stepmother sent the children to boarding school. A needy matriarch sabotaged her children's romances. For much of the time the McQuestens led tragic, dysfunctional lives punctuated by mental breakdown, premature death, religious zealotry, and drug and alcohol addiction. It is one of Whitehern's great ironies that a family who in life discreetly kept up appearances, who presented a rosy front to the public, afterward let their pile of hoarded correspondence expose their most intimate failings for all to see.

In three generations the McQuestens went from riches, to near rags, to a state of recovered respectability. Their turbulent years advanced in four distinct phases, characterized by four succeeding heads of the Whitehern household.

Dr. Calvin McQuesten: Industrialist, Financier, Philanthropist, 1801–1885

Dr. Calvin grew wealthy producing Canada's first threshing machines and cooking stoves in what was to become one of the country's most important industrial centres of the twentieth century. As gifted as he was in industry, however, Whitehern's founder proved unlucky in love.

He was born in 1801 in New Hampshire, a third-generation New Englander. As a young man, he taught school for a couple of years, then studied medicine and became a doctor in Brockport, New York, near Rochester. In 1834, his cousin, John Fisher, settled across the border in Hamilton to start a factory. Dr. Calvin put up $1,500 and, with two other partners, the cousins established an iron foundry called McQuesten & Co. Gradually, Dr. Calvin got more involved. He went on sales trips for the firm, bought raw materials and equipment from U.S. suppliers, and in 1939 quit his medical practice to move to Hamilton as foundry manager.

He made a fortune. He showed a head for business and helped build the company into what would later evolve into the Sawyer and Massey Company and eventually the giant Massey Ferguson farm equipment manufacturer. He got rich on a par with Sir Allan Napier MacNab, who lived across town in his forty-room Dundurn Castle. By comparison, Dr. Calvin's tastes proved modest. In 1852, he settled for an elegant new home on a spacious urban property. Five years later, at fifty-six, he liquidated his business holdings, worth $500,000, and reinvested in banks, real estate, and various industrial enterprises. As a philanthropist, he helped to finance the Wesleyan Female College and several Presbyterian churches, including the nearby

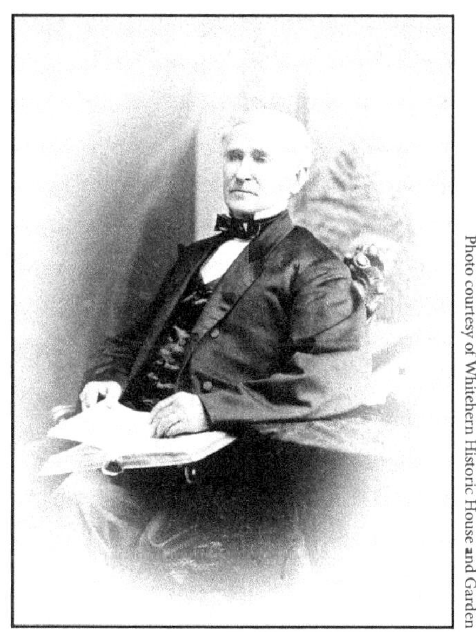

Photo courtesy of Whitehern Historic House and Garden

Dr. Calvin McQuesten co-owned and managed the first iron foundry in the town that was to become "Steel City." As gifted as he was in industry, however, Whitehern's patriarch proved unlucky in love.

MacNab Street Presbyterian Church, which his family attended for more than a century.

Dr. Calvin also married three times — twice tragically and once disastrously. In 1831, while still at Brockport, he married Margarette Lerned (pronounced *LEARN-ed*). The couple lost their first child in infancy, and ten years into the marriage Margarette died giving birth to their third child, who also died.

Heartbroken but pragmatic, as a single father of a young boy, Dr. Calvin proposed marriage to a friend of a friend, Estimate "Ester" Baldwin. Although they scarcely knew each other on their wedding day in 1844, they developed a caring relationship. "Yes, my dear wife, I do feel happy in the thought that our views are so similar," he wrote to her in 1847, "our tender and affectionate regard for each other resting on the solid foundation of true Christian principle."

Misfortune, however, struck again. In 1851, after seven years of marriage, Ester died of tuberculosis. Dr. Calvin was left with three boys — one from his first marriage, two from his second — and in 1853 he married for the third time. Again on the recommendation of friends, he married a Boston woman, Elizabeth Fuller, whom he barely knew, and moved with her and the boys into Whitehern, looking for a fresh start.

"She is amiable, talented, pious, mild and lovely in disposition as in her looks and deportment," an acquaintance of the bride told Dr. Calvin in congratulations. Over time, however, Elizabeth revealed a darker side. Some people came to know her as "cold" and "distant." Others encountered her foul temper. Her face when angry gives "an idea of Hell," Dr. Calvin said after getting to know her. When his eldest son, Calvin, talked briefly of moving back home, the father advised: "It would perfectly ruin you to be brought daily in contact with such a woman." Another son, Isaac, once said: "Threaten her, & she is ugly. Treat her kindly, & she is ugly. Use a middle course, & her native ugliness comes out." In later years family members referred to her irreverently as "the O.L.," meaning "the Old Lady."

Elizabeth could never be called maternal. From day one she instructed the boys to address her as "Mrs. McQuesten," never as "Mother." When she arrived, the boys were sixteen, six, and four years old, and within a year the youngest, David, was dead. He perished in a fire under circumstances not clearly recorded. Afterward, the two others were sent to boarding school. The elder boy, Calvin, went to the United States where he became a doctor, never to return. His younger half-brother, Isaac, departed for a private school in nearby Galt, now part of Cambridge.

Elizabeth took up shopping. She shopped in New York City, Philadelphia, Boston, and sometimes parts of Europe, spending her husband's money on clothes and high-end furnishings. Money tensions permeated the marriage. "Man Wants Little, Nor That Little Long," Dr. Calvin wrote poetically as a young man, the title of an essay he wrote about the corrupting power of luxury. Elizabeth held the opposite view. She wanted much and for as long as possible. Dr. Calvin paid $3,200 for the house. Elizabeth spent $2,000 decorating the drawing room alone. "I did hope to see you at home the last of this week," she wrote to her husband from Boston during their second year of marriage, "but it would be a pity not to spend a little more money, since I [be]came so rich; so I must spend a few days here in order to lighten my purse."

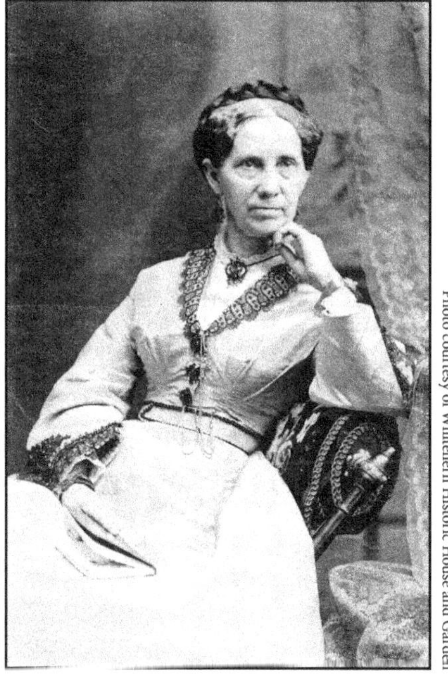

Photo courtesy of Whitehern Historic House and Garden

"She is amiable, talented, pious, mild and lovely," a friend once said of the former Elizabeth Fuller, Dr. Calvin's third wife. Stepson Isaac expressed a darker view: "Threaten her, & she is ugly. Treat her kindly, & she is ugly. Use a middle course, & her native ugliness comes out."

At some point Elizabeth discovered that her husband planned to divide his estate, when he died, between her and his two sons. She wanted everything. She badmouthed the boys, telling Dr. Calvin they were "unworthy of his affection," then tried to blackmail him, saying she would publicly expose the boys' bad behaviour, which she never specified. She nagged her husband to rewrite his will to the point where he complained that she "frequently and at short intervals harassed [him] on the subject." Fed up, he finally did rewrite it, allotting his sons the bulk of the estate and his wife a small annuity. When he died at the age of eighty-four in 1885, Elizabeth left for Virginia never to be seen again. As much as everybody despised her, however, nobody redecorated the house. To this day, much of Whitehern — including the parlour into which she poured so much money — remains faithful to her taste and style.

Isaac McQuesten: Lawyer, 1847–1888

By the time of Dr. Calvin's death, the elder half-brother, also named Calvin, had established himself as a doctor in Manhattan's Upper East Side. The family seat devolved to the younger half-brother, Isaac, although his stewardship was to prove short-lived. Isaac suffered a tormented inner life. As a child, he had endured loss and abandonment. When he was four, his mother died of tuberculosis. When he was seven, his younger brother died in a fire. When his loveless stepmother appeared on the scene, he must have sensed he was unwanted, and his father proved either unwilling or unable to keep the two boys at home.

Isaac left for the nationally renowned but forbidding Galt Grammar School run by William Tassie, described by historian J. Donald Wilson as "an 'old school' educator" — famous for being "aloof" and "a strict disciplinarian." Afterward the boy attended Upper Canada College and later the University of Toronto, where he studied law and threw himself into a high-spirited social life. "A mighty mingler," one friend called him at the time, a "drinker of strong drink."

While studying in Toronto, Isaac also met Mary Baker. She abhorred strong drink, but he hid his habit from her and she agreed to marry him. When she discovered the truth, she broke off the engagement, but he persuaded her that he had quit, and in 1873 they married and moved to Hamilton. Isaac joined a law practice and bought a townhouse on Bold Street around the corner from Whitehern. Within twelve years he and Mary had six children. A seventh died before the age of two. Isaac joined the Liberal Party, served on the local board of education, got elected to the University of Toronto senate, became a director on several boards and a trustee of his church, and as heir to a massive fortune generally assumed his place at the upper echelons of Hamilton society.

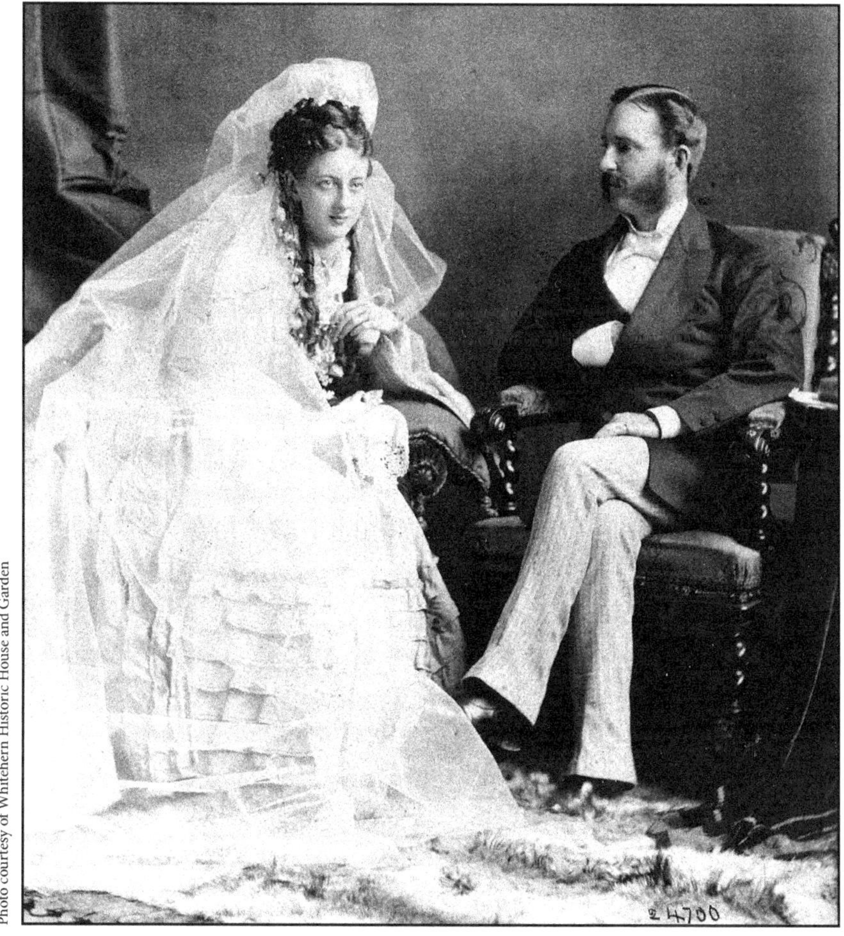

Photo courtesy of Whitehern Historic House and Garden

Mary and Isaac on their wedding day in 1873 appear poised to take their place in Hamilton society. He had graduated in law, stood to inherit his father's industrial fortune, and so far had managed to keep his drinking a secret.

On his father's death in 1885, Isaac moved with his family into Whitehern. He was thirty-seven years old. Publicly he looked to be doing well; privately his life was a mess. He was an alcoholic. He also suffered from depression and insomnia, and complained of symptoms associated with what later came to be called "manic depression" or "bipolar disorder." He described his condition to his brother as "an unhealthy excitement" followed by "sluggishness." His wife called it a "nervous disease." Doctors at the time treated such disorders with Chlorodyne and paregoric, both addictive opiate-based narcotics, or with calomel, a toxic mercury-based drug that could lead to central nervous system damage and personality changes. Isaac developed an addiction to such drugs. He experienced what he called "one long continuous want or craving" for "stimulants." Several times he checked himself into the Homewood Retreat for alcohol and drug addiction in Guelph for treatment by Canada's first addiction specialist, Dr. Stephen Lett.

As he struggled psychologically, Isaac also squandered his inheritance. Years before his father's death he took charge of managing the family capital and through bad investments proceeded to throw good money after bad. He lost money on a new type of railway coupler, on a device for sharpening band saws, on a stoking mechanism for boilers, and on an ambitious five-year plan to establish a knitting mill in nearby Hespeler, now part of Cambridge. No setback or delay could diminish his hopes for windfall profits until one after another the projects collapsed and he lost almost everything. He lost his own inheritance, he lost his brother Calvin's inheritance, and when his wife's father died leaving another small fortune Isaac lost that, too.

As his life spun out of control, Isaac wallowed in self-loathing. From the Homewood Retreat he wrote that the act of taking stock of his life "produced something very near despair." Not long afterward at Whitehern, at around midnight on March 6, 1888, Mary discovered him in the library "lying in an insensible condition," as the *Hamilton Spectator* put it. Deliberately or otherwise — suicide was never ruled out — he overdosed on a sleeping potion meant to treat insomnia. Family members carried him upstairs to bed where he died the next morning at the age of forty.

Mary Baker McQuesten ("Mother"): Single Parent of Six, 1849–1934

Mary watched as the educational, legal, and political elite turned out for her husband's funeral at MacNab Street Presbyterian Church. In the crowd could be seen the principal of Upper Canada College, the vice-chancellor of the University of Toronto, and John Morison Gibson, Hamilton's most prominent Liberal — a provincial cabinet minister at the time and later Ontario's lieutenant governor. Mary took social standing seriously. Despite being financially ruined, she would continue to view herself as somehow aristocratic and would seek for the rest of her life, consciously and unconsciously, to restore the McQuesten name.

She grew up as an only child. Her father was Thomas Baker, an Englishman who ran away to sea at eleven to serve in the Napoleonic Wars and later in the War of 1812 on Lake Ontario aboard the HMS *St. Lawrence*. At twenty-one he quit the Royal Navy to become a Congregational Church minister. He married, had eight children, and when his wife died he remarried within the year. By then his children were grown. Mary was born in Brantford, Ontario, in 1849, when he was fifty-three and his wife, Mary Jane, was forty.

In his daughter Mary, Reverend Baker saw his last chance to mould a child into what he considered to be a proper Christian. His other children had proved a disappointment to him. They had not lived up to his exacting military and religious standards. One daughter, who had married against his wishes, asked to see him as she was dying of complications from childbirth. He refused. "We must be apart from each other," he wrote

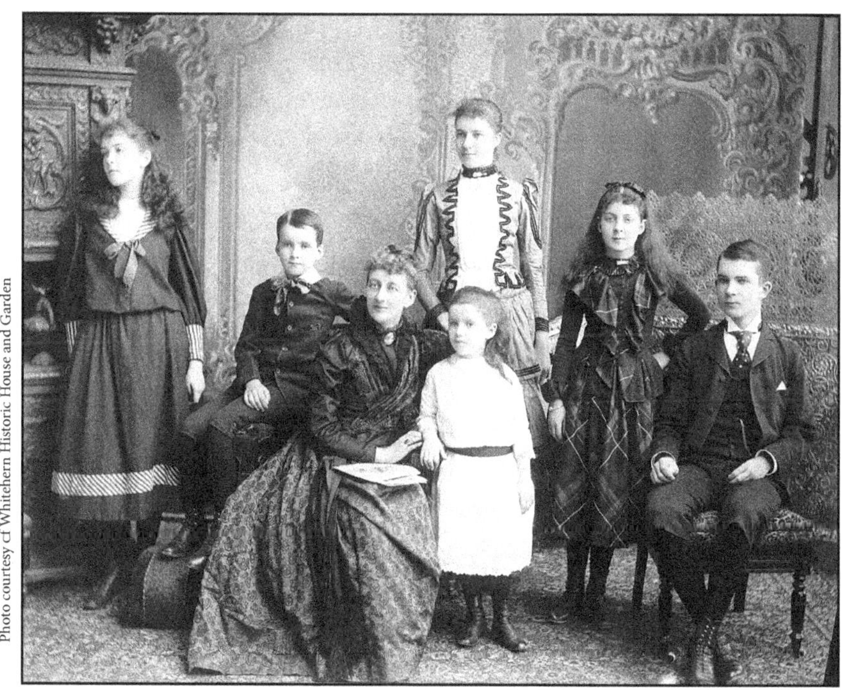

Photo courtesy of Whitehern Historic House and Garden

Clinging by her fingernails to apparent gentility, Mary McQuesten sits for a formal portrait with her six children in probably 1889 or 1890, one or two years after her husband's death. Left to right: Hilda, Tom, Mary (standing), Edna, Ruby, and Calvin.

coldly. "This is very painful, but it is the legitimate consequence of your own conduct." Not only was her illness her own fault, he suggested, but also perhaps God's way of offering her a chance to atone for her sins. "It may be He is now making a last effort for your salvation," he wrote.

Seizing his fresh opportunity, Reverend Baker devoted himself to Mary's education and training. The girl responded well, scoring top grades in Latin and French and finishing first in ancient history and Greek prose composition. Her engagement to a wealthy lawyer who also called himself a committed Christian delighted Reverend Baker, and the father-daughter bond remained close. When Isaac and Mary moved to Bold Street in Hamilton, Reverend Baker and Mary Jane uprooted themselves from Toronto to take the adjoining house. When Isaac and Mary moved to Whitehern, the widower Reverend Baker moved with them. He died in 1887 at ninety-two. Isaac died the following year, leaving Mary a near-bankrupt single mother of six.

She was thirty-eight years old. She kept Whitehern, which had been put in her name. She also retained the two Bold Street houses, which were dilapidated but later fixed and rented. In addition, she held on to investments that gave her an annual income of $1,700 — just enough to cling by her fingernails to apparent gentility. She laid off her last two servants and assigned her children to the household chores. The eldest was thirteen, the youngest two. One daughter learned to cook. Another learned to sew. Both helped to look after the younger children.

Years later Mary mused that holding on to Whitehern rather than move into something simpler might have been a mistake. "It does seem sometimes," she wrote to her son Calvin, "as if it had been a great cross to have been burdened with this property during the best years of our lives."

She clung to the family seat, however, and to everything in it. Dr. Calvin's portraits of British royalty continued to hang in the front foyer. The O.L.'s drawing room remained intact. Reverend Baker's books, paintings, and mementoes occupied the same spaces they always had. Long after their deaths the first generation continued to assert their presence in the home, and not only through their belongings. Like the family china, unhappiness and dysfunction passed intact from one generation to the next.

Mary developed a matriarchal style that resembled her father's patriarchal one. Religiously strict like her father, she devoted herself to evangelical work. In 1893, five years after Isaac's death, she took over as president of the Women's Foreign Missionary Society at her church, and for the next twenty-five years locally and at the national level she organized meetings, gave speeches, and travelled to various parts of the country to inspect missions and promote the society's expansion. At the same time, she indoctrinated her children in Christian righteousness. She turned into another kind of O.L., creating a family system that engendered a strict type of Christian denial. She also put her own emotional needs above those of her children. Although capable of expressing affection and support for her children, Mary demanded unquestioned loyalty from them, going so far as to say that if they did not bring honour to the family she would die.

"I have never been worried with my children's bad conduct," she told her son Calvin after he moved away, meaning that, in fact, she feared they would disgrace her, as her husband had. "That is the thing which would have killed me."

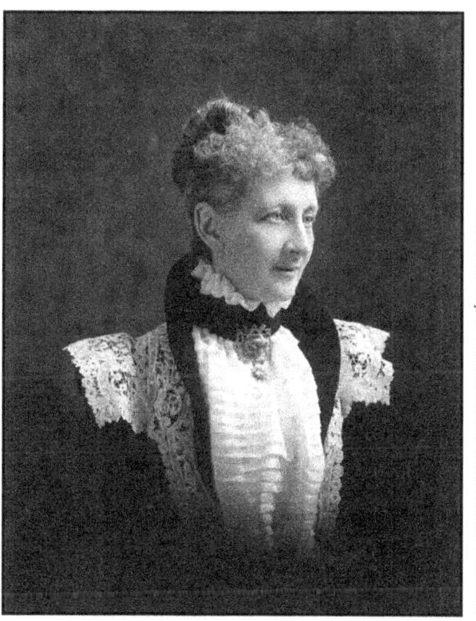

Photo courtesy of Whitehern Historic House and Garden

Often displayed at special events, this portrait of second-generation matriarch Mary McQuesten counts as a museum favourite. It dates to probably 1880, when Mary was thirty-one years old and by all outward appearances happy and thriving.

"She brought on this heart trouble with me," she wrote on hearing that her daughter Ruby was secretly dating a man Mary thought unsuitable.

"I am so very nervous and anxious minded," she wrote to her son Tom, "that if you had been anything else but what you are I would certainly have broken down. If you had been a lazy good for nothing, selfish and unsympathetic, it seems to me I would have died."

The Third-Generation McQuestens

Mary and the children made a good-looking family but an emotionally fragile one. The boys were handsome, the girls beautiful, but they had suffered years of terrible tensions as their father slipped ever deeper into alcohol and drug addiction. Afterward came years of money worries and other stresses. Mary demanded emotional loyalty and got it. None of her six children married. Two of them never left home, and all who did ultimately returned. All pursued self-limiting lives calibrated to their mother's narrow sense of religious propriety and aspirations to social status, although Tom proved uniquely resourceful and imaginative in stretching family constraints to the maximum. Faithful to his mother's demands for self-sacrifice and duty, and accepting little financial reward in return, he rose to the highest levels of political power and status in Ontario, devoted to public infrastructure improvements and civic beautification.

Altogether Isaac and Mary had seven children, the fifth of whom, Muriel, died in infancy. The entire family figures in the museum's narrative, but curators present the house as it looked in 1939. By then, Mary and her two youngest adult daughters had died. That left four adult siblings. Tom, at the height of his career, was living at Whitehern on weekends with his elder brother and two sisters. The three eldest were to live the longest, sharing the house well into old age.

Mary, Eldest Daughter, 1874–1964

"Attractive and intelligent but not scholarly," biographer Mary Anderson says of the eldest daughter, Mary, in *The Life Writings of Mary Baker McQuesten: Victorian Matriarch*. Daughter Mary proved a homebody. She sailed once to Europe and took holidays in Muskoka but otherwise spent her entire life at Whitehern. No evidence exists of any romantic involvements. "Not fitted for [marriage] at all," Mother once confided to her son Calvin. "She has not head enough and there would be trouble." The assessment conveniently left daughter Mary available to look after the house. She died at Whitehern in 1964 at the age of ninety.

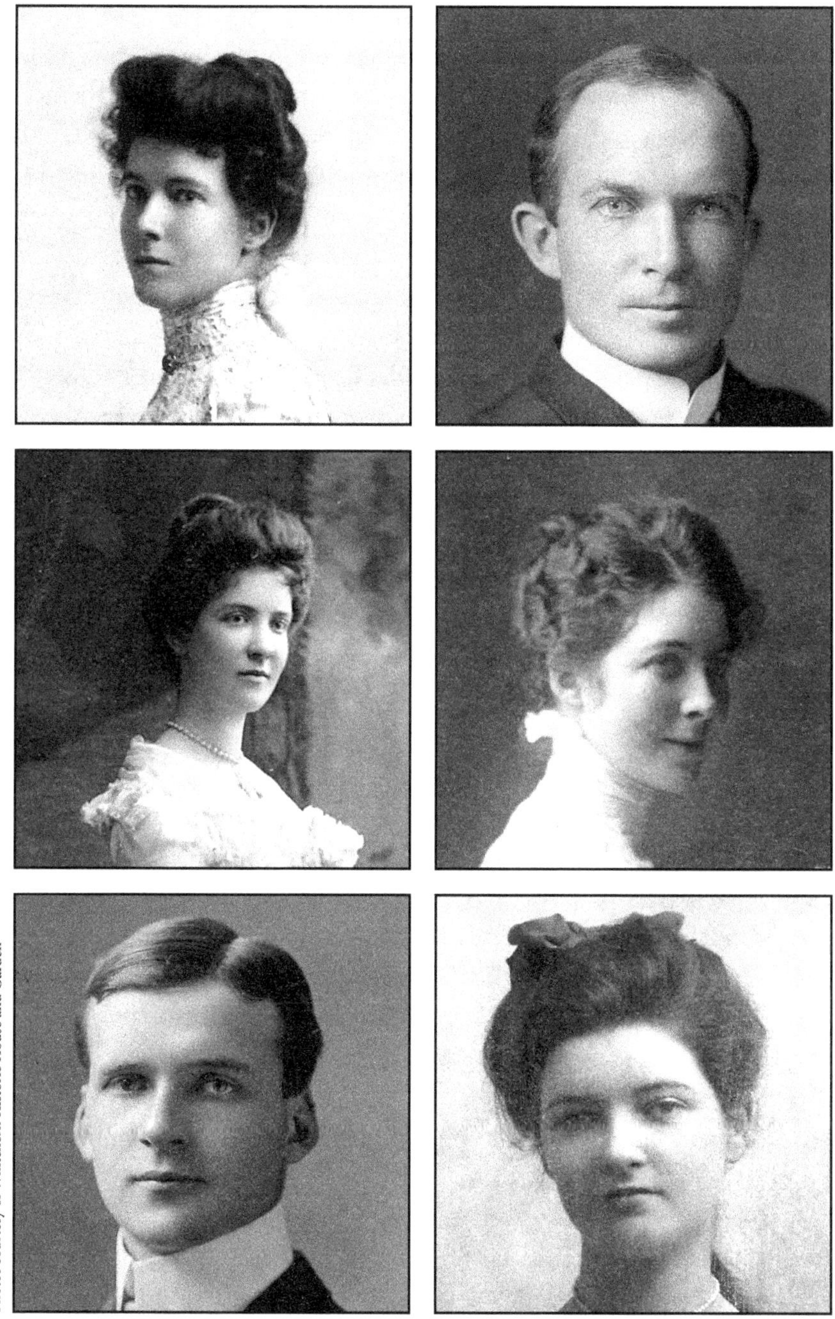

Photos courtesy of Whitehern Historic House and Garden

They made a good-looking family but an emotionally fragile one. Left to right and downward, eldest to youngest: Mary, Calvin, Hilda, Ruby, Tom, and Edna.

Calvin, Second Child, Eldest Son, 1876–1968

Of all the children, Calvin wandered the farthest from home. Between the ages of twenty and forty, he lived out of town and mostly out of province, working first as a journalist, then as a missionary preacher. He wrote columns for the Toronto *News* and later the *Montreal Herald*, but finding the deadlines too nerve-wracking switched to become an itinerant preacher in Alberta, Ontario, and Quebec. At thirty-three he was also ordained in the Presbyterian Church. He struggled financially, however, and suffered mental imbalances. Born with what was described as a "withered" left hand and some paralysis on his left side, he sometimes expressed a low opinion of himself. "You are not to abuse yourself and call yourself slow & stupid," Mother once wrote in response. "You were never either, you were sadly handicapped physically, poor fellow, from the start, and met with some disappointments in your plans, but you bore it heroically and have had to push your way along without assistance from any one."

Mother wrote him twice a week and demanded that he write her back at least once a week. "Her letters acted like a kind of umbilical cord between them," biographer Anderson says. At forty he returned to live at Whitehern, afflicted by psychological problems diagnosed as "nervous prostration" and described as swings from manic activity to depression. For the next thirty years he served as a semi-volunteer chaplain at the Hamilton Mountain Sanatorium. No evidence exists of a serious romantic involvement, but he indulged in his love of the outdoors, particularly by canoeing in the Cootes Paradise wetlands at the west end of Hamilton Harbour. It was Calvin who initiated the move to bequeath Whitehern to the city. He outlived everybody else in the family and died in 1968 at the age of ninety-two.

Hilda, Third Child, 1877–1967

At twenty-four Hilda received a marriage proposal from a commercial traveller in Montreal named Ken Trigge, but Mother objected. "I had to have a very plain talk with him," Mother later wrote. She demanded that Trigge become a teetotaller. He replied that he was a salesman, and that part of his job was to socialize and buy drinks for customers. He could hardly buy drinks for others and not take one himself, he said. Mother told him that he "was making his living by tempting men to do wrong."

She also said: "I could never consent [to the marriage]."

To her son Calvin, Mother confided at one point that she felt "very very sorry, for I think [Trigge] would have suited [Hilda] very well & she seemed quite heartbroken." One week later, however, she hardened her position. "It is a terrible thing for a girl to take a man who has not decided on his principles," she wrote as though thinking of her own marriage to a drinker. A few days later she wrote even more harshly: "I never thought him good enough for her, & I am sure of it now, a poor weak chap and like people with very little brains, hard to convince." Hilda agreed, Mother said.

Like her elder sister, Hilda lived at Whitehern for her entire life, but unlike her sister she exuded charm and demonstrated social skill. As her younger brother's career progressed, she played hostess to his legal and political gatherings, and when Tom became an Ontario cabinet minister, she accompanied him to events. She died in 1967 at ninety, survived only by Calvin.

Ruby, Fourth Child, 1879–1911

"Beautiful, charming, articulate, intelligent, scholarly, artistic, and very loving and caring," biographer Anderson writes of her favourite McQuesten. "The tragic Victorian heroine," Anderson also calls her.

Ruby left home at twenty to teach at the Presbyterian Ladies' College in Ottawa. Much of her earnings she sent home, largely to fund the education of her younger brother, Tom. At the college she met David Ross, son of the college principal. His three sisters also taught at the school. When she was twenty-seven and he twenty-four, he proposed marriage, but Mother objected. "Such a restless jump about," Mother called Ross. She disliked his "weak face," his "presumption," his plans to establish a homestead north of Regina, and especially his failure to rise to the type of man who might be good enough for her daughter. "The more I think of it the less I favour it," Mother wrote to Calvin. "It seems as if [Ruby] were fitted to take a fine place in a higher sphere."

Mother insisted that they break it off for two years to reconsider. When she discovered that Ruby and Ross were still in touch, she complained of Ruby causing her "heart trouble," and the couple ended the relationship for good. Instead of getting married and starting a life of her own, Ruby stayed at the college and continued to send money home. She also developed a talent for still-life watercolour painting and an art form known as "pyrography," which involved creating designs on wood with a hot poker. Exposed at the school to a series of infectious illnesses, she eventually contracted tuberculosis and died at a cottage retreat on the Hamilton escarpment at the age of thirty-one.

Muriel, Fifth Child, 1880–1882

Muriel died at twenty-one months of undocumented causes.

Edna, Youngest Child, 1885–1935

A top student, Edna won a Governor General's Scholarship in Classics to study at Queen's University. Her fragile mental state, however, prevented her from attending. "Never ceases talking," family letters say. "Takes us all to attend to Edna." "Such a miserable state of nervousness and weakness." "Afraid her mind had become unhinged." For many years Edna lived at Whitehern, but at thirty-five, in 1920, she was committed to the Homewood Sanatorium in Guelph where her father had sought treatment for his addictions. She died there at fifty in 1935.

Thomas McQuesten: Sixth Child, Head of Household, 1882–1948

Photographs of Tom invariably portray a smooth, bland face, even in middle age, with no sense of character etched into his skin and no hint of an inner life. Whether he considered himself happy or not is probably irrelevant. To the McQuestens, life was not about happiness. It was about duty, and Tom fulfilled expectations spectacularly. When he was still in university, his sister Ruby spoke of him as a potential instrument of God. "I have wondered if in the course of time you mightn't become a member of Parliament," she wrote to him. "I can't help thinking of you and longing and praying that God … may in His time raise up a saviour."

Tom never ran for federal Parliament or saved the country, but as a Hamilton city councillor and a Member of Provincial Parliament, he helped modernize and beautify the city in ways that can still be seen today. Among his many achievements, he proved instrumental in creating Gage Park and the High Level Bridge, bringing McMaster University to the city, and building the Royal Botanical Gardens. He developed a talent for power. He learned

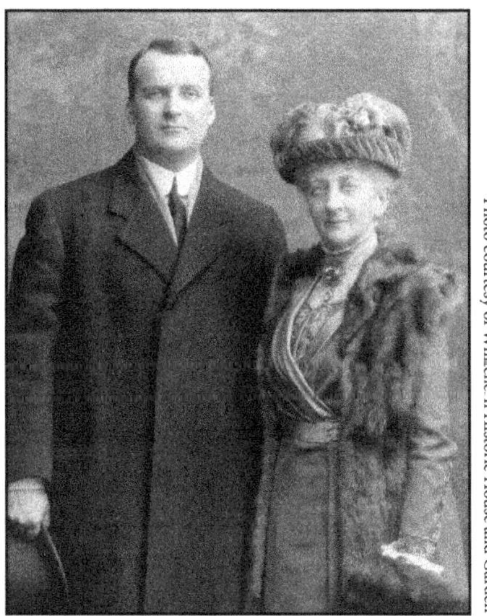

"If you had been anything else but what you are," Mary once wrote to her son Tom, "I would certainly have broken down." She developed a matriarchal style that resembled her father's patriarchal one.

how to get power and wield it, not for personal benefit but as a way to contribute to society. He demonstrated "a genius for bringing schemes to fruition … [for] the betterment of mankind through public duty," writes biographer John C. Best in *Thomas Baker McQuesten: Public Works, Politics and Imagination*. Throughout a career that included directing large government expenditures as Ontario minister of highways and minister of public works, Tom drew praise as "wholesome," "likeable," "level-headed," and "scrupulously honest." He also remained devoted to his mother. In Ottawa, Prime Minister Mackenzie King might have been communicating with his late mother's ghost, but for most of his career Thomas McQuesten actually lived with his mother, and while in cabinet spent almost every weekend with her. She exuded pride in her son, but sometimes worried about his robust contact with the world. She worried that worldliness might distract him from devotion to God.

"The only anxious thought I have for you dearie," she wrote after he graduated from law school, "[is] lest you should by mixing continually with those who have really scarcely a thought of God, you should grow formal in serving Him and not be spiritually minded."

Early Years, 1895–1912

Tom was smart, handsome, and athletic, and from an early age showed an aptitude for the law. When he was thirteen, a winter storm hit Hamilton, leaving a slick of ice on the sidewalk in front of Whitehern. A city employee came by to say that a bylaw obliged homeowners to clear their walks. Tom did his best. He tried scraping off the ice, then laid down salt, but before the salt could take effect five city workers arrived to finish the job and left a bill for $1.50. "I don't know if they will get their money or not," Tom wrote to his elder brother, Calvin, "because the bylaw says that citizens are compelled to clean snow and LOOSE ice, but HARD ice is not mentioned."

In high school, Tom played on a basketball team that won the 1900 Ontario championship. At some point — the period is poorly documented — he also played semi-professional football for the Hamilton Tigers, which later merged with another club to become the Hamilton Tiger-Cats of the Canadian Football League. At the University of Toronto he took a bachelor's degree in English, history, and the classics, and joined the fencing and rowing teams. Afterward he studied law at Osgoode Hall.

Like his siblings, Tom never married, but like Hilda and Ruby he came close. While attending law school, he got serious about a woman identified in family letters as Isabel Elliott. Mother said that she heard from a friend that Tom was engaged. Perhaps Isabel knew of Mother's reputation, because to help smooth an introduction she commissioned an artist to paint a miniature of Mother as a gift. She didn't like it. The lower part of the face was "too heavy altogether," Mother wrote to Tom, and the artist "had worked at the lips and spoiled the eyes." After disparaging artists generally, she also told Tom, "You had better let Miss Elliott know you are not yet pleased with it." Afterward the name "Miss Elliott" disappeared from family correspondence.

In 1907, in his first job as a lawyer, Tom opened an office for a Toronto firm in the Northern Ontario town of Elk Lake during a silver-mining boom. In 1909, however, he returned to Hamilton and Whitehern. He accepted a job from his father's former law partner, James Chisholm, a prominent Liberal who was to become Tom's political mentor. By then brother Calvin was preaching in Saskatchewan and sister Ruby had moved to Calgary for tuberculosis treatment. That meant that Tom moved back with his mother and three sisters — Mary, Hilda, and Edna — as man of the house and sole breadwinner.

In Hamilton, Tom used his professional standing to enter politics. His political career evolved in three main overlapping stages. He began in city politics, rose to become Hamilton's Liberal Party boss provincially and federally, and ascended to the most senior ranks of the Ontario government as a cabinet minister handling several key portfolios.

Hamilton Politics, 1912–1934

In 1912, at the age of thirty, Tom won a seat on Hamilton City Council and immersed himself in public works. In 1914, when the First World War began, he tried to enlist in the army but his mother stopped him, unwilling to risk his death. In 1916, he won an appointment to the Town Planning Commission, and in 1922 landed a seat on the Hamilton Board of Parks Management, an unelected post, where he began to grow his political base.

Tom loved parks. He grew up surrounded by his mother's gardens, which she tended lovingly at Whitehern even in the leanest of times. "The garden is quite a show now with hollyhocks in all types and shades," she wrote to Calvin in 1901. "We have had extremely warm weather for over a week the roses are out in full great quantities of all colours," she wrote in 1909. "The garden is magnificent … such lovely phlox and snap dragons and wonderful salpiglossis," she wrote in 1930. When speaking of gardening, she often mentioned Tom. "Today Tom & I went up to the cemetery to prune the shrubs," she wrote in 1902. "Tom is so pleased to have been able to see the place in spring for the first time in many years," she wrote of him as a young lawyer in 1908. "The dwarf double lilacs are lovely," she wrote in 1916. "Tom found Fonthill near Welland the only good place to get them." By the time he joined the parks management board, Tom associated parks and the protection of natural beauty with human goodness. Parks are, he said at the time, "amongst the really important things which go to the development of the individual as well as the national character."

With Tom's appointment, says biographer John Best, the parks board went from a sleepy committee to a dynamic catalyst for change. The local parks and playgrounds system nearly quadrupled in size, and by 1932 Hamilton had the largest area of developed parkland and playgrounds of any city in Canada.

Tom handled the final arrangements to purchase twenty-five hectares in the city's east end to create Gage Park. He negotiated the 160-hectare expansion of the west end's Cootes Paradise wetland conservatory. He also secured 283 hectares of ravine for King's Forest Park, which included Albion Falls.

For Tom, parks meant not just trees and flowers, they also meant redevelopment on a grand scale. In 1928, motorists from Toronto entered Hamilton through a wasteland. "Billboards, gas stations and run-down dwellings line the High Level entrance — and the gravel pits!" recalls

Leslie Laking in *Love, Sweat and Soil,* a history of the Royal Botanical Gardens. "Below to the west, the tar-paper shacks, boathouses and sheds blotted the eastern shore of Cootes Paradise."

Tom led the parks board in creating what he called the Northwestern Entrance. Over a number of years, he assembled parcels of land to create a welcoming parkland gateway into Hamilton, culminating in the dramatic High Level Bridge across the western end of Burlington Bay to downtown. He also developed a park-like block of land to attract a Toronto Baptist college to Hamilton as McMaster University and led the creation of the Royal Botanical Gardens as a McMaster-affiliated institution.

Grandfather Dr. Calvin helped build the city as an industrial centre; grandson Tom raised it to the next level. "Hamilton has become too much a factory town," Tom said in 1928 when the McMaster deal was concluded. "This is the first break toward a broader culture and a higher educational development."

In all his projects, Tom also drew on the best artistic talent he could find. To design Gage Park, he hired Howard Dunington-Grubb, later known as "the father of landscape architecture in Canada." To build the High Level Bridge, he engaged Beaux Arts architect John Lyle, who had designed Toronto's Royal Alexandra Theatre. To further beautify the city, he commissioned fountains, pillars, and other embellishments created by a circle of artists that included Toronto sculptors Florence Wyle and Frances Loring. At Scott Park he built an indoor swimming pool, still in public use as Jimmy Thompson Memorial Pool, and the nearby Civic Stadium, since rebuilt as Tim Hortons Field — venues that in 1930 played host to the first British Empire Games, now called the Commonwealth Games.

"Tom avoided the spotlight," biographer Best says. Tom got lands assembled, designs approved, contracts tendered, and copious amounts of money allocated, all the while developing the low-profile political style that was to serve him throughout his career. He played the backrooms to smooth opposition and controversy, and he let others take the applause at inauguration ceremonies. Not all recognition escaped him, however. The committee officially formed to bring McMaster to the city credited their success to the "time and skill T.B. McQuesten had devoted to the task," and in 1988, Princess Margaret, Queen Elizabeth II's sister, rededicated the High Level Bridge as the Thomas B. McQuesten High Level Bridge.

Liberal Party Organizer, 1923–1934

Guided by his mentor, James Chisholm, Tom got elected vice-president of the local Liberal Party Association in 1912, the same year that he became an alderman. In 1923, at forty-one, he took over as association president. Until then the Hamilton Liberals had suffered from poor organization and infighting. The party held power federally but not provincially, and at both levels Hamilton voters consistently elected Conservatives. Slowly, in his backroom style, Tom improved the party's chances, and by 1930, biographer Best says, both Prime Minister Mackenzie King and Ontario Liberal Leader Mitchell Hepburn recognized Tom as "Hamilton's undisputed boss." In 1932, Tom also took over as president of the Ontario Liberal Association.

Ontario Cabinet Minister, 1934–1943

Tom ran for a seat in the Ontario legislature in 1923 and lost. For years afterward, elected office seemed not to interest him, but in 1934 he ran again and swept to victory, defeating the Tory incumbent in his riding by one of the widest margins in the province. "More than any other single man he is responsible for the unprecedented Liberal sweep of Hamilton and the Niagara Peninsula," the Toronto *Globe* reported. Conservative Party Leader Mitchell Hepburn won by a landslide.

"The finest gentleman in Canada," Hepburn called Tom, who at fifty-two embarked on the most challenging and productive period of his life. He accepted two cabinet portfolios — highways and public works. Tom also became director of the Niagara Parks Commission, a provincial agency, and took a seat on the three-member Hydro-Electric Power Commission, the provincial electricity company. The jobs did not pay well. Tom would be making less than he did as a lawyer. To honour a campaign promise, Hepburn cut annual ministerial salaries to $8,000 from $10,000 and slashed the hydro commission pay to zero from $10,000.

"His lips are firmly set, indicating inflexible resolution," *Saturday Night* magazine said of Tom as he assumed his posts. "He speaks slowly and deliberately almost icily as if carefully weighing each word."

Tom moved to Toronto for work but returned every weekend to Whitehern. He renovated the basement to create a lounge for himself and visitors, but slept in the same bed he had used since he was five and sat every Sunday in the family pew at MacNab Street Presbyterian Church.

Six months into his first term his mother died. She was eighty-four. At the funeral her long-time pastor spoke ambivalently of her "puritanical sense of right and wrong" and "inflexible integrity." The Hamilton *Herald* cited her influence on Tom, particularly on his "love for beauty that was large enough to spread out and influence the appearance of a great city." She would have been pleased with the turnout. Most of the Ontario cabinet attended, which meant that forty-six years after Isaac's death the McQuesten name had been definitively restored.

Tom served nine years in cabinet — two terms — and spent every one of those years building infrastructure with an eye to human betterment. Traffic deaths sickened him. He called them "manslaughter." He introduced public service campaigns to promote highway safety and proposed a divided superhighway modelled after the new German autobahns. In the mid-1930s, the speed limit in Ontario was fifty-five kilometres per hour. Tom foresaw cars going ninety-five kilometres per hour and proposed what would become the Queen Elizabeth Way, four lanes of traffic divided in half by a grass median stretching between Niagara Falls and Toronto. He wanted to turn Niagara into a gateway from the United States into Canada, the way he had turned the Northwestern Entrance into a gateway from Toronto into Hamilton.

As head of the Niagara Parks Commission, Tom led construction of the ornate Oakes Garden Theatre near the Falls and of the nearby Carillon Tower with its fifty-five bells. He helped build the international Rainbow Bridge, named "the World's most beautiful Bridge" in 1942 by the American Institute of Steel Construction. Along the Niagara River he built the scenic Niagara Parkway, and as monuments to the War of 1812 he restored Fort George, Fort Erie, and Navy Hall at Niagara, and Fort Henry at Kingston. He supervised construction of a memorial arch at Niagara Falls, paying tribute to William Lyon Mackenzie and indirectly flattering Mackenzie's grandson, Prime Minister Mackenzie King, and had the home of Mohawk leader Joseph Brant rebuilt on Lake Ontario at present-day Burlington. Beyond the Niagara-Hamilton region, he also saw international bridges built at Sarnia and Kingston, paved Highway 11 from Toronto to North Bay, and generally upgraded the northern highway system.

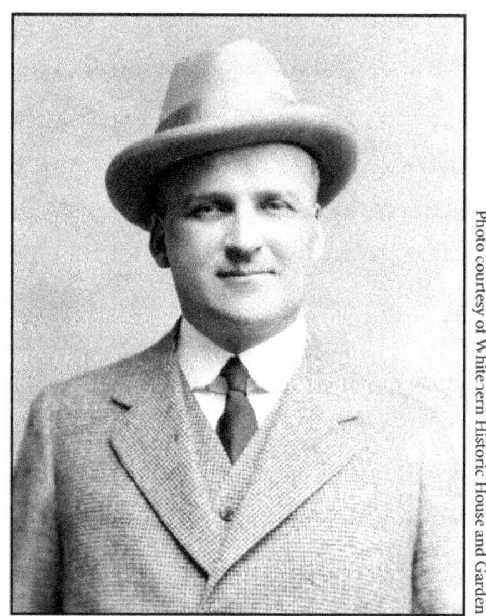

Photo courtesy of Whitehern Historic House and Garden

Photos of Tom invariably portray a smooth, bland face even in middle age, with no hint of an inner life. To the McQuestens life was not about happiness, it was about duty, and Tom fulfilled expectations spectacularly.

The biggest day of Tom's career came on June 7, 1939. King George VI and Queen Elizabeth visited Niagara as part of a month-long North American tour, the first to Canada and the United States by a reigning British monarch. Three months later the Second World War was to begin. At Tom's suggestion the Royals transferred from the train to a limousine at St. Catharines to drive along a completed section of his divided highway. Along the route in the official car the Royals passed between two pillars, breaking an electric beam and causing drapes to fall away from a sign saying QUEEN ELIZABETH WAY. That afternoon, Tom presented his brother Calvin and sisters Mary and Hilda to the King and Queen. He also walked to Table Rock with their majesties and Prime Minister Mackenzie King for a close view of the Falls. "The Queen remarked about the beautiful green of the water," the prime minister wrote in his diary.

In the provincial election of 1943, Tom lost his seat. The Progressive Conservatives regained power in Ontario, and Tom moved back to Whitehern to live with siblings Mary, Calvin, and Hilda. Five years later the City of Hamilton named him Citizen of the Year. A few days after that Tom died at sixty-five of some type of cancer. His net worth amounted to $25,000 plus his share of Whitehern, a testimony to his self-sacrificing ethic. For nine years he had run the government departments most closely associated with graft and corruption, and when the new government audited those departments, looking for scandal, they found none. Tom had lived as frugally as his mother had taught him. He had run a clean administration to the point of maintaining his own car and never submitting expense claims for it even on government business.

It was an unnecessary sacrifice. Thomas McQuesten never freed himself from his mother's emotional grip and never lived the life he might have chosen for himself with Isabel Elliott. Instead, he did his duty, but he interpreted that duty in a grand, imaginative way. He channelled his genius for closing the deal toward the creation of parks, infrastructure, and other public works that proved a lasting benefit to the people of Hamilton and Ontario.

WALK-THROUGH: LIKE A MUSEUM

Whitehern stands on a raised terrace surrounded by gardens and a low stone wall. Although three blocks from the city's main King-and-James intersection, the house seems tucked away behind the old courthouse and next to the back of City Hall. Heritage architects call the place "an outstanding example of a mid-nineteenth-century urban estate." It is built of stone two storeys high, with large windows organized symmetrically and a central portico supported by Ionic columns. Visitors pass through a front gate, make their way around a formal heart-shaped flowerbed, and enter

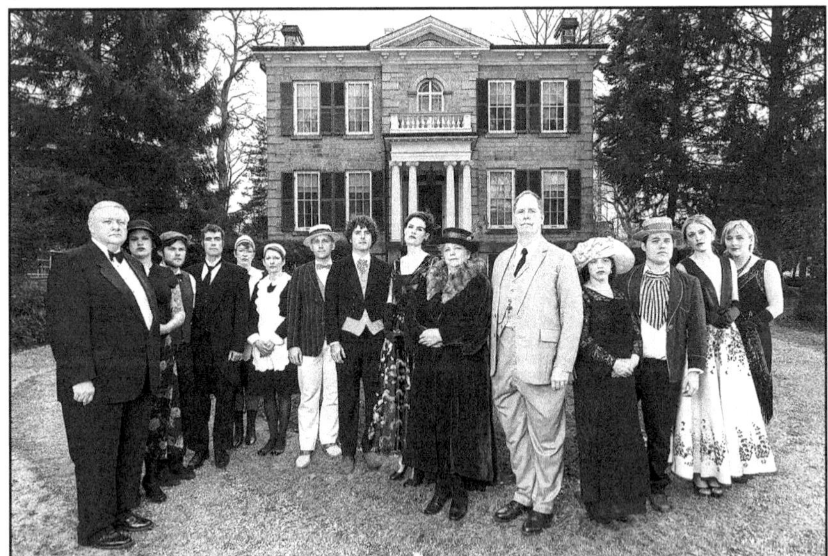

Photo by Jeff Tessier

Whitehern staff members mimic the promotional photo of the British hit television series Downton Abbey. *In the light-coloured suit toward the right stands Whitehern curator Tom Minnes, taking the place of Robert, Earl of Grantham.*

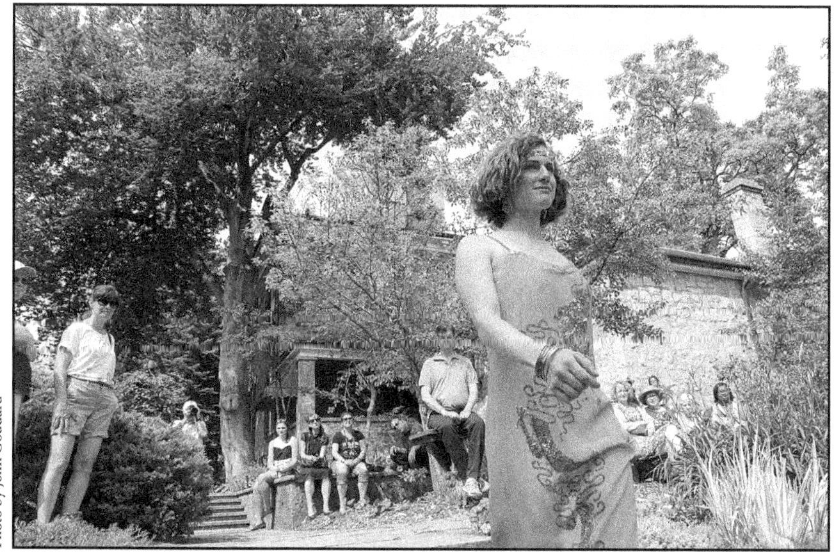

Photo by John Goddard

A model steps into Whitehern's lush back garden in a fashion show set during the period of the British hit television series Downton Abbey. *Ironically for a house whose third generation never married, the garden also serves as a popular wedding venue.*

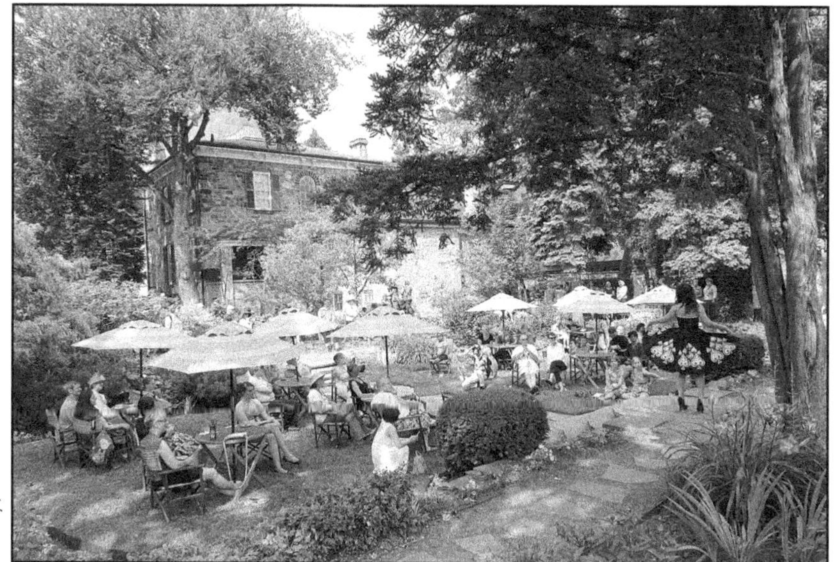

Photo by John Goddard

Whitehern's back garden makes an ideal venue for a summer show of period fashions. To design the garden, Tom McQuesten hired Howard Dunington-Grubb, the father of landscape architecture in Canada.

the house as the McQuestens and their guests did, through the front door.

Most heritage-home museums come to the public stripped of original contents, but Whitehern is different. It came complete with thousands of family artifacts, everything from furniture to bobby pins, and including diaries, paintings, photographs, nail scissors, and can openers. Three generations of the McQuesten family lived here from 1852 to 1968.

Curators present the house as it looked in 1939 on the eve of the Second World War and at the pinnacle of Thomas McQuesten's political career. Four McQuestens occupied the house at that time, two sisters and two brothers: Mary, sixty-five; Calvin, sixty-three; Hilda, sixty-two; and Tom, fifty-seven. As a senior Ontario cabinet minister, Tom kept a Toronto residence but spent weekends at Whitehern, and returned permanently in 1943. Photographs from the time have enabled curators to lay out rooms exactly as they were, with everything from table forks to sewing boxes located to within a centimetre of where the family placed them.

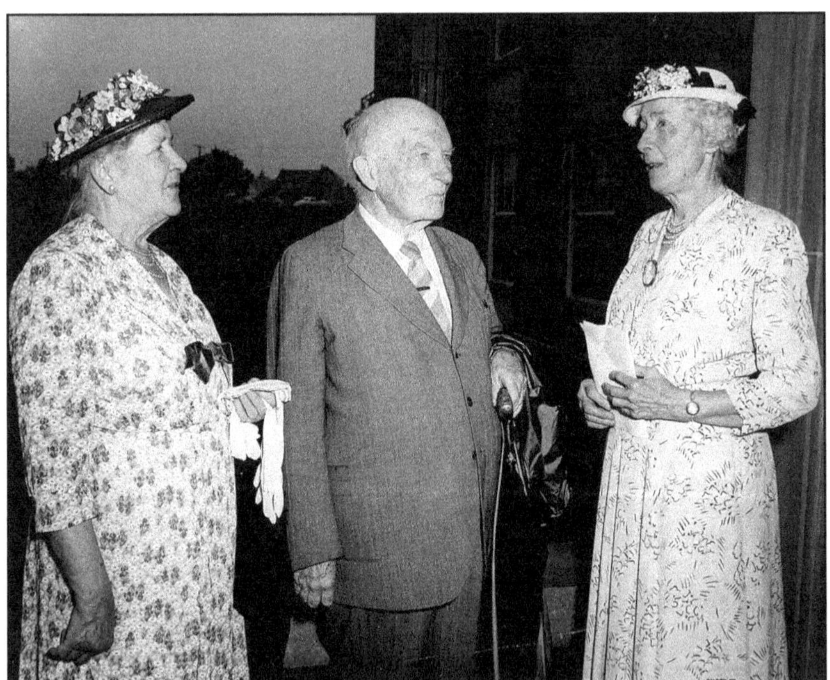

Photo courtesy of Whitehern Historic House and Garden

Siblings (left to right) Hilda, Calvin, and Mary attend a ceremony in 1959 marking their bequest to the City of Hamilton of Whitehern and all its contents. Calvin outlived his sisters and was the last McQuesten to reside in the family home.

To say "1939" might be misleading. Much of the house looks frozen in the 1880s. Even in 1939 it was like a museum. The library, dining room, and drawing room barely changed from the first generation to the last. While other families embraced Modernism or Art Nouveau, the McQuestens remained stuffily attached to the over-decorative cluttered taste of the mid to late Victorian era. Mother Mary McQuesten's room in particular was locked in time, maintained exactly the way she left it the day of her death on December 7, 1934.

In 1959, Mary, Calvin, and Hilda McQuesten bequeathed Whitehern to the City of Hamilton, effective the day the last of them expired. In 1962, the property was declared a National Historic Site. In 1968, when Calvin died, it devolved to the city, and in 1970, Governor General Roland Michener officially declared the museum open.

Upstairs: Hallway

Museum tours usually start in the spacious upstairs hallway where curators have arranged photographs on the wall like a family tree. At the top, Dr. Calvin occupies a place by himself. Below him can be seen his successive wives, Margarette, Ester, and Elizabeth. Guides often apologize for the unattractive grimace in Ester's portrait, but it is the only known picture of her. Below them hang Margarette's son Calvin, who became a doctor in New York, and Ester's two boys, David, who died at five in a fire, and Isaac, who succeeded Dr. Calvin as Whitehern's proprietor. Next to them Isaac is pictured with his wife, Mary Baker McQuesten. Off to one side are her parents, Reverend Thomas Baker and Mary Jane Baker. Below Isaac and Mary can be seen their seven children, six of whom survived to adulthood — a good-looking family but emotionally fragile.

Upstairs: Flash Glass Window

Look back at the stairwell to see how Dr. Calvin's third wife, Elizabeth, had part of the back wall knocked out for a decorative window that she commissioned from the Hamilton Glass Company, one of her few local purchases. The window is called flash glass rather than stained glass. Thin layers of red and blue glass, imported from England at considerable expense, were flash-heated and laminated to a thicker body of clear glass, with a design etched with acid into the coloured panes. The middle pane depicts a crane among reeds and foliage. The top panel shows a small bird on a stylized branch.

Upstairs: Tom's Room

In 1939, as Ontario minister of highways and minister of public works with enormous budgets and huge staffs and as host to King George VI and Queen Elizabeth, Thomas McQuesten continued to sleep in his childhood bed in a room essentially unchanged since he was five. By then he was spending much of his time in Toronto and travelling around the province, but on weekends his driver returned him to Whitehern.

He took over the bedroom from his maternal grandfather, the former British Navy officer and Congregational Church minister Thomas Baker. It still looks like Baker's room. The bed dates to the 1870s. The floor-to-ceiling bookcase against the far wall was Baker's, as were most of the books. The framed pictures on the walls were also his, most of them conforming to the twin naval and religious themes of his life.

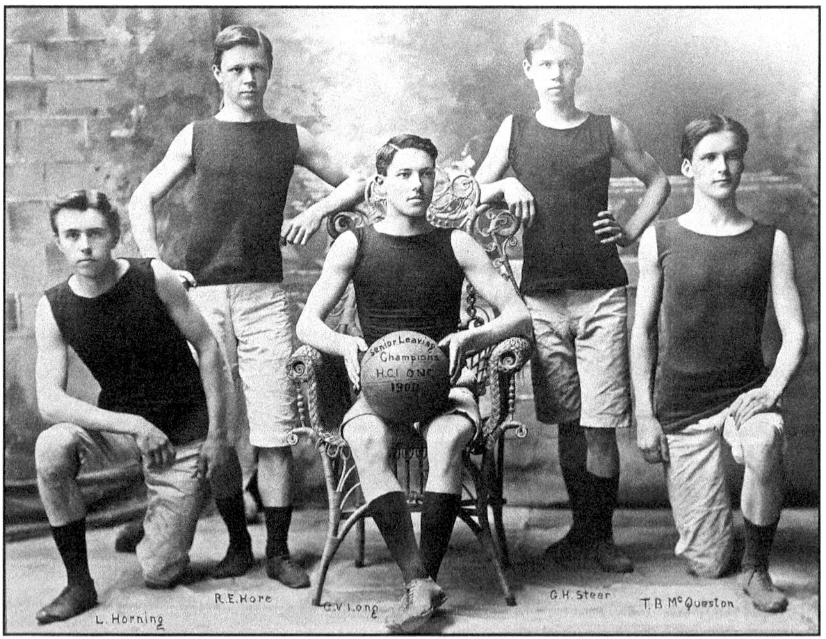

Photo courtesy of Whitehern Historic House and Garden

A photograph in his bedroom shows Tom, far right, looking handsome and athletic with his Ontario championship high school basketball team of 1900. He strove to embody what the Victorians thought of as "muscular Christianity."

A few of Tom's belongings can be seen. The gold pocket watch carries an inscription indicating that it was a twenty-fifth birthday present. A framed photo shows Tom and his mother in the Whitehern gardens, probably in 1934, the year of her death. He wears a black top hat and tails, she a flowered hat and what looks like a satin gown with a sash of white lace. The grey top hat on the oval table is the one he wore on June 7, 1939, when he accompanied King George VI and Queen Elizabeth to Niagara to open the Queen Elizabeth Way and the Oakes Garden Theatre, among other landmarks. The ashtray next to the hat belonged to him. Tom was a smoker and died at sixty-five in 1948 of cancer. He was also a sportsman and strove to embody what the Victorians thought of as "muscular Christianity," with a commitment to both piety and physical health.

A photograph shows him with his Ontario championship high school basketball team. He also played semi-professional football with the Tigers before the team merged with another club to become the Hamilton Tiger-Cats. A prized football is on display. As a politician, he continued to attend games, and in 1933, after a win over the Toronto Argonauts, Hamilton Tigers football hero Brian Timmis had the ball signed by the Hamilton players and gave it to Tom.

Upstairs: Calvin's Room

Across the hall, Calvin's room reflects a love of the outdoors, especially canoeing. Despite a withered left hand and weak left side — schoolboy classmates called him "chicken hand" and he referred to himself as "crippled" — Calvin canoed in Hamilton's Cootes Paradise wetlands park twice a week into his late eighties. He stopped when he was ninety. Visitors to the museum have recalled watching him haul a canoe by himself at various times from lakes in Algonquin Park, and from Buckhorn Lake in the Kawarthas. Such exercise apparently helped keep him healthy. He outlived everybody else in the family, eventually dying in 1968 at the age of ninety-two. Toward the end of his life he spent time in a care facility, but he is thought to have died in this room.

Framed artworks on the walls romantically depict the northern wilderness and the lives of early Canadian voyageurs, mostly in reproductions of paintings by Arthur Hemming, Calvin's favourite artist. Hemming dramatized wilderness canoeing with powerful stylized images, and Calvin asked that after he died his bedroom become an Arthur Hemming gallery.

Partly he got his wish, but other items arouse possibly higher interest. Three pieces of art from his sister Ruby can be seen: the small watercolour of a river above the bedside table; a montage on the same table showing a Canadian Red Ensign flag, maple leaves, and a black-and-white photograph of Calvin; and an oval-shaped framed photograph of Ruby below the reading light. She decorated the frame by applying a hot poker to the wood to create burn marks, an art form known as pyrography. The box decorated with First Nations quillwork, also on the side table, is thought to be a gift from a tuberculosis patient at the Mountain Sanatorium where Calvin served for thirty years as chaplain. The binoculars are the ones he used for birding in Cootes Paradise and elsewhere as president of the Hamilton Bird Protection Society.

Upstairs: Mary's Room

What a beautiful space, with two large front windows and a massive walnut wardrobe that comes apart in three sections. As children all four girls shared this bedroom. Their dollhouse, with its miniature handmade furnishings, now occupies the front right-hand corner to symbolize those early days, and every Christmas curators bring out dozens more of their childhood toys, once preserved in chests in the attic.

By 1939, this room belonged to Mary, the eldest. The scholar Mary Anderson portrays her as a bright and attractive-looking woman, but shy and unworldly. When her father died after squandering the family fortune, she was thirteen, obliged by her mother to help care for the younger children and take over some of the domestic chores as servants were let go. Mary lived to be ninety. As far as anybody knows, she never developed a serious romantic relationship and never left home — "except for brief vacations in Muskoka, or other parts of Ontario, and a trip to the Continent in July 1914," Anderson says.

A pair of tennis rackets against the far wall represents Mary's fondness for the game. A grass tennis court occupied the west lawn where Mary in her shyness could engage with others without having to converse. On the desk can be seen a number of personal items, including original notepaper with the Whitehern letterhead. The paintings on the walls are mostly Ruby's. Most are still-life watercolours rendered by a woman with a sense of cheerfulness and beauty. Either shortly before or shortly after her death from tuberculosis at thirty-one in 1911, the family had them mounted in gold-coloured frames.

Upstairs: Hilda's Room

This small space off the master bedroom once served as Dr. Calvin's dressing room. Its large window overlooks the front balcony above the portico. When she was in her fifties, Hilda, the third child after Mary and Calvin, claimed it as her bedroom after decades of sharing a bed with Mary.

Hilda was a competent woman. "Beautiful, charming, and a gracious hostess," Anderson calls her. As a child, after her father died, she learned to cook and sew. When the family could no longer afford new clothes, she remodelled and repaired existing ones, a challenging job at a time when women's clothing still called for six or seven metres of fabric. Notice her hand-held sewing machine on the dresser, and on the side table to the right of the bed a gorgeous papier mâché sewing box decorated with images of pagodas and still holding Hilda's needles, threads, and bobbins.

In 1902, when Hilda was twenty-five, a salesman named Ken Trigge proposed marriage, but Mother disapproved because he admitted to drinking socially with clients. No other serious romance presented itself, although Hilda remained interested in a wider world. She wore Shalimar perfume from France, an extravagant choice for a woman from a pious Presbyterian family. In 1928, when Tom bought the first family car, Hilda took driving lessons, and when the unmarried Tom needed her as a companion at various political functions, Hilda would take his arm. She died at Whitehern at ninety in 1967.

Upstairs: Mother's Room

In the film *Psycho*, Norman Bates preserved his mother's bedroom exactly as she had left it, and at Whitehern the McQuesten children did the same. After their mother died in 1934, Mary, Calvin, Hilda, and Tom, in their fifties and sixties, maintained the master bedroom as a shrine to her memory. Hilda continued to occupy her cubbyhole. Tom resigned himself to his boyhood room. Mary and Hilda used Mother's room as a thoroughfare to the en suite washroom installed in the 1920s, but nobody ever slept here again.

Dr. Calvin occupied the room first. Isaac and Mary took it over in 1885 when they moved from nearby Bold Street with their six children — the youngest, Edna, born three days after Dr. Calvin's death. The bed is one that Isaac and Mary brought with them. Calvin once said that he and his sisters were all born on that bed, and Tom was born at a summer cottage near Hespeler, now part of Cambridge. Isaac is said to have died in the bed, as did his wife, Mary.

The fireplace is the only one on the floor. The other bedrooms used small wood stoves and after 1939 hot-water radiators. The sturdy piece of mahogany furniture in the corner was likely Reverend Baker's, a "campaign chest" that opens as a desk with drawers and can be taken apart for a military officer to take on campaign. Notice the petit point slippers, skillfully made by Hilda. The telephone dates to the 1930s, although the McQuestens had a phone in the house as early as 1886.

On the wall outside the door, a photograph shows Mary Baker McQuesten as a girl standing between her parents, one hand resting

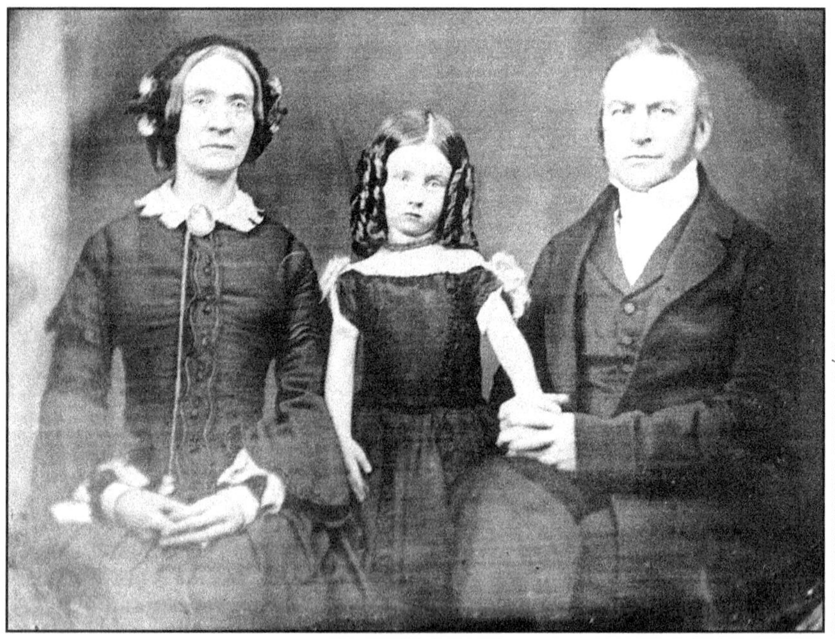

Photo courtesy of Whitehern Historic House and Garden

Little Mary Baker, later Mary McQuesten, stands between her parents, one hand folded within her father's, the other pressed to her side. A later photo hanging in the upstairs hall outside Mary's bedroom door displays a similar family dynamic.

affectionately on her father's shoulder, the other dangling at her side. Her parents look as though they might be her grandparents. When she was born, her mother was forty, her father fifty-three. The children and grandchildren from his first marriage he had essentially disowned.

Main Floor: Library

An entire wall of books stands opposite the front window in the family's official library to the right of the main front entrance. The collection includes forty-one Bibles in different languages, a set of first editions of Charles Dickens novels, one of six known copies of the world's first printed cookbook from France, and an array of popular novels, children's stories, and political and legal texts. There are books on dog breeds, and Canadian Automobile Association maps from 1911. Curators sometimes display an oversized text in Latin printed in 1569.

The doors have been taken off for museum purposes, but Dr. Calvin had lined them with baize, a sturdy green cloth the Victorians used as

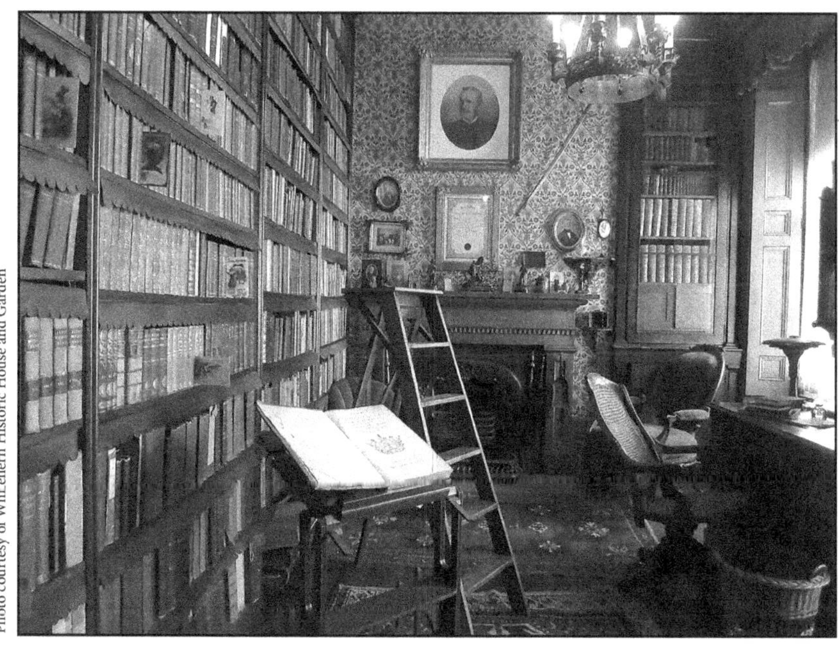

Photo courtesy of Whitehern Historic House and Garden

Isaac McQuesten's portrait hangs prominently in the library, where he is believed to have taken his fatal sleeping potion in 1888 at the age of forty. The book collection includes forty-one Bibles in different languages.

soundproofing. It is easy to imagine him retreating to the room to read quietly or otherwise get away from O.L. His son Isaac is said to have drunk his fatal sleeping potion in this room. That is Isaac's portrait on the far wall, and below it a certificate of condolence to his wife from the University of Toronto senate, on which Isaac had sat. The sword on the wall was Isaac's as a young soldier in the Queen's Own Rangers. Son Calvin, the last surviving family member, wrote sermons in this room when he lived in Hamilton, and his sisters Mary and Hilda gave lessons to students learning English as a second language.

Main Floor: Drawing Room

As a young man, Dr. Calvin wrote an essay about the corrupting power of luxury entitled "Man Wants Little, Nor That Little Long." His third wife, Elizabeth, loved to shop. In 1852, he paid $3,200 for the entire house. In the 1850s, she spent $2,000 decorating this room alone.

On a trip to New York, she bought the rosewood piano in the far back corner for what it would cost to buy several Hamilton workers' cottages. The youngest daughter of the third generation, Edna, played and gave lessons on the piano for a while. The lamp on the piano was converted from the original gas version, its gas spigot still intact at the base. Similarly, the chandelier was converted to electricity around 1908.

Above the mantelpiece hangs a spectacular curved mirror in an ornate frame. Its reflection shows a painting on the opposite wall, and above the painting a patch of original wallpaper, which featured staggeringly expensive hand-applied gold leaf. On the mantelpiece, under glass, stand two carved alabaster ewers or water pitchers. They match the giant one standing between the two front windows, except the giant one has grown darker over the years without the protective glass.

The priciest piece in the room might be the Victorian rosewood étagère, or shelving unit, purchased in New York City. The prettiest item might be the fretwork desk near the door, a twenty-first birthday gift to the eldest third-generation daughter, Mary. The painting of Native chiefs at Niagara Falls over the piano and below the Dr. Calvin portrait is thought to have been a gift to Tom for his work on the Niagara Parks Commission.

Main Floor: Dining Room

This is the largest room in the house and bright in the afternoon sunlight. The ceiling is spectacular. The home's builders cast it in wet plaster on the floor in sections, which they then raised and fastened in place with brass nails. Visually, the fireplace attracts the main focus. Its wood finish extends around the walls in a painted *trompe l'oeil* effect, a two-dimensional surface appearing as a three-dimensional trim to almost halfway up the walls. Normally, the dining table would have been set for four at its minimum size without the leaf extensions.

At one end of the room a mounted Roosevelt elk's head symbolizes man's superiority over nature, a gift from Mary Baker McQuesten's half-brother, who hunted it in northern Washington State. At the other end can be seen a number of prized items, including the nine-piece silver tea service and a platter bearing the inscription "Mary Baker from her father, June 18th, 1873 [her wedding day]." Along the sideboard a row of desserts is laid out. The charlotte russe, a version of sponge cake, was a favourite. According to family lore, handed down from Reverend Baker, the knife box next to the table was fashioned by a ship's carpenter out of wood from a Spanish ship destroyed in the Napoleonic Wars.

Main Floor: Sitting Room or Family Room

Guests sometimes sat here for tea or a light lunch, but mostly family members retired here after dinner. From a chair at the far end of the room, Mother listened to the radio, sitting closer and closer to the set as her hearing deteriorated. Later the three surviving family members watched black-and-white television.

Reverend Thomas Baker left behind a few naval artifacts. An artwork shows the Duke of Wellington in his dining room at London's Apsley House with the officers he led during the Napoleonic Wars of 1792–1815. A Union Jack on the wall includes lettering that reads, "We are proud to be Canada, God Bless the British Empire." The model sailing ship, perhaps the most fascinating item in the room, was fashioned in England by a French prisoner of the Napoleonic Wars. Prisoners built and sold such products for extra rations and other privileges. Wood from the hull came from a shipwreck. Pieces of chicken, mutton, and fish bones from prison dinners form such details as the masts, spars, and nearly sixty miniature cannons. Human hair forms the rigging.

In front of the model lies a ship's spyglass. So does a chunk of wood with a brass plaque from the 1930s honouring Thomas McQuesten in memory of his Grandfather Baker. The wood was recovered from the sunken HMS *St. Lawrence*, built on Lake Ontario for the War of 1812 and the largest warship ever built on the Great Lakes during the age of sail, with 120 guns. Commanded by Royal Navy Captain James Lucas Yeo, it ensured British superiority on the lakes. Baker served on it as a junior officer, a midshipman.

Next to the door stands an especially beautiful Victorian teapoy, a lockable rosewood box and pedestal for storing different varieties of tea, which was expensive. Above it a photograph on the wall depicts the widowed Mary with her six children in their garden about two years after Isaac's death. Nearby hangs a portrait of Isaac taken the year before he died at the age of forty.

Main Floor: Back Addition

In 1935, the year after Mother's death, Tom added a kitchen and servants' quarters to the back of the house and hired a housekeeper and cook. The housekeeper, who was married, continued to live off-site. The cook, Anne Vallesi, got both bedrooms as an apartment. When she started in 1935 at the age of eighteen, her mother took a photo of her in the garden wearing the black-and-white maid's uniform of the type she was to wear for more than two decades. The museum's female guides wear a copy of the same outfit.

Anne had a boyfriend. She wanted to marry him, but he worked for the electrical company and got electrocuted. Not until 1957, at the age of forty, did she find a husband and leave her job, meaning she served the McQuesten siblings for twenty-two years through the height of Tom's political career and for a considerable time after his death in 1948.

To the museum staff, she has proved a rich resource. Some of the rooms had been photographed for insurance purposes in 1907, and all were documented when the three remaining family members signed an agreement in 1959 to donate the property to the city. Anne has filled in much of the rest. She knew when Hilda moved into the cubbyhole. She confirmed that Mother's room was kept undisturbed from the day she died. She knew the family's favourite desserts, what dishes they used for what occasions, and that although generally they were "meat and potatoes" eaters they loved her Italian mother's spaghetti and meatballs recipe. Vallesi cooked it once a week, and "they just devoured it," she told the museum staff.

The McQuestens treated her well, she said. Sometimes they took her with them to restaurants. They treated her to vacations, once to Banff, another time to Chicago. When she retired, they gave her an electric sewing machine and several thousand dollars toward a house. They also gave her a monthly pension, which the estate is obliged to pay until her death.

The kitchen displays milk bottles from 1939, vintage magazines, and a refrigerator at a time when an iceman still delivered ice to most of Hamilton's homes. The extra bedroom contains the Singer sewing machine that Anne used for her own needs and a radio the family provided. She can be seen in photographs on a table in her sparsely furnished bedroom.

Cellar Lounge

As part of the 1935 renovations, Tom converted the Victorian basement kitchen into a lounge where he could socialize with political friends and colleagues on weekends, or simply retreat from his sisters and brother. "One of Ontario's first rec rooms," the museum guides call it. The room is at once modest and indulgent. By then Tom had the money to buy the latest furniture, but instead reupholstered family chairs from the 1870s. "Man Wants Little, Nor That Little Long," his paternal grandfather once wrote, and Tom subscribed to a similar standard of frugality. At the same time ashtrays betray Tom as a heavy smoker. As for the highball glasses carrying Tom's etched signature, Anne Vallesi, the cook, says political friends gave Tom plenty of alcohol for Christmas, but he never touched a drop.

The space doubles as a political trophy room. On the wall to the left of the mantelpiece hang the honorary keys to Fort Henry in

Kingston, which Tom was instrumental in conserving, along with Fort Erie and Fort George in Niagara. Above and to the left hangs a painting of the Rainbow Bridge at Niagara Falls, one of three bridges to the United States that Tom helped get built as Ontario highways minister. A photograph on the mantelpiece shows Tom, third from left, with provincial cabinet colleagues and, sixth from the left, Liberal Premier Mitchell Hepburn.

Royal mementoes stand out. Below the mantel hangs a colour portrait of King George VI and Queen Elizabeth. Their faces also appear on covers of the *Star Weekly*, and next to them a ceramic model of the imaginatively landscaped Oakes Garden Theatre, whose construction Tom oversaw as Niagara Parks Commission chairman between 1935 and 1937. A special place of honour goes to two elaborately carved oak chairs at the right-hand end of the room on either side of Tom's desk. Tom provided the chairs for the Niagara leg of the 1939 Royal Tour, meaning that each chair was graced by a royal posterior. Formalities included the

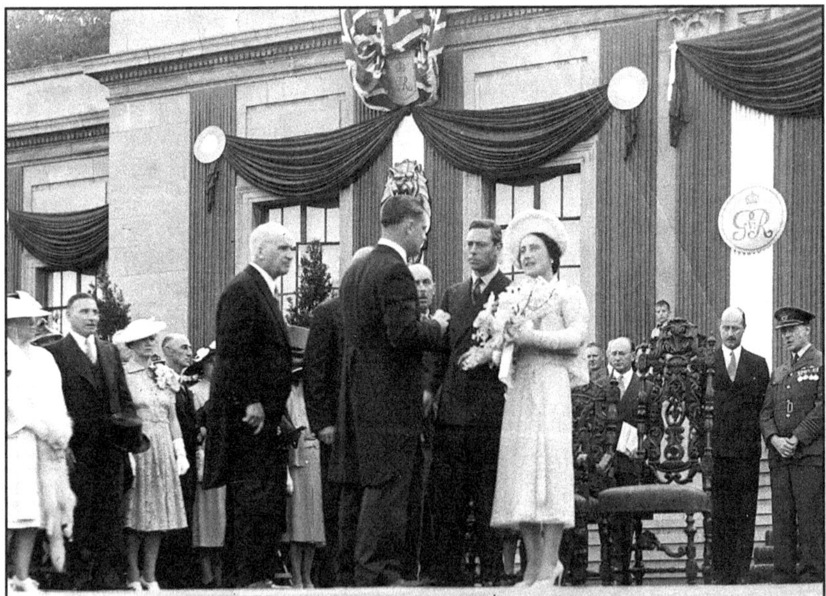

Photo courtesy of Whitehern Historic House and Garden

King George VI and Queen Elizabeth, holding flowers, receive well-wishers at Niagara Falls on June 7, 1939, as Tom McQuesten, with short white hair, stands slightly to one side. Behind the Royals can be seen the two carved oak chairs now in Tom's cellar lounge.

dedication of the Queen Elizabeth Way, the high-water mark of Tom's tenure as highways minister and of his career.

Cellar Hallway

Three lithographs passed down from Tom's maternal grandfather, Reverend Baker, show Hamilton at progressive stages of development: 1848, the time of Whitehern's construction; 1859, the year the first Hamilton waterworks opened to give the city running water; and 1883, the year Tom was born and Hamilton reached a population of fifty thousand people. A hooked rug depicts the Queen Elizabeth Way, the median of trees and shrubs dividing the opposing lanes of traffic. On the same wall, a photograph shows Tom and Hilda at a social occasion probably in 1940 with Hamilton city solicitor A.J. Polson.

Cellar Exhibition Room

Behind the stairs a room provides space for rotating exhibitions. Shows have included the McQuestens' children's toys, their extensive collection of dishes and silverware, and selections from their vast archive of family photos.

Cellar Storage Rooms

In 1935, two servants' bedrooms devolved into storage rooms for a family that liked to save everything. A peek into the first reveals a travelling trunk from 1907, vintage garden furniture, the dumb waiter that once rode between the basement kitchen and dining room, and the original panel of servants' bells used to summon servants from the cellar when needed. The other room stores old crockery, chamber pots, and wash basins. Sisters Mary and Hilda also continued to use the room for making and storing preserves. Children tend to especially like the humane mousetrap on the floor. Resembling a miniature motel, it imprisoned the mouse for later release. It did not, however, catch every mouse. "Alice [a servant] as usual meandering at midnight went into the cellar … saw a mouse jump out of a basket, fell and broke her wrist," Mother wrote in 1929.

THE ENDURING LEGACY OF THOMAS MCQUESTEN

1. MacNab Street Presbyterian Church:

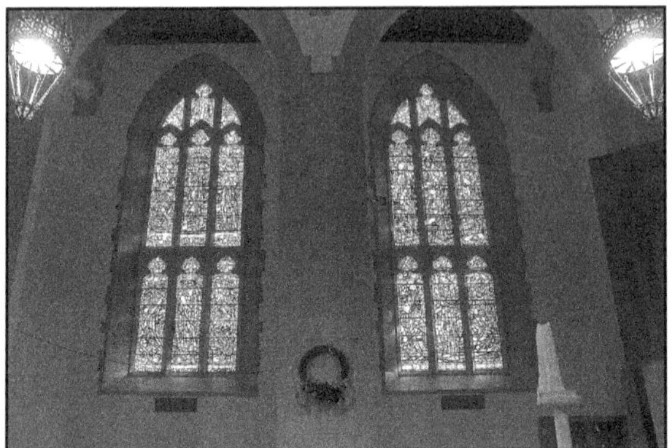

Photo by John Goddard

Patriarch Dr. Calvin financed construction of a church at nearby 116 MacNab Street South that the family attended for more than a hundred years. Two stained-glass windows are dedicated to family members. On the left, "Baptism of Jesus/Temptation on the Mountain," was unveiled in 1935, a gift from Tom McQuesten in memory of his parents, Isaac and Mary. On the right, "Miracle at Cana/Healing the Six," was unveiled in 1936, a gift from the third-generation McQuestens to honour Isaac's parents, and their grandparents, Dr. Calvin and his second wife, Ester.

2. Hamilton Cemetery:

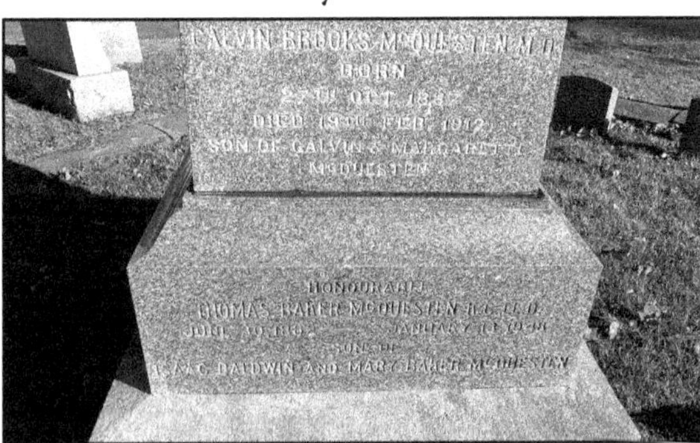

Photo by John Goddard

Tom McQuesten lies buried in Section D5 of Hamilton Cemetery, across the road from Dundurn Castle. Listed above him is his Uncle Calvin, Isaac's elder stepbrother, who moved to New York. The entire cast of

McQuesten characters can be found in the same family plot, including the in-laws Reverend Baker and his wife, Mary Jane, although not Elizabeth "The O.L.," who died in the United States.

3. 15 Bold Street, Hamilton:

The twin townhouses around the corner from Whitehern now go by the collective name of Hereford House and serve as head office to the law firm Turkstra Mazza. The houses were built in 1862, and Isaac McQuesten bought them in 1875, the firm's website says, meaning Tom spent his first seven years here. In one half lived Isaac, Mary, and their children, and in the other half Mary's parents, Reverend Thomas Baker and Mary Jane Baker. In 1885, the family, including Mary's widowed father, moved to Whitehern. The McQuesten estate sold the building in 1969, one year after the death of the last surviving family member, Calvin McQuesten.

4. Royal Botanical Gardens (RBG):

The jewel in the crown of Tom's beautification efforts, the RBG is the largest botanical garden in Canada and a National Historic Site. Among its distinctions, it is home to the world's largest lilac collection, with more than six hundred lilac varieties among its one thousand or so lilac plants. Its centrepiece remains the Rock Garden, a former gravel pit and the first area to be developed. "Last evening Tom took us all to see the Rock Garden," Mother wrote to her son Calvin in July 1930. "It is all beyond description simply amazing."

5. High Level Bridge:

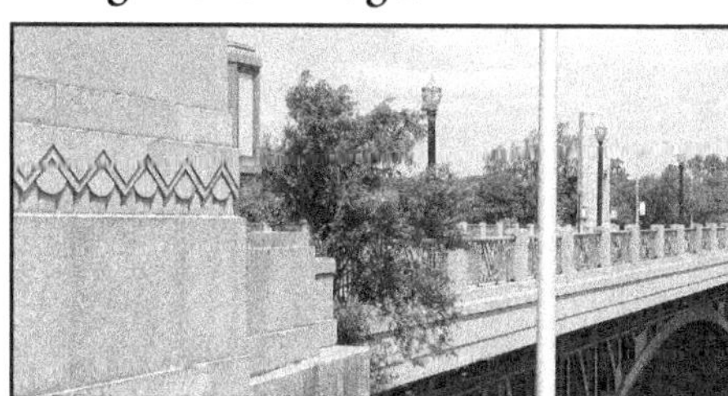
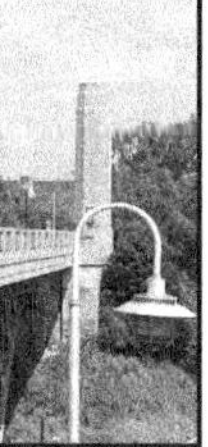

Photo by John Goddard

In 1988, with Princess Margaret officiating, the bridge that formed part of Tom's grand entrance into Hamilton from Toronto formally took the name Thomas B. McQuesten High Level Bridge. Designed by architect John Lyle, also known for Toronto's Union Station and Royal Alexandra Theatre, the bridge is distinctive for its steel arch and four decorative pylons, one at each corner. Each carries the Hamilton coat of arms with its motto COMMERCE, PRUDENCE, INDUSTRY. "Had it not been for Tom's foresight in insisting that the bridge be built to a four-lane width," writes biographer John C. Best, "the original structure would likely have given way long ago to one of the drab structures which have dominated modern highways."

6. Gage Park:

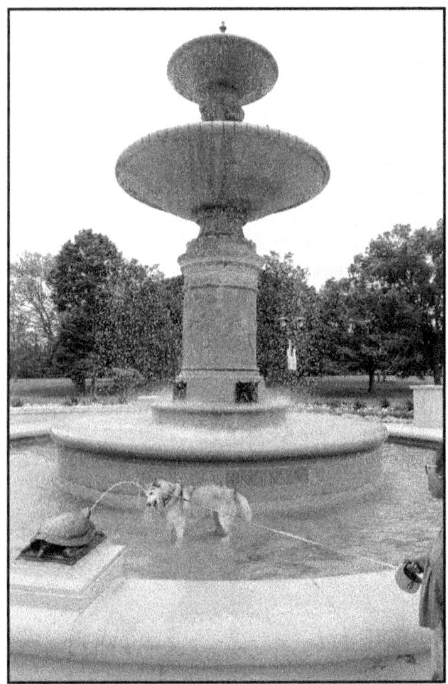

Photo by John Goddard

John Lyle also designed the Gage Park Fountain, featuring a limestone double bowl and water spouting from bronze turtles and ducks. Tom hired Lyle after handling the final negotiations of the 1918 land purchase in Hamilton's east end. The park honours Robert and Hannah Gage, descendants of Stoney Creek's William and Susannah Gage.

7. T.B. McQuesten Community Park:

It is not grand and not his creation, but Hamilton named a park after Tom on the Hamilton escarpment at Upper Wentworth Street and Limeridge Road East. The site includes a baseball diamond, a soccer field, a "creative play area," and asphalt paths suitable for rollerblading.

8. Lion Monument:

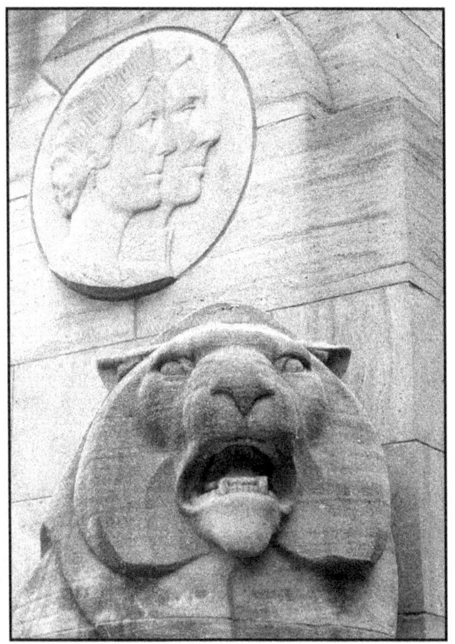

Photo by John Goddard

Tom commissioned a decorative stone pillar to mark the Toronto entrance to the Queen Elizabeth Way near the Humber River. At the monument's base, Toronto sculptor Florence Wyle carved circular medallion-like reliefs of King George VI and Queen Elizabeth. Wyle's life partner and fellow-sculptor, Frances Loring, fashioned the monument's most distinguishing feature, a statue of a pugnacious lion "rising to its feet and roaring splendidly — the traditional symbol of England rising from slumber to meet the challenge of the Second World War," in the words of Wyle and Loring biographer Elspeth Cameron. The lion became one of Loring's most famous works — "a Toronto landmark," Cameron says. Children passing it in cars said, "Hello, lucky lion," and "Goodbye, lucky lion." It stands today on the east bank of the Humber River in Sunnyside Park.

9. Henley Bridge:

One of Canada's most beautiful bridges when King George VI and Queen Elizabeth opened it in 1939, the Henley Bridge consists of twin spans over Twelve Mile Creek at St. Catharines. They carry traffic in either direction on the divided Queen Elizabeth Way. The highway's later expansion compromised much of the original design, but artistic flourishes can still be seen, the most prominent being the twin stone sculptures in the median at either entrance. Each protrudes like the stylized prow of a ship and features four back-to-back lions facing in the four main directions of the compass. All the lions bear ceremonial shields.

10. Oakes Garden Theatre:

Across from the Rainbow Bridge at Niagara Falls, the terraced garden with ornamental iron gates and a limestone wall marks the gateway to the park leading to Table Rock at Horseshoe Falls. Local millionaire Sir Harry Oakes donated the land. To create the park, Tom engaged his usual crew of artists, including architect W.L. Somerville, landscaper Howard Dunington-Grubb, and sculptors Frances Loring and Florence Wyle. Tom attended the opening gala in 1937.

11. Rainbow Tower Carillon:

Marilyn Monroe, as Rose Loomis, runs up the tower steps to escape her husband, played by Joseph Cotten, in the 1953 film noir *Niagara*, but he catches her and strangles her beneath the bells. "I loved you, Rose, you know that," he says when she is dead. Tom had the tower built at the Rainbow Bridge as a welcome to American visitors, with fifty-five bells weighing a total of thirty-nine metric tonnes. For years a resident carillonneur played the bells on a series of oak levers and foot pedals. Today an automated system plays the bells three times a day: noon to one o'clock, three to four o'clock, and six to seven o'clock.

**12. Pieces of the Memorial Arch,
Formerly at Niagara Falls, Now in Toronto:**

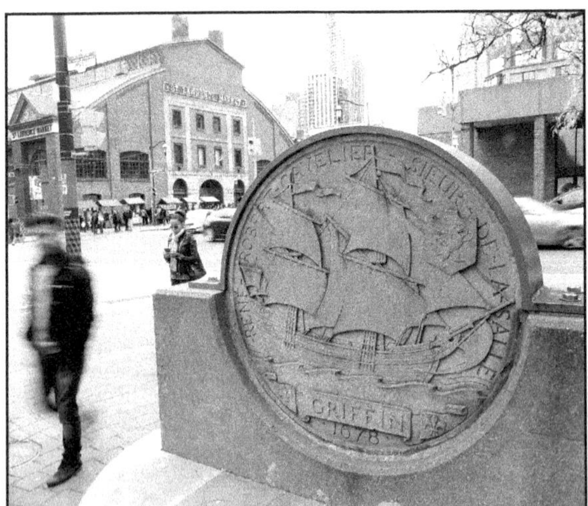

Photo by John Goddard

To commemorate certain pre-Confederation events, Tom McQuesten led the construction at Niagara Falls of what he called a Memorial Arch. It marked the War of 1812, paid tribute to United Empire Loyalists in the American Revolution, and honoured rebel leader William Lyon Mackenzie, grandfather to Prime Minister Mackenzie King. The arch opened in 1938 and was torn down in 1967, but parts of it can still be found at two Toronto locations. The courtyard of Mackenzie House museum, just off Yonge-Dundas Square at 82 Bond Street, displays panels dedicated to Mackenzie and his 1837 Upper Canada Rebellion. A monument at the northeast corner of Front and Jarvis Streets showcases two medallions scavenged from high on either side of the arch. One medallion depicts *Le Griffon*, the first sailing ship on Lake Erie, launched in 1679 by French explorer René-Robert Cavelier, Sieur de La Salle. The flip side shows the HMS *St. Lawrence*, built on Lake Ontario for the War of 1812 and the largest warship ever built on the Great Lakes in the age of sail. Tom's grandfather, Thomas Baker, served on it as a midshipman.

Why Go?

Nowhere else in North America can you see a giant steam engine in its original location still running as though it were pumping water. When the twin waterworks engines commenced operation in 1859 to supply the City of Hamilton with fresh, safe, running water, they counted as the largest, most powerful steam engines ever constructed in North America. Local craftsmen built them into the floors and walls of a limestone building designed almost like a chapel, which also still stands. Hamiltonians felt justly proud. The size and power of the engines, and the beauty of the masonry, spoke of the city's boldness, modernity, and ambition. A plaque on an outside wall reads: "This dignified building … houses one of Canada's greatest surviving engineering achievements of the mid-19th century." It is a National Historic Site.

Address

900 Woodward Avenue, in the northeast end of Hamilton next to Lake Ontario.

Getting There by Public Transit

From the Hamilton GO Centre, the No. 4 bus gets you there in forty minutes without changing buses. You can also catch the No. 4 on Bay Street between Hunter Street West and York Boulevard. Another handy stop is opposite the Hamilton Market entrance at York Boulevard and MacNab Street North. Get off at Glow and Woodward Avenues and walk two blocks north to the museum.

HAMILTON MUSEUM OF STEAM AND TECHNOLOGY (THE WATERWORKS)

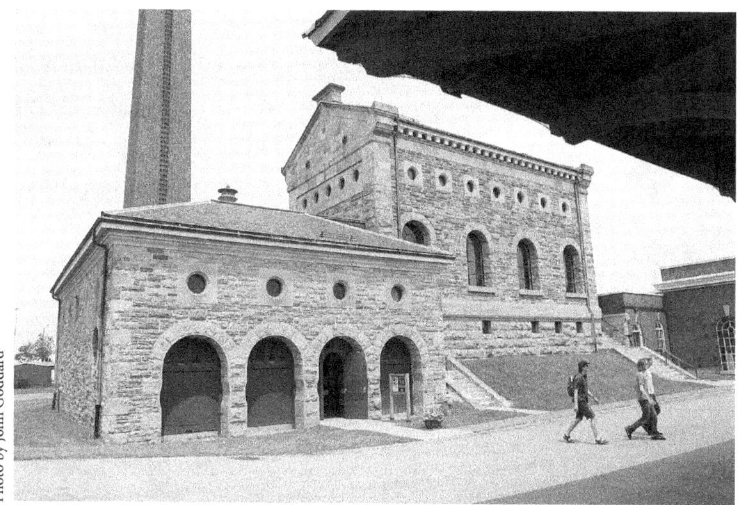

Photo by John Goddard

"All the character and dignity of a North Italian chapel and campanile," writes classical scholar Alexander McKay. The site includes the storage overhang, tall chimney, boiler house with four doors, and vaulted pump house with two steam engines built into its floors and walls.

THREE CANADIAN HEROES: KEEFER, GARTSHORE, MCFARLANE

Hamilton needed fresh, clean, running water. In the mid-1800s, residents still drew water from five community wells for drinking, cooking, and washing. They hauled it by hand in buckets or paid to have it delivered by horse-drawn cart. With no handy water supply, they could not dampen the city's unpaved streets. Every passing carriage tossed up swirls of dust that settled over furniture, clothing, and fruit and vegetable stalls, and got drawn into the throat and lungs. Fire posed a chronic threat. Wooden shops and houses periodically went up in flames, and all that firemen could do was pump water by hand from horse-drawn trucks, or form people into lines with pails to toss water at the blaze.

Worst of all, when immigrant ships docked at the busy port, infectious diseases spread to the harbour's outhouses and into the city's groundwater. The wells turned into transmission sites for deadly diseases, including dysentery, typhoid, and especially cholera. During a single eight-week period in 1854, cholera killed 552 people out of a population of twenty thousand — one in forty residents.

Nobody knew about germs and microbes, but they knew that their wells were tainted and that they needed a clean water source. They knew that to transform Hamilton from a disease-ridden firetrap into a city with a future they needed a means to pump water from a nearby river or lake. A waterworks would be expensive to build at a time when the city was overextended with railway construction. It would also be technologically daunting at a time when nobody in North America had ever tried to forge castings as massive as those needed for water-pumping steam engines. But civic leaders persevered. They had to. They gathered the brightest talents they could find and set them to work, and in 1860 Queen Victoria's eldest son turned a handle to start two of the biggest steam engines ever built to that time in North America.

"They move with great smoothness, and are very well finished," one reporter said of the machinery in 1860.

"The best engine house in the country," John A. Macdonald, attorney general for Canada West and future Canadian prime minister, said on a tour of the works in 1859.

"The best piece of hydraulic masonry to be seen anywhere," the *Canadian Illustrated News* said of the building in 1863.

Credit fell mostly to three genuine Canadian heroes. In their drive for technical precision and civic beauty, they not only built a waterworks but also set a national standard for industrialization. Chief engineer Thomas Keefer designed the system and oversaw its construction. Foundry owner John Gartshore oversaw the forging of the giant boilers and engines. James McFarlane helped forge the machines, took charge of installing them, and for the next fifty-one years kept them running.

Thomas Coltrin Keefer, Designer, Chief Engineer, Project Manager

Keefer first made his name as a transportation visionary. In 1850, when he was twenty-nine, he published a booklet called *Philosophy of Railroads*, quickly followed by *The Canals of Canada.* In his first treatise, bursting with optimism, he conjured up a Canada transformed by the prosperity that would come from what he called "the civilizing tendency of the locomotive," and urged that the Province of Canada, as Ontario and Quebec were then called, build railways at a pace set by the United States.

"We are placed beside a restless, early-rising, 'go-a-head' people," he wrote of Americans with his own typical energy and verve, "a people who are following the sun Westward, as if to obtain a greater portion of daylight: — *we* cannot hold back — we must tighten our own traces or be overrun — we must *use* what we have or *lose* what we already possess."

Keefer came by his industriousness naturally. He was born in 1821 at Thorold, Ontario, near Niagara Falls. His father, George, was to serve as first president of the Welland Canal Company, helping to construct the first shipping canal between Lake Ontario and Lake Erie. One of his older brothers, John, was to own the local general store and post office, and in 1866 would build the grand house that stands now as the boutique tourist hotel, the Keefer Mansion Inn.

Young Thomas, like his father, went into engineering. In 1838, fresh out of Upper Canada College, he took a job as an apprentice on the Erie Canal in New York State. Afterward he served as an assistant engineer to help deepen the Welland Canal, and later took charge of timber slides and river improvements at Ottawa, then called Bytown.

In 1850, he published his transportation booklets and went on to distinguish himself in Montreal as a pioneer in Canadian waterworks design. He worked as a harbour and shipping canal engineer, and designed the city's first waterworks by harnessing the flow of the St. Lawrence River to help pump water to reservoirs on Mount Royal.

In 1854, he arrived in Hamilton. Civic leaders were holding a waterworks design competition and had hired Keefer to judge it. He was thirty-three years old, an independent engineering consultant. An illustration from the time shows him with dark eyes focused on the distance, longish dark hair parted smartly on the left, and a bushy moustache bridging two prominent mutton chops. Surrounding him are scaffolding, ladders, pulleys, shovels, and a number of novel engineering works, including the Welland Canal and a city fire hydrant. "By far the ablest man to be found on the continent for the work," Hamilton Water Commission chairman Adam Brown was later to say of him.

Six designers entered the contest. Keefer awarded third-, second-, and first-place prizes and pronounced the winning submission viable. Ultimately, however, questions arose over the proposed use of Burlington Bay. The marshes of nearby Cootes Paradise turned the bay cloudy at certain times of the year, leading city commissioners to ask Keefer to research other potential sources instead, including river systems. When he recommended Lake Ontario as the cleanest, most dependable long-term source, the commissioners asked him to personally design and build a system with the lake in mind.

In early 1857 he got to work. Hamilton's population at the time stood at twenty thousand people. He would create a waterworks to serve more than double that number, one that would supply eleven million litres a day for residents, businesses, and industry.

Keefer started with a large filtering pond. Next to the lake, workers dug a basin that gradually filled with water filtered by the sand, free of weeds and fish, and suitable for drinking. The idea was to pump the basin water through pipes to a reservoir on the Niagara Escarpment. From there gravity would take the water through other pipes to houses and businesses in the city below.

To move the water uphill, Keefer would need a pump house. He chose a site near the lake and basin outside the city limits among farmers' fields, then designed and oversaw construction of four main structures. Square timbers held aloft a large roof canopy to protect construction machinery and later to shelter coal for the boilers. A red-brick chimney rose forty-six metres to become the area's tallest landmark, a reference point for Lake Ontario sailors. Between the canopy and the chimney, workers constructed the pump house, consisting of two adjoining buildings of brick and cut greystone. One half housed the boilers, the other half the giant steam engines.

The pump house wowed critics when it was first built and continues to captivate visitors today. In his 1967 booklet *Victorian Architecture in Hamilton*, classical scholar Alexander McKay likened it to Roman and Italian landmarks. "Classical in design, the rounded arches recall the proud aqueducts which had stalked across the Roman Campagna," he enthused. "The Old Pump House," he also said of the buildings and chimney, "has all the character and dignity of a North Italian chapel and campanile [bell tower]." In another allusion to Italian classicism he wrote, "The splendid cast iron columns [of the engines] recall the equally impressive Roman underground cisterns around Naples."

John Gartshore, Foundry Owner

A photograph taken late in life shows John Gartshore as a powerfully built man with a grizzled beard, swept-back dark hair, and an expression of calm determination. Nothing stopped him. No setback seemed to even slow him down. In 1833, he left Scotland for Upper Canada. In 1834, he got married in Toronto, and within months lost his bride to cholera. In 1835, he built a house and flour mill at Fergus on the Grand River, and the following year remarried. In 1837, his new flour mill burned down. He moved to Dundas, now a suburb of Hamilton but at the time the more promising industrial centre, with rivers for ready power and easy shipping access to Lake Ontario through the Desjardins Canal. In 1838, he built a foundry. In 1846, the foundry burned down in its entirety — two-storey main building, woodworking shop, pattern shop, stove assembly shop, moulding and blacksmith shops, and all the workmen's tools, as well as books, plans, and drawings. He rebuilt, this time raising a handsome two-storey stone structure that still stands as a renovated office and retail space at 64 Hatt Street.

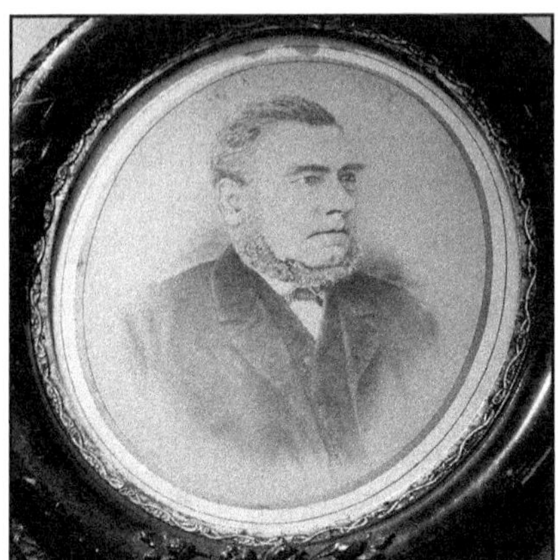

Photo by John Goddard courtesy of the Dundas Museum & Archives

A photographic portrait at the Dundas Museum & Archives shows John Gartshore as a powerfully built man of calm determination. Nothing stopped him. No setback seemed to even slow him down.

In 1857, when Keefer started his designs, Gartshore was forty-seven years old. His Dundas Iron and Brass Foundry stood as the town's top employer and as one of the largest and most innovative manufacturing plants in Canada West. It was producing stoves, steam boilers, machinery for sawmills and gristmills, marine engines for the rapidly developing steamship industry, and a special Treble-suction Smut Machine that cleaned mould from wheat. The foundry also functioned as an unofficial trade school for mechanics and other workers who would then take their skills to other parts of Canada and to the United States.

Gartshore's business was thriving, and when Hamilton tendered the contract for its waterworks, he placed a bid. The project would be his biggest challenge ever and would solidify his name as one of the great foundry owners of North America. He had never forged iron castings of the size the Hamilton engines would require, but neither had anybody else on the continent.

Keefer had assumed the castings would come from Great Britain, but Gartshore made an offer the city could not refuse. He offered to be paid in debentures, meaning that he would front all the costs of materials and labour, and accept deferred payments. His bid proved wildly generous. Gartshore would spend a small fortune building and installing the boilers and giant engines, and overcoming unprecedented technical challenges, and the city would never fully reimburse him. In 1862, two years after the waterworks' official opening, Hamilton would go bankrupt from overspending on railways and other infrastructure. The Dundas foundry would struggle afterward as a result, but to this day the owner's name shines from a polished brass plaque on each engine: "John Gartshore, Contractor & Builder, Dundas Foundry C.W. [Canada West]."

Gartshore built the twin stream engines that Keefer designed. Each was gigantic, modelled on those installed in 1852 to supply water to London, England. Each of four boilers weighed eight metric tons, nearly the weight of two fully grown African elephants. On each engine the flywheel, which steadied the pump's velocity, spanned more than seven metres in diameter — nearly three storeys high. Each weighed twenty metric tons or more than four elephants. On each engine, the "walking beam," a teeter-totter type beam that connects the flywheel to the pump, weighed almost thirteen metric tons — nearly three elephants — and somehow each had to be positioned high near the pump-house ceiling, one of the toughest jobs of all.

Gartshore executed his job perfectly. The building contractor, George Worthington, was running four months behind schedule, eating into Gartshore's time to install and test the machines, but Keefer never appeared to worry. "From the character of the work furnished by Mr. Gartshore," the chief engineer wrote in one of his progress reports to the water commissioners, "I have no doubt we shall be able to maintain an uninterrupted supply [of water] within a week after the Engines are started."

He was right. The first time they were started in 1859 both performed flawlessly. They did so again on September 21, 1860, when nineteen-year-old Albert Edward, Prince of Wales — Queen Victoria's eldest son and heir to the throne of the British Empire — officiated at the opening ceremony. Albert Edward was later to become King Edward VII, great-grandfather of Elizabeth II.

"Who living in Canada had not heard of the Hamilton waterworks — of the large amount of money spent upon them, and of their final success as an engineering work?" an official account of the ceremony reads. "Proceeding at once to the engine-house, there was His Royal Highness. To the left of the double flight of broad stone steps giving entrance to the building, a square platform had been erected, ornamented with cedar and with wreaths of flowers. Over it stood a canopy of a very handsome design. The floor was nicely carpeted and furnished with chairs."

On one of those chairs sat Sir Allan Napier MacNab, Dundurn Castle's proprietor and former premier of the Province of Canada. He had hosted Prince Albert Edward at lunch that day. Water Commission chairman Adam Brown made a speech, then the prince entered the pump house through its red double doors.

"He started the engines simply by turning a small handle," the official account says. "The steam passed into the cylinders, and they immediately commenced working."

From the nearby beach artillery guns fired. The official entourage descended the steps to a fleet of carriages. Once the party reached the shore, they stepped onto a long carpet spread over the sand, mounted a specially installed floating wharf, and boarded a small steamer, the *Peerless*.

Historic accounts also like to mention little Johnny Gibson. Chairman Brown had asked the principal of Central School to appoint his most promising pupil to be the first person to officially turn on a city tap. The principal chose well. The schoolboy grew up to become Sir John Morison Gibson, lawyer, businessman, politician, and tenth lieutenant governor of Ontario, serving as vice-regal representative to the same Albert Edward, or King Edward VII. Gibson also appears in the second chapter of this book attending Isaac McQuesten's funeral.

James McFarlane, Foundry Foreman, Installations Manager, Waterworks Engineer

For Thomas Keefer and John Gartshore, the Hamilton Waterworks proved a career highlight. For James McFarlane the project proved a career. He came to Canada in 1854 from Glasgow, Scotland, where he had trained as an engineer. After a brief stay in Montreal, he moved to Dundas where he took a Scottish-born bride and landed a job at the Dundas Iron and Brass Foundry. He was twenty-nine years old. A drawing of him five years later depicts him as strong and commanding, leaning against the second-floor balustrade of the pump house while wearing a seaman's-type cap, a black beard with no moustache, and a suit of clothes compete with vest. When the pump-house contract came through, Gartshore put McFarlane in charge of casting the boilers and steam engines, then installing them with a workforce that varied between fifty and one hundred men.

"For this job McFarlane's talents were admirably suited, for he was a man of uncompromising standards," William and Evelyn James write in their 1978 book *"A Sufficient Quantity of Pure and Wholesome Water": The Story*

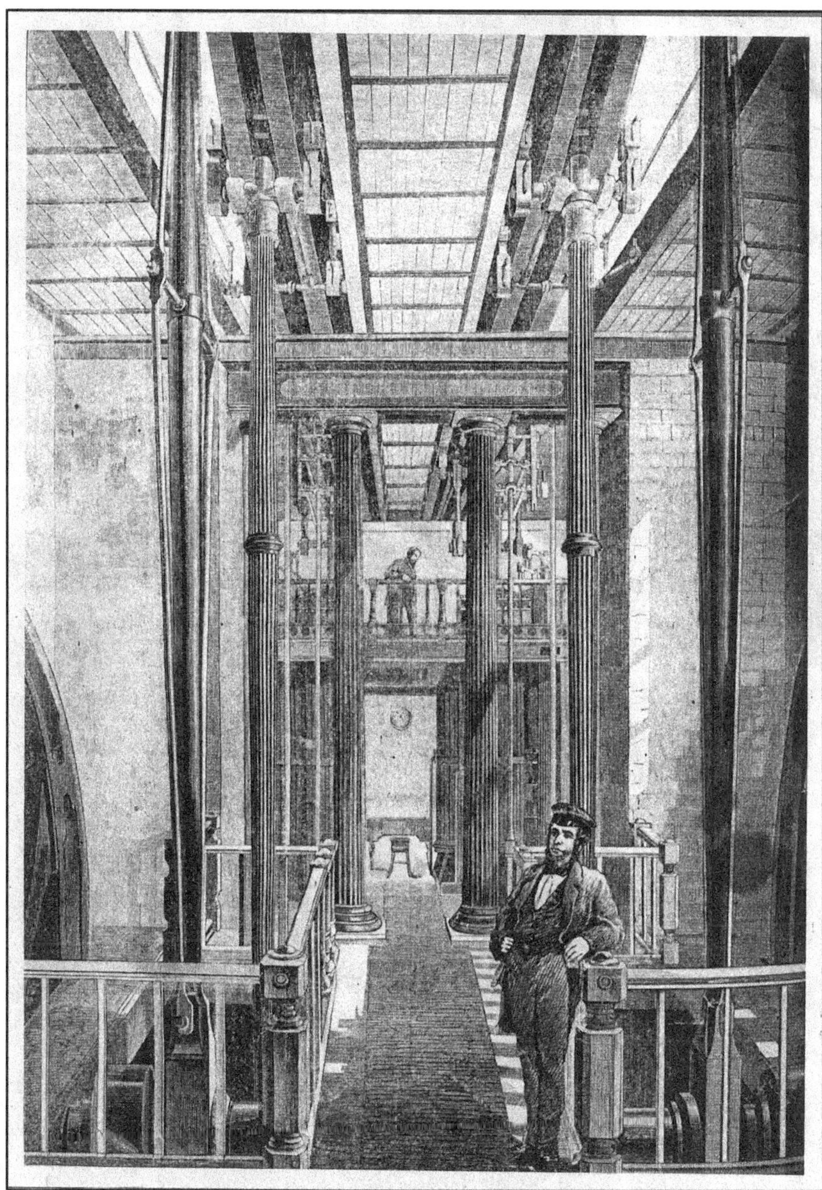

Image courtesy of the Hamilton Steam and Technology Museum

A sketch from the early days of the first Hamilton Waterworks depicts James McFarlane as both relaxed and commanding against a second-floor railing. He cast the steam engines, installed them, and ran them for fifty-one years.

of Hamilton's Old Pumphouse. McFarlane built the engines into the building's framework as it was taking shape, the authors also say, "so that both stonework and machinery grew together, with absolute precision and minimal delay." In other words, he built the pump house and the engines as one — the main reason they survive today. Anybody tempted to sell the engines for scrap would have had to first separate the engines from the building.

On enormous sleds drawn by teams of horses, McFarlane gingerly hauled the outsized castings to the pump-house site. As heavy and strong as cast iron is, it is also fragile. Under stress it does not bend, it shatters. At some point one of the enormous flywheels slid off the sled and sank into the mud on Beach Road. McFarlane could not retrieve it until the soil dried in late spring, but it remained intact.

Much of the credit for the waterworks rightfully went to Thomas Keefer and John Gartshore for their vision, determination, and managerial talent, but generous praise also fell to McFarlane for his rigorous attention to detail. So pleased were Hamilton's water commissioners with his standards that when the job was done they hired him to run the pump-house site as engineer and building manager. They also held him to a demanding job description.

"The Engineer," McFarlane's original one-year contract reads, "shall and will preserve and keep the engines and machinery in perfect working order and in neat and clean condition ... [and] shall and will during such periods take good and sufficient care of the buildings, filtering basin and grounds ... and also of all coal, wood, oils, tools and other stores."

To be available at all times in the rural setting, McFarlane moved into a large brick home on the site, since demolished, with his wife, Mary Fraser, and their seven children. After Mary died in the late 1860s, or perhaps 1870, McFarlane married the farmer's daughter next door, Sarah Lottridge. Together they had four more children, and authors William and Evelyn James say that a number of second-generation marriages developed between the McFarlanes, the Lottridges, and another neighbouring farming family named Bates. Early photographs show the families picnicking together and punting on the nearby creek.

Essentially, the pump house was a family-run operation. McFarlane's wife and daughters provided three meals a day to employees living in a second on-site residence. On the kitchen stove, they also boiled the engine-lubricating oil — often linseed oil or, more commonly, animal fat. All six McFarlane boys worked in the plant when they turned eleven or twelve, shovelling ash from the fires and helping in other ways.

Late in life the youngest child, Blair, wrote a brief reminiscence for an engineering club newsletter. He paid tribute to his father, James McFarlane, who was sixty years old when Blair was born. "He was among the most knowledgeable and proficient then in his line, equally able to work in wood as well as metals," the son wrote. "A strict disciplinarian, he had to have unbounded patience, and exercised it, in rearing and laying the foundations for training a young monkey like me."

Blair mentioned swimming with buddies in the filtering basin — the city's drinking water — and sneaking up to the fourth floor of the pump house to ride one of the enormous walking beams as it rocked up and down above all the other machinery, a dangerous stunt. "I always knew where my father was," he wrote in 1975 at the age of eighty-six, suggesting he never got caught.

The Hamilton Waterworks brought cholera under control. Never again did the city experience a serious outbreak. The waterworks also helped keep street dust in check and protected the city from fire, reducing fire losses and fire insurance rates. In the short term, the city struggled financially, declaring bankruptcy in 1862, two years after the teenage prince presided at the opening ceremony, and residents started to move away. The city took years to recover, but over the longer term it grew and prospered, and within thirty years of the waterworks' opening its population quadrupled in size to eighty thousand people.

The waterworks helped transform Hamilton into one of the dominant manufacturing hubs of pre-Confederation Canada. For twenty-eight years, beginning in 1859, the twin engines took turns pumping fresh water to the city. In 1887, a supplementary pump house opened next door to help meet demand. In 1910, fifty-one years after the waterworks opened, the steam era ended. Electric pumps took over and McFarlane retired at the age of eighty-one. Until 1928, however, the old steam engines served as backups, and as late as the end of the Second World War they were maintained in operating condition. In 1965, the supplementary pump house was demolished, but nobody moved to scrap the Keefer-Gartshore-McFarlane original. In 1971, the Historic Sites and Monuments Board of Canada designated it a National Historic Site. In 1983, the site reopened as a museum to commemorate the age of steam-powered industrial transformation.

WALK-THROUGH: INGENUITY AND ELEGANCE

The name sounds a bit dull — "Hamilton Museum of Steam and Technology." Some people prefer "The Old Pump House," which sounds warmer and friendlier, or "the Steam and Tech," which sounds diminutive and affectionate. I call it "the Old Waterworks," or just "the Waterworks," but probably no name could adequately evoke the ingenuity and elegance attached to this once-rural collection of pre-Confederation buildings that helped transform Hamilton into a modern city and primary manufacturing hub.

Four main components make up the site. All belong to the original 1857–59 construction:

- the woodshed that sheltered wood, then coal, for the boilers;
- the chimney that carried smoke away from the boilers;
- the boiler house that produced steam for the engines; and
- the pump house, or engine house, that harnessed steam pressure to pump water from Lake Ontario to the Niagara Escarpment.

Two subsequent buildings stand nearby: a carpenter's shed that serves as a staff office, and a 1913 waterworks building due to reopen eventually as an exhibition space showcasing Hamilton's industrial past. Visitors head first to a reception desk in the boiler house. The guided tour begins at the woodshed.

Woodshed

Some buildings have an overhang; this overhang has a building. Thick square timbers hold aloft a broad roof without walls, the first structure built on-site in 1857. Originally, it sheltered equipment and machine parts. Once the waterworks were built, the canopy protected a woodpile used to fuel the boilers. Within months, coal arriving by train from Pennsylvania replaced the wood, and the space became known as "the coal shed." In 1916, workers added walls to the back half of the structure as a maintenance shop. Today the shop serves as the museum's orientation room. It includes several highlights:

The Gore Park Model: As a centennial project in 1967, Hamilton bus driver Meryn Fortney built a scale model of the city as it appeared in photographs at the time of Canadian Confederation. The entire model spans four metres. In the smaller section on display, British Union Jacks fly from the windows of downtown Victorian shops and office buildings facing Gore Park, whose central fountain, built in 1859, served to showcase the city's brand-new waterworks.

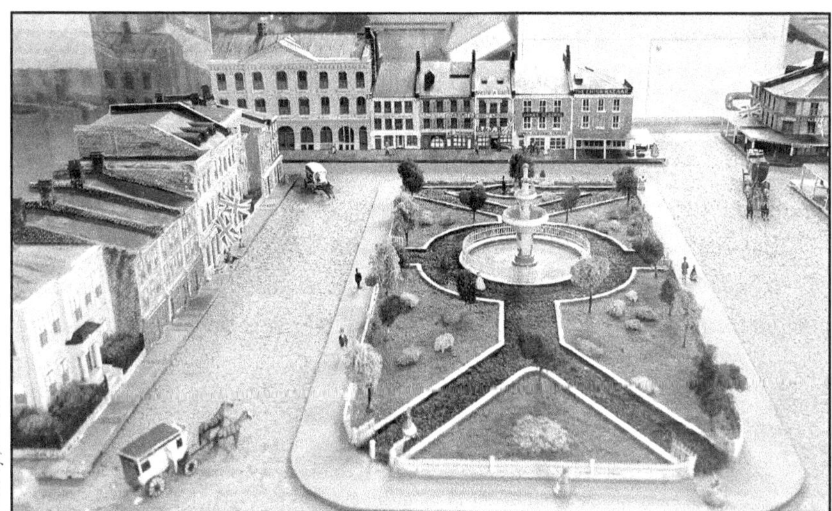

Photo by John Goddard

Union Jacks fly from downtown Victorian buildings facing Gore Park in Meryn Fortney's scale model depicting Hamilton in the year of Canadian Confederation. The fountain, built in 1859, showcases the city's abundant supply of running water.

Keefer Pump-House Model: Behind the Gore Park display stands a brilliantly engineered scale model of the Keefer-Gartshore-McFarlane twin steam engines, with the pump-house walls cut away to demonstrate how the engines worked. Joe Newton, a retired technician at McMaster University's chemical engineering department, built the model in the early 1980s as a member of the Hamilton Model Engineering Club. The original engines took less than two years to build. Newton devoted more than six years to his replica, working meticulously in his basement with a lathe, milling machine, and drill press to produce a precise working facsimile. No matter how small or fiddly, every detail of the big machines can be seen in Newton's miniatures, right down to the old-fashioned square-headed bolts and the dozens of egg-cup-like brass funnels used for oiling the machine parts.

"When it's done, I'm going to present it to the Hamilton Museum of Steam and Technology at the old pump house as a complementary tool," Newton told the *Hamilton Spectator* in 1983 when he was half finished, "something visitors can look at to get an overall picture of its workings before viewing the real thing."

Gratefully, the museum accepted the donation. A visitor can press a button to start an electric motor, which simulates high-pressure steam travelling through an overhead pipe from the boiler room to the engine house and into the giant cylinders. Each cylinder contains pistons that rise and fall under the steam pressure, controlled by a series of valves and cams. When the cylinders fall, they pull down one end of the walking beam, the massive teeter-totter-like beam built of cast iron. When the walking beam falls at one end, it rises at the other, forcing up the pump. When the pump rises, it sucks water from the lake. When it falls again, it pushes water up toward the reservoir on the Niagara Escarpment. Along the wall, the enormous flywheel steadies the operation. Its sheer weight and momentum smooth out dips and peaks in steam pressure, and keep the pump moving at an even speed.

Information Panels: Chief engineer Thomas Keefer and Dundas foundry owner John Gartshore appropriately star in the information panels on the walls. Recognition is also paid to William Hendrie, who laid the water pipes to the escarpment and the city, and George Worthington, who constructed the waterworks buildings. For the boiler house and engine house, he hauled limestone and sandstone from the escarpment, and used local bricks. "Each building stone was cut on site," one panel says. Other panels explain why the waterworks was necessary and how the system worked.

One panel, entitled "Architecture and Landscape," merits special attention. A sketch shows what early visitors to the waterworks would have seen as they approached from the lake or chimney side of the site. In the background, they would have seen two sizable houses — since demolished — one for the workers, the other for waterworks chief engineer and manager James McFarlane and his large family. Gardens, walkways, and ornamental trees covered the area. In the foreground, visitors would have seen the grand waterworks themselves — "an important civic structure built to announce to the world that Hamilton was a modern growing city," the panel says. "The Italianate style was the fashion for civic buildings in the 1850s," it also says. "The style is typified by the arched pump house windows and the rough stone walls with carefully finished corner pieces. Also notice the intricate brickwork at the top of the chimney, which is intended to suggest a bell tower."

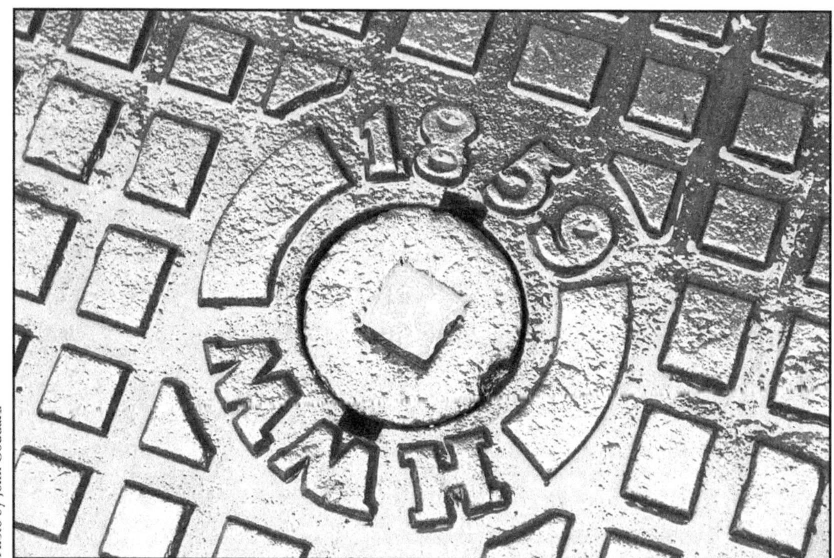

Photo by John Goddard

One of Thomas Keefer's one hundred or so manhole covers from 1859 can be seen next to one of his original fire hydrants outside the boiler house. The letters "HWW" stand for "Hamilton Water Works."

On leaving the woodshed, take a moment to study those features — the rough walls, the finished corners, the intricate chimney top brickwork. To the right, the pump house appears to be built on a grassy mound, which, in fact, are earthworks created to stabilize the already solid stone structure. Notice also the 1859 fire hydrant and manhole cover to the right of the boiler-house entrance. Keefer installed one hundred hydrants throughout the city to immediately reduce loss of life and property through fire.

Boiler House

Enter the building. In Thomas Keefer's time, heat would have hit you like a wall. Interior temperatures soared to around forty-five degrees Celsius. Coal fires heated water to its boiling point in iron tanks, turning the water into steam, which expanded through pipes with such force that it drove the engines. The higher the boiler-room temperature, the easier to convert water into steam. The room was not only hot, it was also smoky and dirty, filled with soot. A person could hardly breathe, but the workers wore no masks, no protection of any kind.

The room contained four boilers, each the size of a school bus and each corresponding to one of the building's four red entrance doors. In 1882, after twenty-two years of operation and with Hamilton's population nearly doubled to thirty-five thousand people, renovators jacked up the roof by one and a half metres and replaced the four original boilers with two larger ones.

On the left-hand wall toward the front of the building, a large round window remains the only one of the original four. Higher up, a row of four smaller windows dates to the 1882 renovation. They provided light and minimal ventilation. Tin sheeting on the ceiling helped reflect the rising heat downward again.

At any one time four to five workers manned the room. In the first three years, when demand was less than capacity, the boilers and engines ran intermittently, so as not to overflow the reservoir. Every day an employee living at the reservoir walked five kilometres down the Niagara Escarpment to tell James McFarlane the water level. When telephones became available, he and McFarlane got one of Hamilton's first sets to spare the reservoir watchman the daily journey.

After three years, the boilers and engines ran twenty-four hours a day. The boiler-house crews took turns working one of two shifts — an eleven-hour day shift and a thirteen-hour night shift. "Firemen" shovelled coal into the boilers, which every day consumed more than two metric tons. "Stokers" tended the fires. Apprentices, usually boys, carried out the ash. It was sweaty, dirty work in a dark room. A fireman might earn $1 a day and a stoker seventy-five cents — "barely enough to support a small family," a panel in the orientation room says.

Today the boilers are long gone. The museum uses the room mostly for temporary exhibitions. To the right of the front entrance, a wall displays part of a boiler similar to those used after 1882. To the left can be seen a permanent collection of small steam engines. A guide will demonstrate them. Several are models sold in toy shops. One is designed to drive a textile loom, another to turn a ship propeller, such as that used on the *Titanic*. Soldiers in the Second World War used the small portable steam engine to generate electricity when no other source could be found.

The largest steam engine on the table was built from scratch a century ago by Percy Ford-Smith. When he finished school at the age of twelve, he apprenticed in a Hamilton machine shop for eleven years. For his final project as an apprentice, he built this model based on the steam engine in the factory where he worked. It still runs. Ford-Smith went on to establish

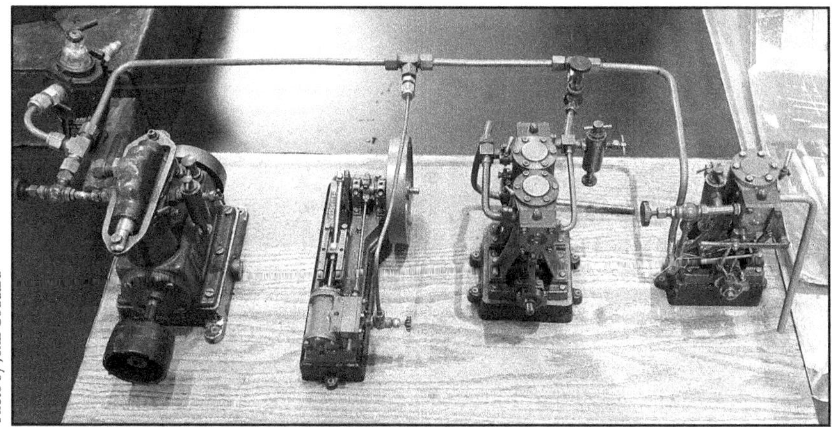

Photo by John Goddard

A permanent exhibition of miniature steam engines occupies the north end of the former boiler house. The one on the left is an actual-size steam-powered engine that generated electricity for mobile Second World War soldiers.

a machinist shop, which exists today in neighbouring Stoney Creek as the Ford-Smith Machine Co., Ltd., manufacturing cranes, hoists, and lifts.

Pump House, First Floor

The term *pump house* can apply collectively to the site or to this section of the building alone, also called the "engine house." A stone wall one metre thick divides the boiler house from the engine house. A thick iron door once separated the two adjoining buildings, as well, to protect the engines in case of an explosion. Mount the steps and pass through the doorway to enter the first floor, a confined area enclosed by engine parts.

You have entered a type of time capsule. You are glimpsing the original twin Gartshore steam engines of 1859, the first giant steam engines fully built in Canada and the only waterworks steam engines left in North America still running in their original location as though they were pumping water. Everything you see is original, not new and made to look old. Some upstairs balustrades were replaced in 1863, the second-floor pressure gauges were replaced in 1882, and a few carpets and stair railings have been installed for visitor safety. Otherwise, everything is as it looked on September 21, 1860, when Prince Albert Edward, the future King Edward VII, turned a throttle and officially declared the waterworks open.

Overhead, the large cast-iron pipe from the boiler room delivered pressurized steam to the large vertical cylinders in full view here. The pipe split left and right, capable of directing steam to either the north engine on the left or the south engine on the right. Normally, one engine ran at a time. The other stood by as a backup.

Pump House, Second Floor

This is the main floor, with the best view of the machinery. Symmetry reigns. The twin engines mirror each other, their respective giant flywheels flanking opposite walls. Notice the columns. Some hold up the building. Others constitute engine parts. All contribute to the overall stylishness of the setting. If not designed by Thomas Keefer, the supporting columns might have focused solely on function, but here they appear as fluted Doric pillars painted forest green with striped black hollows. Some engine parts are also fluted to accentuate the overall esthetic.

Handsome wood insulation encases the engine cylinders. A brass nameplate on each large cylinder reads: "John Gartshore, Contractor & Builder, Dundas Foundry, C.W. [Canada West]." The smooth, curvaceous 1863 balustrades kept workers from falling to the floors below.

The highlight of the tour comes when a guide flicks on an electric motor to start the north engine. The south engine is now dormant, but the north one stays oiled and operational to demonstrate how it once moved under steam. The motor engages the enormous flywheel, which sets everything else in motion. The flywheel rotates counterclockwise, the overhead walking beam rocks back and forth like a teeter-totter, and various columns move up and down, including the all-important pumping column, sucking water up from the lake 545 litres at a time and pushing down to force the water five kilometres up pipes toward the reservoir on the Niagara Escarpment. The engine pumps air instead of water now, and at a rate of three pumps a minute rather than the original fifteen, but little else is left to the imagination.

Visitors sometimes ask what the engines sounded like. Were they loud? No, they were steam engines. They hissed and puffed and moved

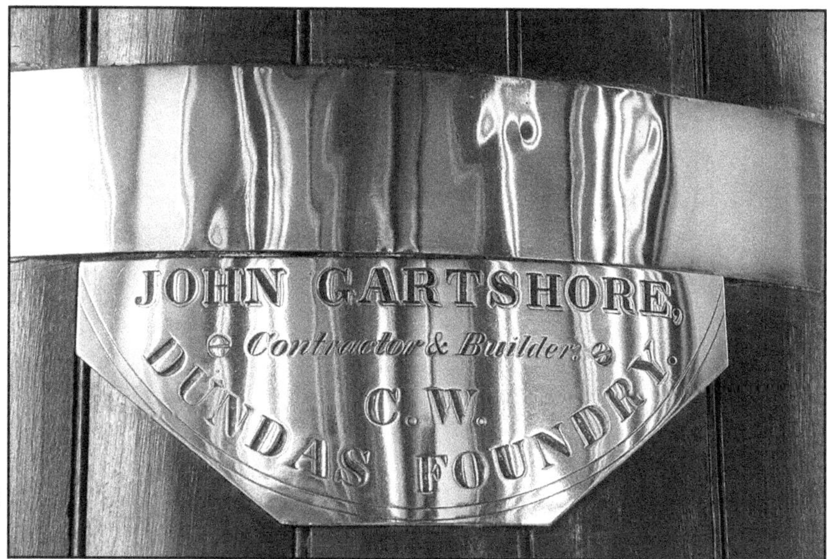

Photo by John Goddard

A polished brass nameplate on the main pillar of each engine still shines for John Gartshore, who forged some of the largest iron parts ever cast to that time in North America. He spent a small fortune and the city never fully repaid him.

with little vibration. The loudest sounds came from the pumping action below. Blair, the youngest of the McFarlane children, long afterward described the sounds as pleasant ones. "I know what it feels like," he wrote of a time after 1883 when more than one engine could run at once, "to sit on your front porch (300 ft away) on a balmy summer evening and hear those two old engines thumping away in the dark."

At the far end of the room stands the main public entrance to the building, a double set of heavy oak doors, painted red, in an arched doorway. A brass plate on the outside arch honours "Thomas C. Keefer, Esq., Chief Engineer, 1859, Hamilton, C.W." The word *Thomas* looks like a correction, as though somebody might originally have written *Tom*. Prince Albert Edward entered through these grand double doors. At the opening ceremony in 1860 he strode through the entrance, passed between the two great engines, stopped toward the far end near the pressure gages, and turned a polished wrought-iron throttle to start one of the pumps. Outside in the yard an open valve sputtered to life as an improvised fountain.

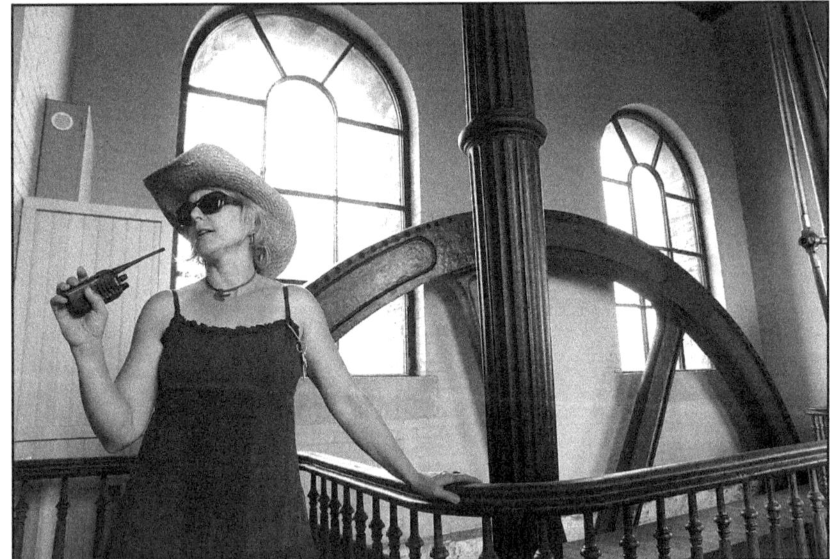

Photo by John Goddard

One hand on a walkie-talkie, the other on the 1863 balustrade, historical interpreter Nancy Prochuk shows off the enormous flywheel that once steadied the rhythm of the north steam engine. The flywheel weighs nearly as much as three full-grown elephants.

Directly opposite the red doors, at the farthest end of the room, James McFarlane's desk still occupies the spot where it served the pump-house chief engineer for fifty-one years. The chair is also original to the property, although not the one used at that desk. A photo on the desk shows McFarlane on the outdoor steps in retirement, looking like an ancient mariner with a full white beard and peaked cap. A sketch shows him leaning proprietarily against the balustrade at the north engine. Also on the desk lies a photocopy of McFarlane's 1861 logbook penned in the beautiful, cursive handwriting typical of the time.

Pump House, Third Floor

The third level offers an intimate view of the cylinders and external piston rods. Each engine has two cylinders, small and large. Steam first enters the small cylinder under high pressure, continues into the large one under lower pressure, then exits into a condenser to be recycled as warm water back into the boilers. The cylinders drive the huge vertical piston rod between them, moving it up and down to drive one end of the walking beam. Look at it rock overhead, an iron casting that weighs almost thirteen metric tons, nearly the weight of three African elephants.

Cast iron is iron that has been melted and poured into a mould to create its shape. Wrought iron has been heated and worked into shape with tools. On the engines you can easily distinguish between both types, with cast iron having a matte finish and wrought iron a polished one.

Look at the large nuts on the cylinders. Each is made of cast iron. The process began with a pattern maker fashioning the shape of the nut from a block of wood. Next, the wooden shape was pressed into a type of wet sand, known as "green sand," to create a mould. Molten iron was then poured into the mould and cooled to create the finished nut. Samples of a wooden bolt and a finished cast-iron bolt can be seen on the nearby desk. At the Dundas Iron and Brass Foundry, James McFarlane served as chief fabricator, whose responsibilities included casting the walking beams — the biggest part of each engine and at the time the largest ever cast in North America. Until McFarlane's achievement at the Gartshore foundry, such enormous pieces had to be imported from Great Britain.

Notice the old-fashioned oil cans on one of the cylinders and on nearby shelves, as well as the little brass cups here and there on the engine parts. The engines needed almost continuous oiling. In the early days of the waterworks, oil meant linseed oil or, more commonly, animal fat heated to boiling. Petroleum-based oils were unheard of. At the pump house an employee called an "oiler" clambered around the engine as it was moving and poured boiling oil into the 105 egg-cup-like openings, finishing one round in about an hour, at which point he would begin again. It was dangerous work.

The engines ran five times as fast as they do now under the museum's electric motor. The oiler climbed into their tight, dark spaces. As safety equipment, he wore a homemade square paper hat, which prevented boiling oil from dripping on his head as he passed under freshly treated engine parts. Otherwise, his only protection was his nimbleness and agility. No injury records were kept, but the oiler constantly risked crushing an arm or losing a finger.

Pump House, Fourth Floor

Here, from a dizzying height, young Blair McFarlane performed his daring rides on the walking beam running at full speed. As far as anybody knows, he never fell and never got caught. "I always knew where my father was when I got on one of the beams for a ride," he recalled at the age of eighty-six, suggesting he never got caught.

The floor is relatively bright, with porthole windows along all four walls and broad, uncarpeted floorboards. Heavy winches at

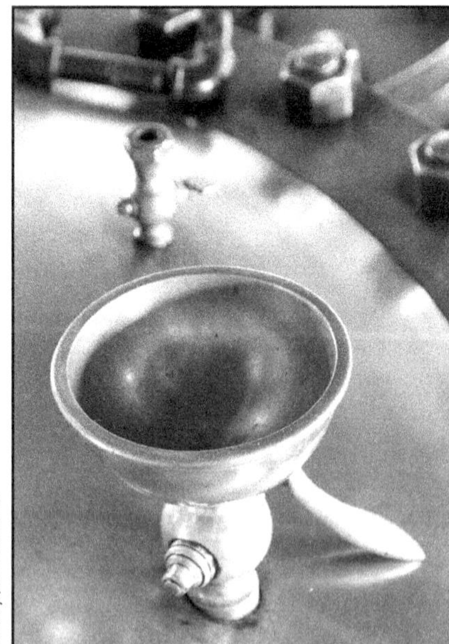

Photo by John Goddard

Brass cups on the engine parts acted as oil funnels, fed almost continuously by an oiler wearing nothing for protection but a paper hat.

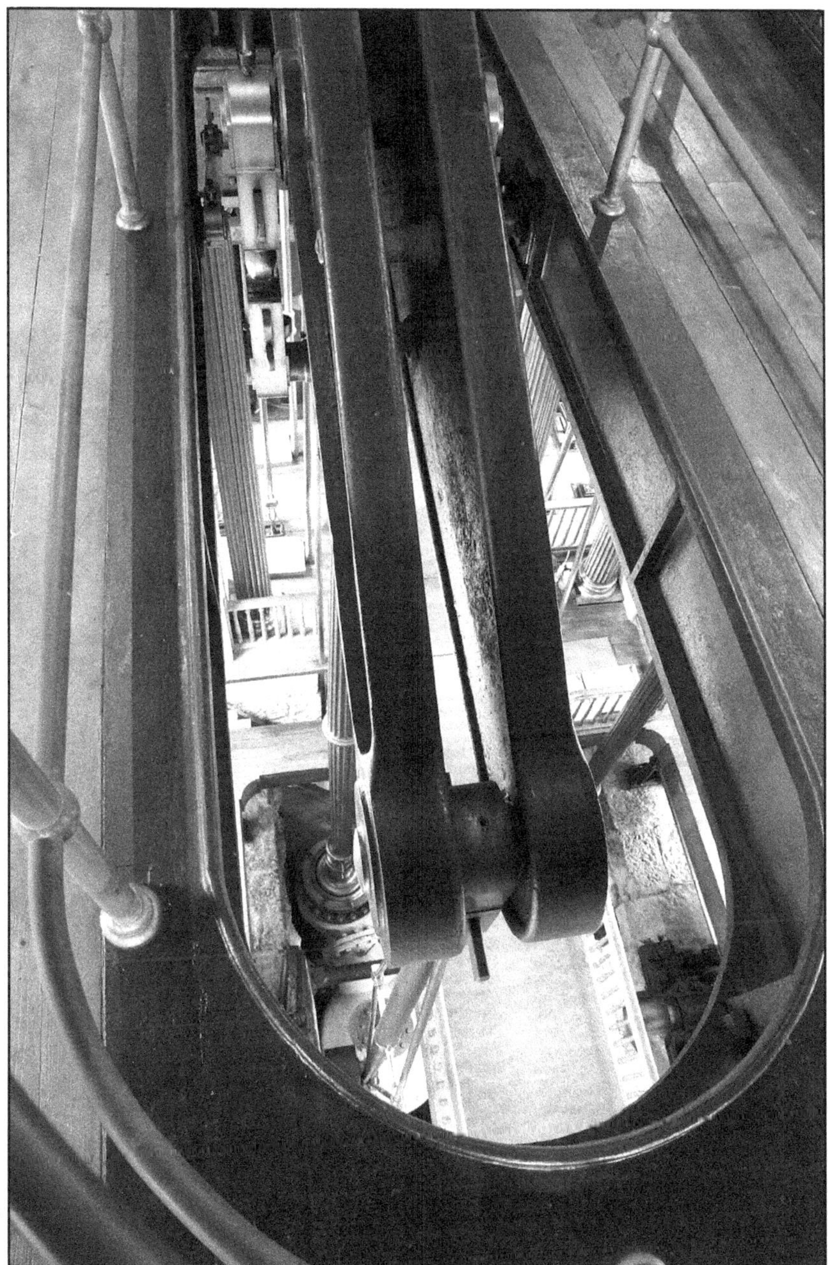

Photo by John Goddard

From an opening in the fourth floor, young Blair McFarlane would climb onto one of the walking beams as it pumped up and down, five times faster than it does today.

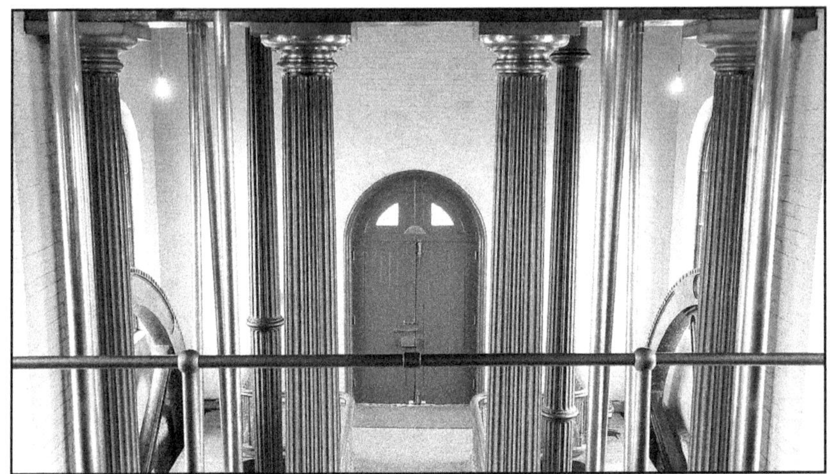

Photo by John Goddard

In the pump house, symmetry reigns. The twin engines mirror each other, their respective flywheels flanking opposite walls. Every pillar and engine part contributes to the overall stylishness of the setting.

one end once held machine parts aloft during maintenance. The walking beams project through gaps in the floor, which are ringed by brass railings with decorative touches that only the workers would have seen — hidden flourishes that speak again to the overall pride of workmanship.

As the walking beam pokes through the gap in the floor in its teeter-totter way, notice how close its bearings come to the floor edge. They almost brush it. In 1859, they came within three millimetres and today they come within the exact same narrow margin. Since the beginning of operations more than 150 years ago, throughout decades of pumping Lake Ontario water to the Niagara Escarpment for the residents and businesses of Hamilton, the Keefer-Gartshore-McFarlane pump house and engines have shifted not one single millimetre.

GOLDEN HORSESHOE LIVE STEAMER DAYS

The term *steam and technology* suggests old trains to some people and conjures up chugging, puffing locomotives. Museum visitors

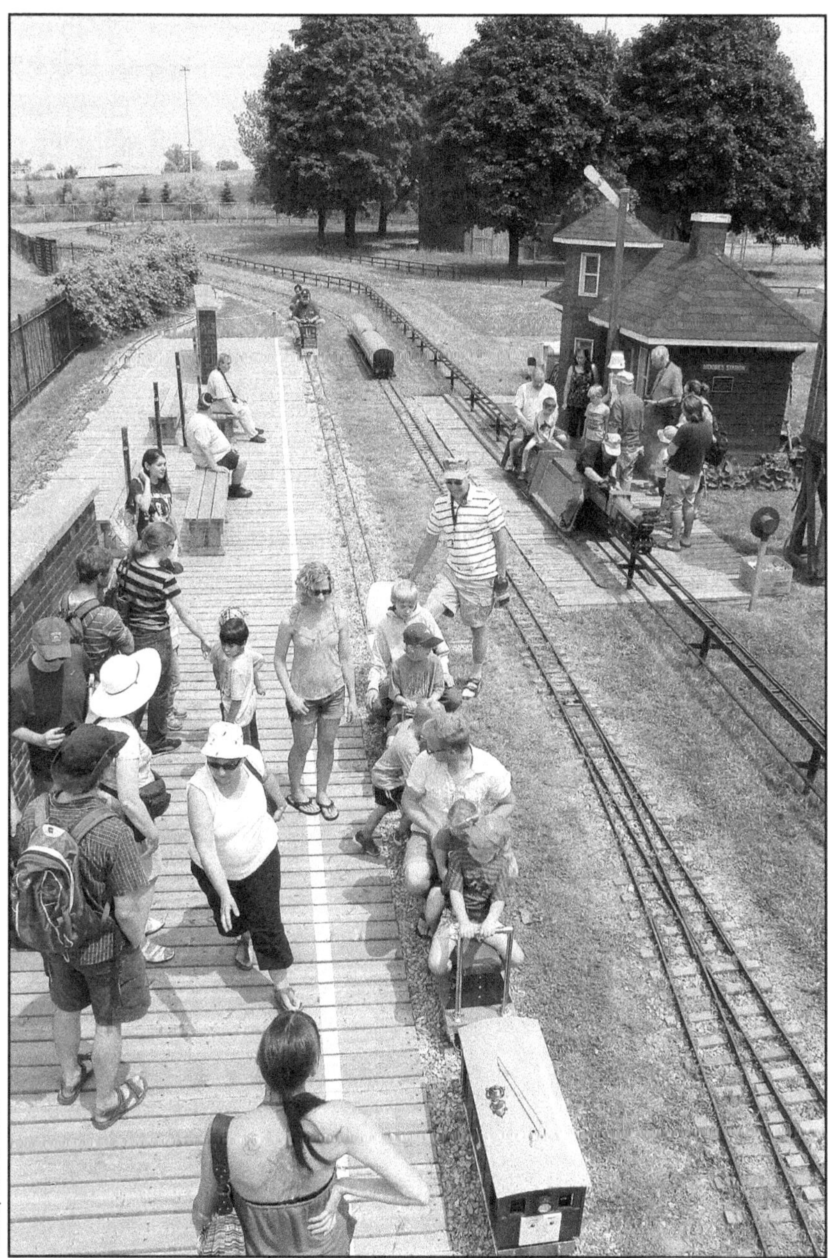

Photo by John Goddard

Ron Watt, in striped shirt and engineer's cap, invites museum visitors to board his train as Fred Eagle, also wearing a cap, hunches to stoke his wood-burning steam engine in front of a miniature railway station.

sometimes arrive expecting to see steam-powered trains, which has led curators to develop a train tradition at a site that had no historic connection to such engines, other than those delivering coal from Pennsylvania. In 1990, a club called the Golden Horseshoe Live Steamers built a track next to the old waterworks and invited the public to take rides.

"We typically attract about four hundred people over the day," says club president Russ Millard. "If we happen to get a bit of publicity, say from CHCH-TV or the *Hamilton Spectator*, the turnout will be more like eight hundred or a thousand."

"Live steam" is steam under pressure obtained by heating water in a boiler. The term *live steam engine* usually applies to a scale model engine running on steam as opposed to a model that resembles a steam engine but uses electricity. In the case of the Golden Horseshoe Live Steamers, most members operate steam-powered trains, although a few run electric ones. The steam engines burn a variety of fuels, usually coal, wood, and propane, although one uses dried corn niblets — "the cleanest fuel of all," says long-time member Steve Bratina.

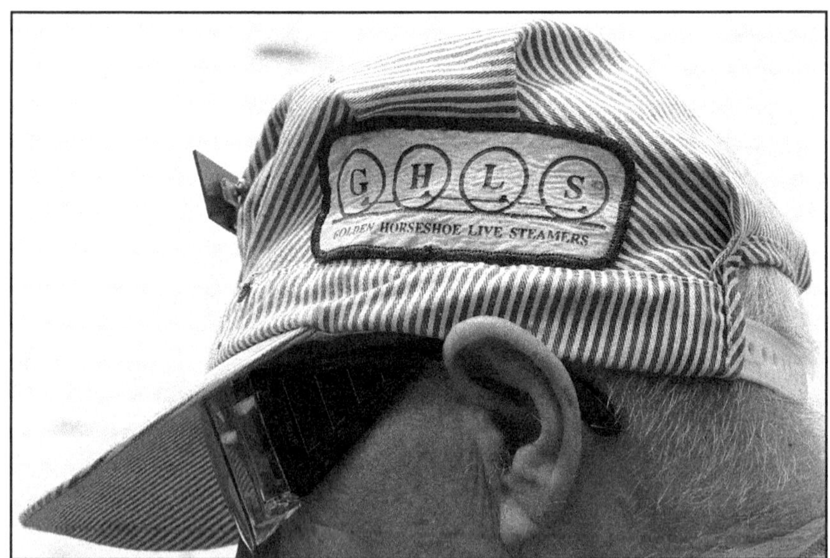

Photo by John Goddard

GHLS member Fred Eagle wears a specially appointed train engineer's cap at one of the Steam and Technology Museum's "Live Steamer Days." He runs a wood-burning steam engine on a high-level track.

The trains are miniatures but big enough for people to sit on. Over the years, club members have expanded the track network. Some tracks lie flush to the ground, while others stand at "high level," like a monorail, so that people can ride with their legs hanging over the side rather than folded in front of them.

"The rides are always free," Millard says, "although we encourage donations to help expand and grow the operation."

The Golden Horseshoe Live Steamers hold their "Live Steamer Days" on select Sundays between May and September. Check the museum website for dates.

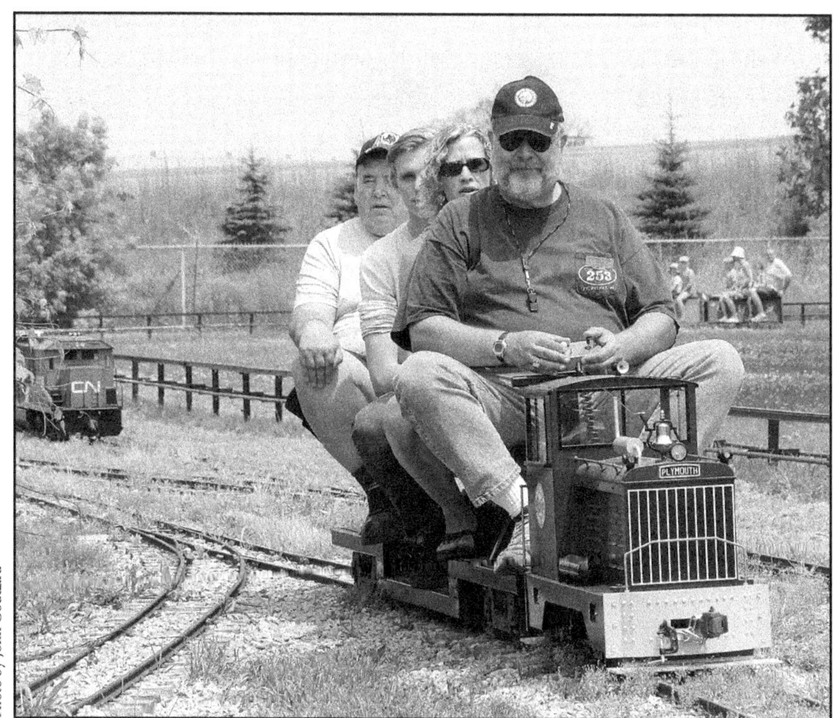

Photo by John Goddard

Chuck Lawrence handles the controls of his electric-powered model train at one of the museum's "Live Steamer Days," generally held twice a month from May to September. Adults flock to the rides as much as children.

Why Go?

Battlefield House Museum and Park commemorates the British victory at the 1813 Battle of Stoney Creek that stopped the American army from capturing Upper Canada. In early June, two days of celebrations and battle re-enactments mark the high point of the museum's calendar. The museum also illuminates the lives of the James and Mary Gage family, whose lands formed part of the battlefield.

Address

77 King Street West, Stoney Creek.

Getting There by Public Transit

From anywhere along Main Street in downtown Hamilton, catch the No. 5 Delaware, Jones Street. Make sure it is going to Stoney Creek. After about fifty minutes, the bus stops at the Battlefield Park entrance.

BATTLEFIELD HOUSE MUSEUM AND PARK

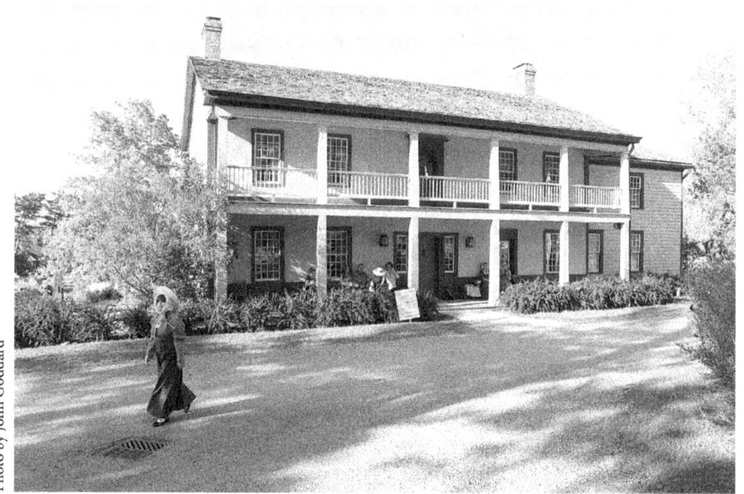

Photo by John Goddard

A woman in period dress walks past the former residence of James and Mary Gage, one of Hamilton's oldest homes. On the day of the Battle of Stoney Creek, on June 6, 1813, the family lived in some version of their original log cabin and stone cellar.

SERGEANT FRASER STEPS FORWARD

Both armies retreated thinking the other had won, yet the battle proved decisive. In the middle of the night, in almost total confusion, British and American forces fought for possession of Upper Canada, sometimes firing on their own lines. Only at sunrise did the British troops realize they had prevailed. Stragglers watched the American enemy scramble away, never again to penetrate so deeply beyond the Niagara River. For their heroism two men in particular distinguished themselves. One was Billy Green, nineteen years old, the first white settler born in the Stoney Creek area. Out of eagerness to aid the British, he contributed a key piece of intelligence to help take the Americans by surprise. The other was British Sergeant Alexander Fraser, twenty-three, a soldier of exceptional boldness and valour. At a pivotal moment, when the battle appeared lost, he led an almost suicidal charge on the U.S. artillery position, managing to silence the guns and almost single-handedly capture both American generals.

The events leading to the Battle of Stoney Creek began on June 4, 1813, at around noon. Teenage Billy Green was hiking along a Mohawk trail on the Niagara Escarpment east of Stoney Creek where Grimsby now stands. He had always been a restless boy. He loved to roam the woods, and knew the trails. With him were his older brother, Levi, and a friend named Sam Lee. Below them they spotted a column of American soldiers on the road, marching from the U.S. border at Niagara to the main British encampment beyond Stoney Creek at Burlington Heights.

One year earlier U.S. President James Madison had declared war on Great Britain, his stated goal to conquer British North America. After a disastrous beginning, the Americans were gaining the upper hand. That spring a U.S. navy fleet had attacked York — present-day Toronto — and captured the British Forts George and Erie at either end of the Niagara River. The British had retreated to Burlington Heights at present-day Hamilton where General John Vincent judged his chances of fending off an American assault to be near zero. He commanded 1,800 men; the U.S. invaders numbered 3,500. Vincent was making plans to retreat all the way to Kingston, leaving most of Upper Canada to the Americans.

The weather was wet, with more rain expected. The Americans were marching, riding, and hauling supplies and artillery pieces through mud. The Green brothers and their friend hooted and shouted at them from behind trees, pretending to be Mohawk warriors. "I tell you them simples did run," Billy recalled six years later in an interview with local historian S.D. Slater. To further harass the soldiers, Billy and Levi dropped to the road. "Levi ran across a fellow with his boot off, putting a rag on his foot," Billy told Slater. "The soldier grabbed for his gun, but Levi hit him with a stick."

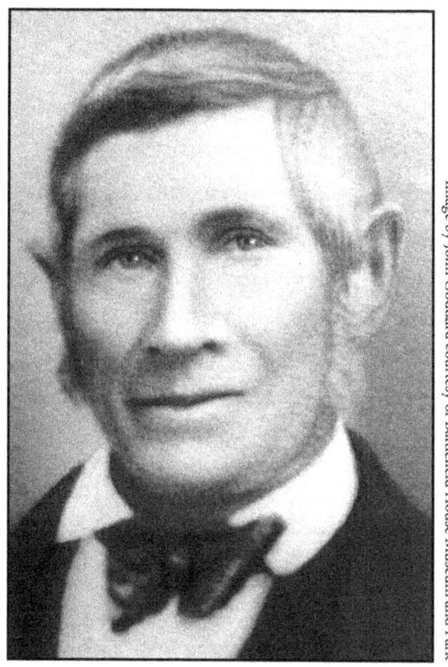

Image by John Goddard courtesy of Battlefield House Museum and Park

Billy Green's mischievous smile in old age hints at his younger self when he hooted at U.S. troops from behind trees, pretending to be a Mohawk warrior. "I tell you them simples did run," he once recalled.

Afterward Sam Lee returned home. Billy and Levi went to Levi's house, on the side of the escarpment with a good view of the road. For a while, with Levi's whole family, they stood outside to watch the military procession until two or more soldiers fired on them. A musket ball struck a rail next to where Levi's wife, Tina, was sitting with their daughter Hannah, and everybody except Billy went back into the house.

Billy decided to check on his sister Keziah and her husband, Isaac Corman. They lived nearby. When he reached their house, his sister said that the Americans had arrested Corman for refusing to answer questions and had led him north to "the Beach," a spot that today lies at the entrance to Hamilton Harbour. Billy followed the trail, making bird calls along the way, and at one point heard an owl-hoot in reply. It was Corman. The Americans had let him go.

"The major and I got to talking," Corman told Billy as Billy recalled years later. "He said he was second cousin to General Harrison [U.S. General

William Henry Harrison, who was leading the war on the American frontier]. I said I was a first cousin of General Harrison and came from Kentucky."

Corman was indeed from Kentucky, and genealogists have since confirmed he had Harrison family connections on his mother's side. To get through the American lines, Corman also told Billy, the friendly major gave him a secret password, which by coincidence was based on General Harrison's name. When an American sentry challenged him, Corman was told to answer, "Will-Hen-Har."

Billy decided to give the British the password. He harboured bitterness against the Americans. Three of his uncles had gone to prison for their loyalty to the British during the U.S. War of Independence, and one had died in prison. Billy's father, Adam Green, had also sided with the British and was forced to abandon his large spread in New Jersey in exchange for a much smaller farm near Stoney Creek as a United Empire Loyalist. Billy, the family's eleventh child, was born at the family's new cabin in Upper Canada. Within a year of his birth, Billy's mother was dead.

"Away I went," Billy later recalled of his mission. He returned to Levi's house, borrowed Levi's plough horse, Tip, walked the horse to the top of the escarpment, and rode to Burlington Heights. When he arrived, it was late, about eleven o'clock. The British took him for a spy, but he won them over, telling Lieutenant-Colonel John Harvey the American password and everything else he had learned that day of the enemy's movements.

Harvey had been doing his own reconnaissance. He knew the Americans were camped at Stoney Creek between the escarpment and lake on roughly cleared farmland owned by James Gage and his nearest neighbour and uncle, William Gage. Harvey also knew the Americans were sloppily organized, with their cavalry camped too far back to protect their artillery position. With the British outnumbered and their ammunition low, Harvey proposed a surprise night attack, their only chance to defeat the Americans. The alternative was to retreat to Kingston and give up most of Upper Canada. General Vincent agreed.

Harvey roused seven hundred troops for the march to Stoney Creek. The number included a small band of Mohawk fighters led by Scottish-born Mohawk leader John Norton. The British would be outnumbered 3,500 to 700 — five to one — but if they got past the sentries and caught the

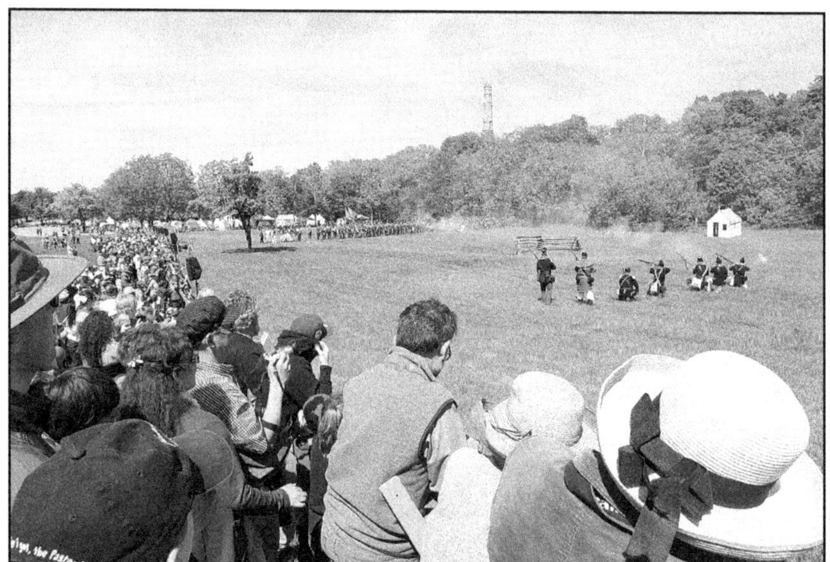

Photo by John Goddard

A line of British troops in the background advances on the Americans in a field next to Battlefield Monument during War of 1812 re-enactment events that attract thousands of spectators annually over two days. The original twenty-minute battle took place in pitch darkness.

Americans sleeping they had a chance. Harvey asked Billy if he knew the way. "Yes, every inch of it," Billy replied. Harvey gave him a uniform and a sword, and by about 11:30 p.m. the eleven-kilometre trek began. Billy could hardly contain himself. "Sometimes I would get way ahead and go back to hurry them up," he later recalled. "I told them it would be morning before we got there. Someone said that would be soon enough to be killed."

On the way the troops encountered a light shower. The rain stopped but cloud cover remained heavy. The night was pitch-black. As the British approached Stoney Creek, Billy spotted an American sentry crouched or leaning against a tree. Billy told the soldier behind him to shoot, but Colonel Harvey said, "No, run him through," and the soldier used his bayonet. As the British approached the Methodist church, now the site of Stoney Creek Cemetery, another sentry fired his musket and challenged Billy for the password. Billy walked up, gave the password, grabbed the sentry's gun with one hand, and used the other hand to slice the sentry with the sword Harvey had given him. The teenager was obeying orders but later said he always felt bad about killing the man after disarming him.

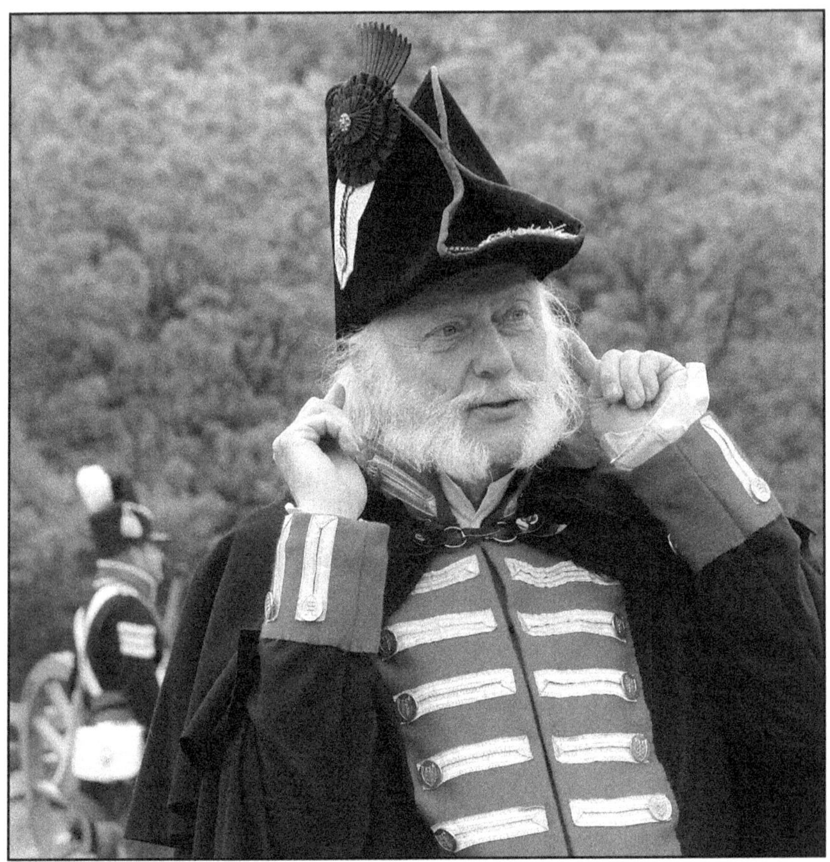

Photo by John Goddard

Dressed as a British field commander, Andre Stewart Reed of Burlington, Ontario, alerts spectators to the imminent firing of the field artillery. Soldiers grew side whiskers to hide facial burns caused by the flare of a musket to a soldier's left, leading to the term "sideburns," he says.

The British overran other sentry posts. They approached to within three hundred metres of the sprawling American camp. They could see cooks preparing the next day's food on open fires burning on fence posts from the Gage farms. All was going according to plan — approach by stealth until close enough to bayonet the enemy in their beds. Harvey had even ordered his men to remove the flints from their muskets to prevent anybody firing accidentally. On reaching the cooking fires, however, British discipline broke down. Some men started cheering and hollering. Quickly, the Americans rose to their feet and fired from the darkness at figures silhouetted against the fires, as the British scrambled to reattach their flints.

The battle lasted twenty minutes. It went from 2:40 a.m. to 3:00 a.m. on June 6, 1813. With only a sword as a weapon, Billy stayed behind the line, shouting what guidance he could. In another part of the field, British Major Charles Plenderleath, leader of the 49th Regiment, watched the British line disintegrate under heavy musket and cannon fire.

Plenderleath knew the artillery guns had to be taken. He called for volunteers, and Sergeant Alexander Fraser stepped forward. He was twenty-three years old, an exceptionally large man, and fierce. A photograph taken of him in old age reveals a glimmer of his youthful audaciousness. In it Fraser stands tall and proud, decked out in a ceremonial Scottish kilt, tunic, sash, and bonnet, and in his right hand he holds a sword with its tip to the ground, as might a prince or a pirate. How much more imposing he must have looked in his sergeant's uniform in the heat of battle, preparing to charge. His brother, Corporal Peter Fraser, stepped forward with him, as did others. Various accounts put the number in the party at between fifteen and thirty. Fraser later put the figure at forty-six starting out, reduced to twenty-five by the time they reached the guns.

Major Plenderleath and Sergeant Fraser led the way in the dark over uneven farmland encumbered by brush, stumps, and fence rails. They fixed their bayonets. At one point the Americans fired their cannons simultaneously. When they began to reload, the British sprang. Sergeant Fraser bayonetted seven men, his brother four. Plenderleath, riding a horse, took two musket balls in the thigh. His horse took six shots and fell. As Sergeant Fraser went to his commander's aid, American Brigadier-General John Chandler stumbled onto the scene.

"Where's the line, where's the line!" one witness later recalled the U.S. general shouting, or as Chandler himself was to recall, "I hobbled in amongst them and began to rally them."

To the American general's dismay, the troops he was trying to rally were British. They pointed their bayonets at him, and Sergeant Fraser took him prisoner.

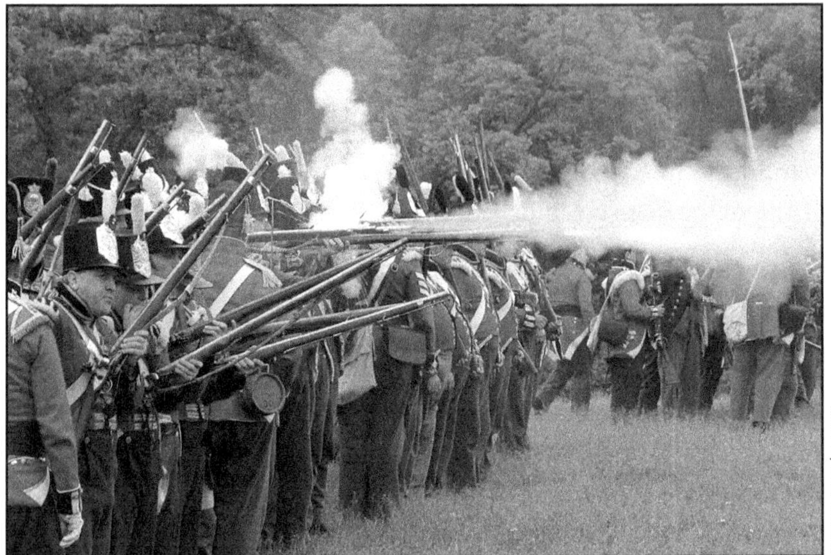

Photo by John Goddard

Re-enactors take turns firing volleys and reloading in the style so successful for the British in the War of 1812. Smoke, flame, and loud musket explosions added to the confusion in the original skirmish that saw both sides retreat from the battlefield.

Minutes later U.S. Brigadier-General William Henry Winder similarly stumbled onto the scene shouting, "Come on, my brave fellows, they are routed!"

When he similarly realized his brave fellows were British, he pointed his pistol at Sergeant Fraser, who held a bayonet to Winder's chest and said, "If you stir, sir, you die."

Fraser had just bayonetted seven other men. Somehow Winder knew to take him seriously. The U.S. general dropped his pistol and handed his sword to Fraser.

In that single daring British raid, the Americans had simultaneously lost their main firepower and top leadership. The British had captured three six-pound guns, one brass howitzer, several ammunition carts, nine artillery horses, and a number of U.S. prisoners, including both American generals. In theory the Americans could still win. They still outnumbered the British and most of the British were in retreat. Without leadership, however, the Americans scattered in disarray.

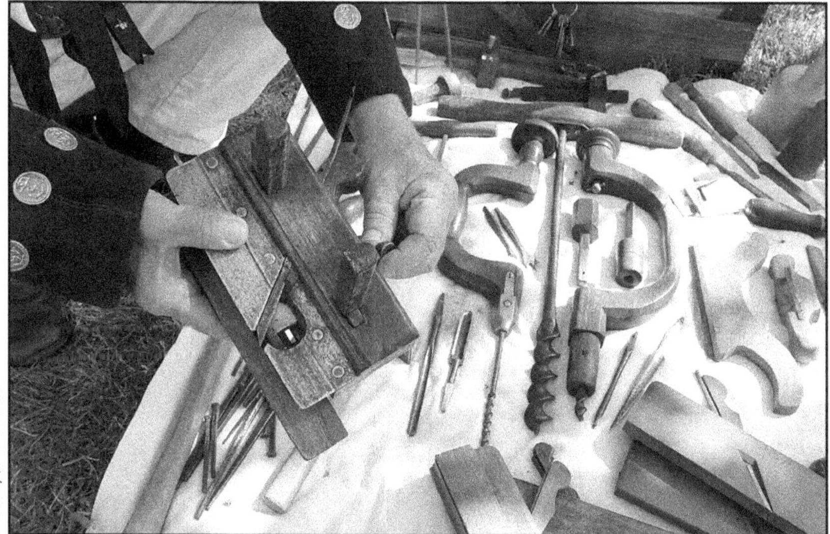

Photo by John Goddard

Fritz Steele, of Brampton, Ontario, re-enacts the role of ship's carpenter, displaying a collection of tools from the War of 1812 era. He holds a plough plane used to produce a groove of a given depth and distance from the edge of a piece of wood.

"When it commenced to get daylight," Billy Green later said, "we could see the enemy running in all directions."

Never again would the Americans penetrate so far into Upper Canada. The following year the two sides signed a peace treaty at Ghent in the neutral country of Belgium. All territories captured by either side in the war reverted to their original owner. Upper and Lower Canada survived as part of British North America, and its citizens developed a sense of identity distinct from that of the United States.

Postscript: The Battle of Billy Green

Nearly two hundred years after the Battle of Stoney Creek, a skirmish erupted over the Billy Green story. A leading champion of the account changed his mind without explicitly saying so. In 1994, James Elliott, a *Hamilton Spectator* reporter turned author, published a twenty-four-page illustrated book called *Billy Green and the Battle of Stoney Creek, June 6, 1813*. The book lists the Stoney Creek Historical Society as publisher and copyright holder. At the back, credit is also given to Elliott's newspaper.

"The *Hamilton Spectator* is proud to support the Stoney Creek Historical Society and help tell the story of Billy Green with the drama and substance it deserves," the acknowledgment says. "By donating the time and talents of journalist/author James Elliott, we hope to foster an appreciation for Canada's rich and fascinating history."

In 2009, Elliott published a second book, *Strange Fatality: The Battle of Stoney Creek, 1813*. It offers an excellent account of the battle and does especially well bringing attention to the heroics of British Sergeant Alexander Fraser. In an appendix entitled "Billy Green: The Scout and the Rout," however, Elliott trashes the Billy Green story. "The persona of Billy Green the Scout was cut from whole, or nearly whole, cloth to create a Stoney Creek hero who could stand beside Laura Secord," he says. Secord was the Niagara-area woman who two weeks after the Stoney Creek battle warned the British of a surprise attack at Beaver Dams. Elliott says that three books, numerous magazine and newspaper stories, and the Stan Rogers song "Billy Green" depict Green as a hero, but the story is a myth. He neglects to mention that he wrote one of the books.

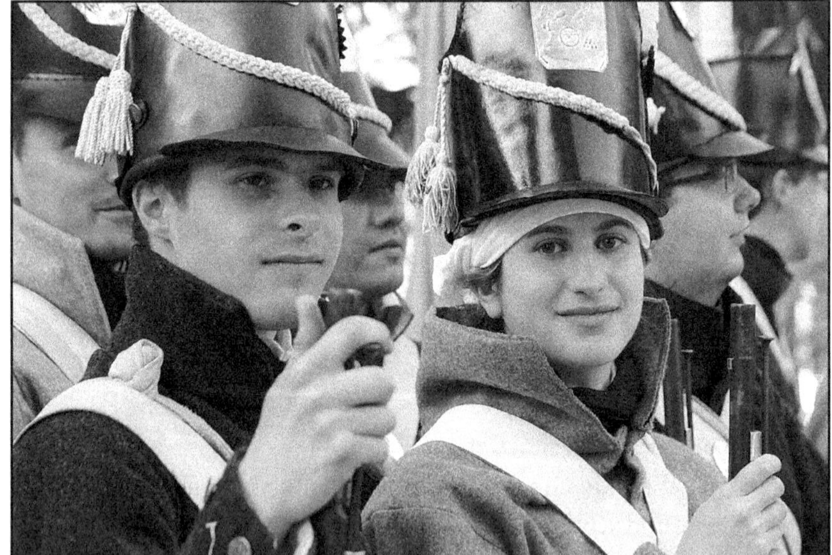

Photo by John Goddard

Historical accuracy bends slightly to welcome women into the ranks of War of 1812 re-enactors at Battlefield Park. John Raso (left) and Sarita DeLaurentiis of Old Fort Erie in Niagara portray U.S. soldiers of the 11th Infantry Regiment, 1st Brigade (Scott's), Left Division (Brown's), 9th Military District.

In response, the historical society published two papers. The first, in 2011, ran to thirty-five pages under the title "Billy Green and Balderdash: A Presentation of the Facts." The second, in 2012, ran to twenty-seven pages under the title "Billy Green and More Balderdash." The titles derive from a story Elliott wrote for the *Hamilton Spectator* under the headline "Is the Billy Green Story Balderdash?" The papers' authors were listed as David Clark, M. Lubell, and Douglas Green. Green is the fourth great-grandson of Billy Green.

"As we approach the bicentennial celebrations of this important battle," the first paper begins, "the Society wishes to clarify the heroic role of Billy Green and to respond appropriately to recent attempts to downgrade his importance." Meticulously and point by point, the authors correct what they say are Elliott's many factual errors and address every doubt he has expressed. They make a persuasive case. Elliott has never responded. In its gift shop, the Battlefield House Museum sells all four publications.

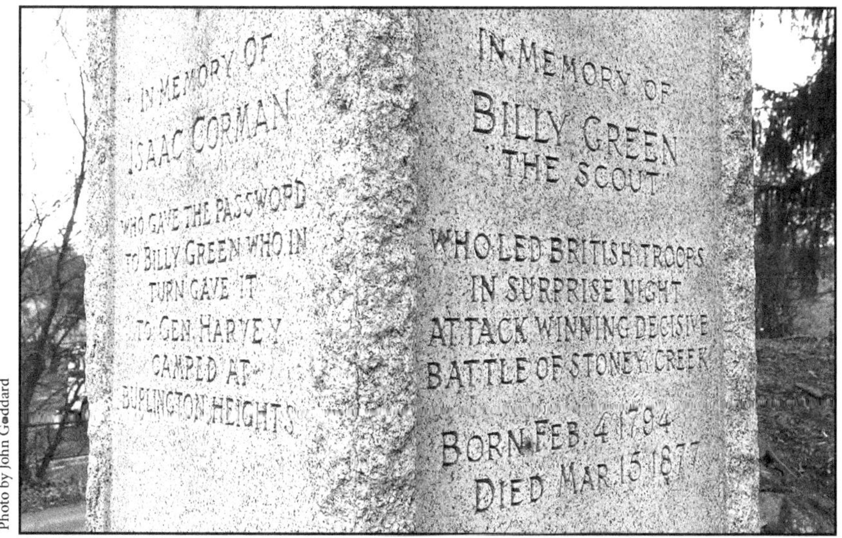

Photo by John Goddard

At Stoney Creek Cemetery next to Battlefield Park a stone memorial credits Isaac Corman for giving Billy Green the American password and Green for leading the British to the American camp. A third side pays tribute to British Lieutenant-Colonel (later General) John Harvey for his victory.

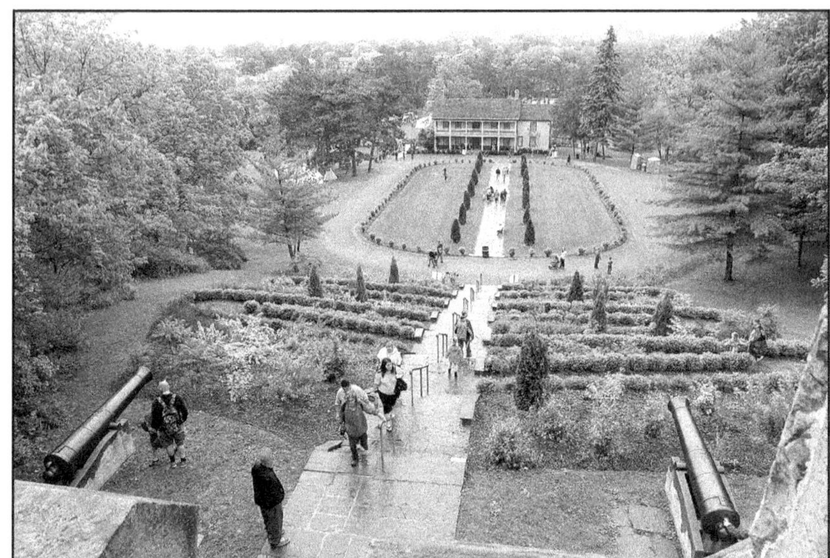

Photo by John Goddard

Visitors climb the steps to Battlefield Monument, uphill from Battlefield House, or Gage House. Exactly one hundred years after the Battle of Stoney Creek, Queen Mary pressed an ivory telegraph key in England to unveil the tower.

WALK-THROUGH: CAUGHT IN THE BATTLE

Battlefield House Museum and Park commemorates the 1813 Battle of Stoney Creek and illuminates the lives of the James and Mary Gage family, whose lands formed part of the battlefield. A visit takes in four main structures: the Nash Jackson House, which serves as a reception centre and gift shop; the Gage farmhouse, one of Hamilton's oldest homes; the Battlefield Monument tower opened in 1913, a century after the battle; and the nearby Battlefield Cemetery at Smith's Knoll, a memorial to the 1813 war dead. Once a year, on the weekend closest to June 6, a field on the property becomes the stage for an anniversary re-enactment of the Battle of Stoney Creek. The creek, while stony, is named for a Mr. Stoney.

Nash Jackson House

A visit starts at the Nash Jackson House, a Georgian-style frame house that began as the nearby home of Samuel and Susannah Nash. Susannah

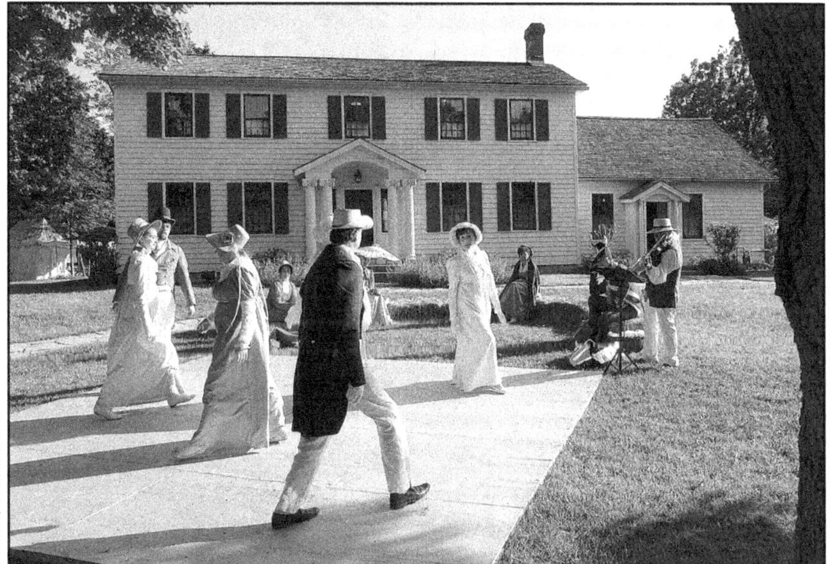

Photo by John Goddard

Plywood laid in front of the Nash Jackson House makes an improvised stage for English country dancers at 2015 re-enactment events. The house began as the nearby 1818 home of Samuel and Susannah Nash, relatives of James and Mary Gage.

was the daughter of William Gage and his wife, also named Susannah, who lived on the neighbouring property at the time of the battle. The two Gage families were closely related. Two brothers married two sisters. James Gage's father and William Gage were brothers. James's mother and William's wife, Susannah, were sisters. (The Gages of Gage Park were descendants of William and Susannah Gage.) The earliest rooms of the house date to 1818. The building was moved to its current location in 1999 to serve as a reception centre, gift shop, and administrative office.

Several maps on display show the positions and movements of British and American forces in the early morning of June 6, 1813, when they fought their twenty-minute battle for Upper Canada. One panel, titled "The Turning Point," honours British Sergeant Alexander Fraser and those he led in what the display calls "a wild bayonet charge directly into the mouths of the American guns."

Gage House or Battlefield House

Mary Gage, Sr., arrived in the area around 1790 with her two children, James and Elizabeth, both teenagers. Mary's husband, the children's father, had been killed fighting on the American side in the Revolutionary War against the British. At Stoney Creek the family declared allegiance to the British crown, and as United Empire Loyalists received two land grants of eighty hectares each. It helped that Mary's brother was Augustus Jones, the land surveyor, who allocated the family a desirable homestead at the foot of the Niagara Escarpment, with a stream flowing through it now known as Battlefield Creek. In 1796, both children married. Elizabeth moved west with her husband to Brant County. James stayed at Stoney Creek with his wife, also named Mary.

The Gage farmhouse began as a log cabin with a stone cellar. An 1816 tax assessment describes the Gages as living in a frame house of one and a half storeys on the same stone foundation. Sometime in the 1830s the house was expanded to two storeys, either by the Gages or the people who bought the house from them in 1835. The two-storey house is what stands today. On the day of the battle — June 6, 1813 — James, his mother, Mary, his wife, Mary, and five or six of the couple's eventual ten children lived in some version of the original log cabin.

American officers commandeered the premises. They imprisoned James somewhere nearby and locked the women and children either in the cellar or the attic. The battle unfolded partly on what looks to be the family's front lawn, between the house and present-day King Street, although, in fact, the house faces away from the street toward the escarpment for the southern exposure. The battle was also partly fought on the land of their closest neighbours, William and Susannah Gage.

Cellar

The two Mary Gages and the five or six Gage children spent the day of June 5, 1813, and much of the night, confined to either the cellar or the attic as the Battle of Stoney Creek raged around them. James Gage is believed to have been held in a nearby outbuilding.

Notice the thick wooden beams. A few steel supports were added recently as reinforcements, but the original beams and supports were hand-hewn with an adze before the first sawmill appeared in the area in the early 1800s. The exposed stone walls are original. When the Gages lived here, the floor would have been dirt. Originally, the foundation supported a log cabin. The frame house came later.

The cellar is displayed as it might have looked in 1813. Wooden barrels hold root vegetables stored in sand to ensure preservation and to keep out mice. A pierced tin lantern would have been used outdoors or in the barn at night, the tin box protecting the candle flame from wind and rain. The metal cylinder with a latch is called a candle safe, for protecting candles from vermin overnight. Candles were made of tallow, or boiled beef fat, which mice and rats would eat if they got the chance.

Main-Floor Hallway

James Gage appears as a droll-looking fellow with arched eyebrows, heavy eyelids, and a wry, knowing smile in a portrait painted of him in middle age. Beside him, his wife, Mary, appears quietly delighted, as if in on his secret. The twin life-size portraits from the 1830s grace the front hallway, the artist unknown. The couple had ten children — four boys and six girls — all of whom survived into adulthood. James worked the family farm and owned a general store. At one point he and his sons started a lumbering business and owned several grist and lumber mills. In 1835, when Sir Allan Napier MacNab and others founded the Gore

Images by John Goddard courtesy of Battlefield House Museum and Park

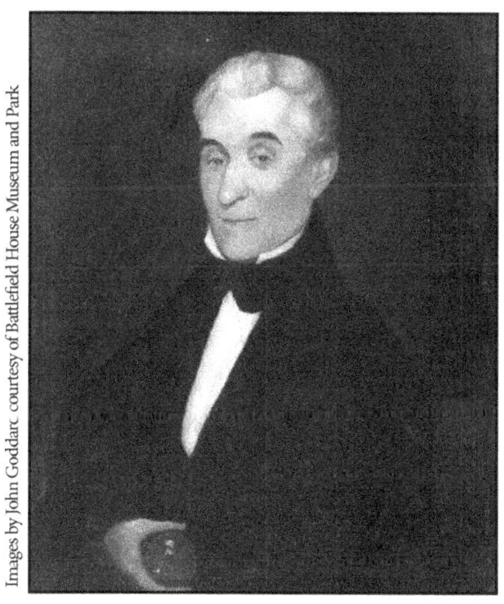

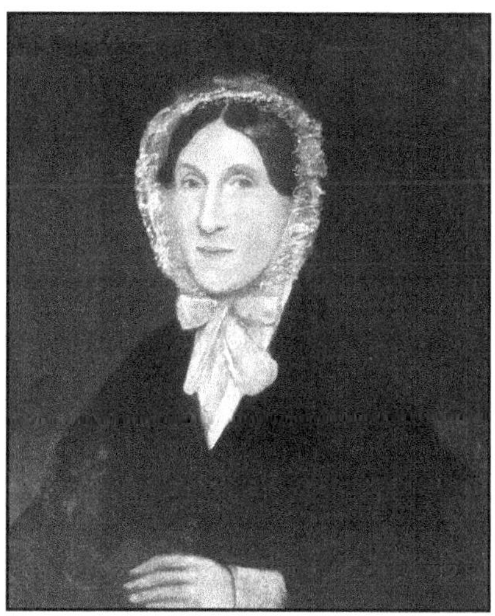

Twin life-size portraits of James Gage and his wife, Mary, from the 1830s grace the front hallway, the artist unknown. They raised ten children, all of whom survived to adulthood.

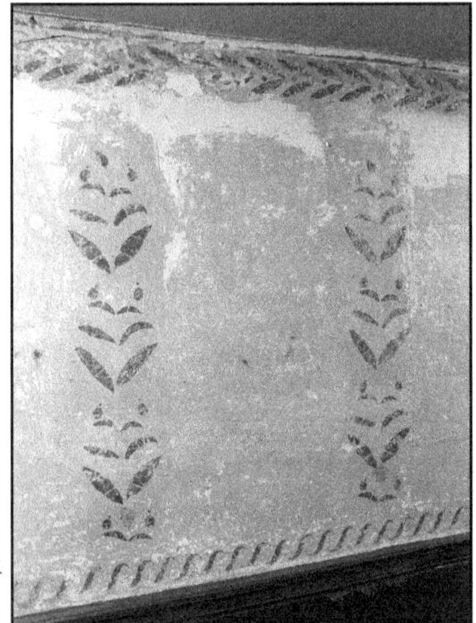
Photo by John Goddard

The removal of wallboard and several layers of paint in the hallway reveal the original plaster and stencils that the Gage family enjoyed. The leaves are green, the berries red.

Bank, James sold the homestead and moved the family to downtown Hamilton where he became one of the bank's directors.

Mary died in 1853 at seventy-five, James in 1854 at seventy-nine. They are buried in Hamilton Cemetery across the street from Dundurn Castle.

"Being very kind in his manners and generous in his disposition, he was not only generally esteemed but loved," the Hamilton *Gazette* wrote of James on his death. "We never heard of his having an enemy."

In recent years, restoration architects have stripped the hallway walls to their original two-hundred-year-old plaster and decorative stencils.

Keeping Room

Some people might call it a kitchen, others a housekeeping (or keeping) room. This is where the Gages cooked their meals and did their chores. The most essential feature might be the fireplace crane, a large iron bracket hinged to the interior of the open hearth, allowing a cook to swing her cooking pots over the fire and away from it again instead of reaching into the hearth. To the cook, fire was a constant hazard. In the Upper Canada of the early 1800s, infections from burns killed women at a rate second only to childbirth. "Died by cooking fire" is sometimes seen on tombstones of the period.

On the mantelpiece rests a maple sugar mould made of cast iron. Maple trees were tapped in spring, sap was reduced to thick, sugary syrup over a fire, and the syrup was poured into a mould to harden. It was a cheaper alternative to the imported product sometimes displayed on the corner cabinet, a cone of white sugar refined in England from cane grown in the Caribbean or the southern United States.

A yoke for fetching water lies on the floor next to a pair of buckets. The house had no running water. To wash dishes, somebody heated water over the hearth and poured it into the basin in the dry sink, which stands in one corner. The soap in the nearby dish was made from ashes and tallow.

On one of the sideboards sits a tea brick, a pricey imported item from Central Asia or China. This is a modern replica. A tea brick is made of ground tea leaves that are steamed, pressed into a decorative mould, and left to cure until the leaves become a solid block. To make a pot of tea, Mary Gage would have broken a chunk from the brick and grated it into a powder.

Larder

Located off the keeping room lies the larder, or food storage area. The tall candle holder belonged to the Gage family, as did the small casks, or firkins, which would have stored butter or salt, or sometimes fish or liquids.

Parlour

Here the Gages entertained visitors, took tea, and sometimes dined. The fireplace frame is painted to look like marble, conforming to contemporary taste. The firedogs, supporting the logs in the fire, belonged to the Gages. So did the stencilled "fancy" chairs, the small wicker box on the settee, and the nearby King James Bible. James and Mary Gage were Methodists, a denomination that later helped form the United Church. The framed piece of needlework on the stand between the settee and fireplace is called a pole screen and dates to the early 1800s. When a woman sat near the fire, the screen shielded her face from the heat.

Upstairs Main Hallway

A painting by Toronto artist J.W.L. Forster, acclaimed for his portraits of such luminaries as Timothy Eaton, Sir Wilfrid Laurier, and Queen Victoria, dominates the upstairs hallway. It is of Sara Calder, the museum's founder. She was also James and Mary's granddaughter, the daughter of

James and Mary's youngest child, Ann Eliza Gage. By all accounts persuasive and untiring, as founder of the Women's Wentworth Historical Society she campaigned for twenty years to reacquire part of the Gage property, restore the Gage home and grounds as one of Canada's earliest museums, and build the Battlefield Monument on the rise above the house. "It can be done, it must be done, and it will be done," she would say, and she did it. The artwork next to the portrait is of the Gage home, painted in the 1890s by Calder herself.

Master Bedroom

The centrepiece high-post walnut bedstead was donated by Sara Calder and is believed to have belonged to James and Mary. The washstand next to it, made in the Niagara area in the early 1800s, still has its original brass pull. A cradle, much like the one on display, would have been kept near the parents' bed. The decorative armchair in the corner doubles as a toilet. The fabric seat cover flips off to reveal the lid to a cavity holding a chamber pot.

Children's Bedroom

Twenty-one years separated the eldest and youngest of the ten Gage children, and most of them would have been grown by the time the second storey was added to the house. The room is set up like a children's bedroom typical of the early 1800s. Crowding was standard. This room features a trundle bed in which a second bed rolls out from under the first to expand the sleeping space.

On the far wall hangs a sampler meant to demonstrate a girl's or young woman's needlework skills. This one was produced in 1816 by Catherine Gage, James and Mary's second child and eldest daughter, when she was fifteen or sixteen. Typically, a sampler included a verse, this one about parents ridding children of their faults and improving their virtues.

> Happy the child whose green unpracticed years,
> The guiding hand of parent fondness rears,
> To rich instruction ample field removes,
> Prunes every fault, and every worth improves.

A second sampler in the museum's collection, not on display, originates from one of James and Mary's twenty-five granddaughters, Cynthia Mills, when she was six and seven. She was the daughter of James and Mary's third child, Andrew Gage. "There is an interesting story behind it," museum staff member Sandy Shichowy says of the sampler. Cynthia's future husband would be murdered, making all the more poignant the verse about the preciousness of life that Cynthia chose to embroider as a child.

> To waste precious time we can never recall,
> Is waste of the wickedest kind.
> An instant of life is more value than all
> The gold that in India we find.

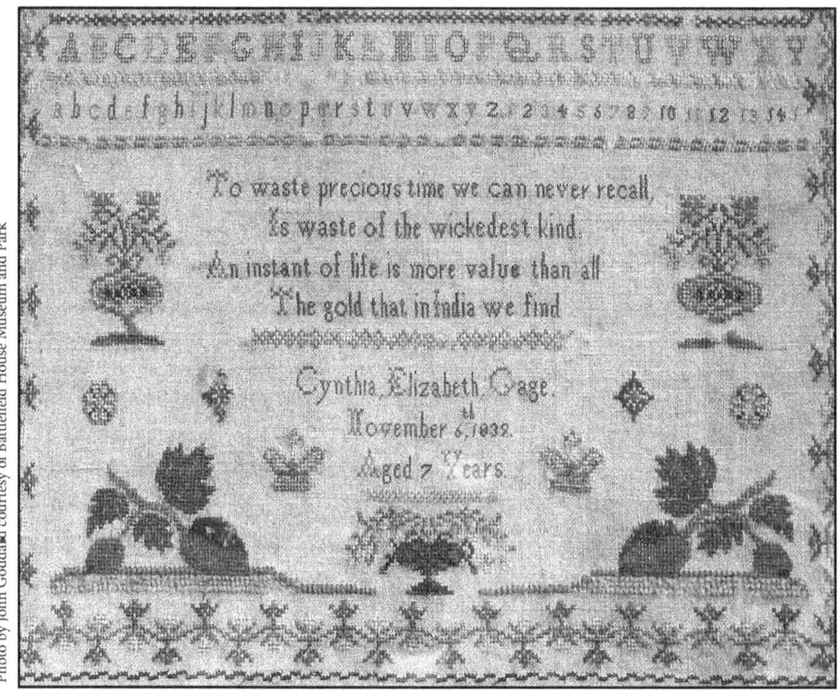

Photo by John Goddard courtesy of Battlefield House Museum and Park

"An instant of life is more value than all," seven-year-old Cynthia Mills, granddaughter of James and Mary, wrote in a verse as part of her needlework sampler. Later in life a butcher murdered her husband in the street.

Cynthia married Nelson Mills of Hamilton, who owned several properties, including a butcher shop in the Hamilton market. The butcher, Michael McConnell, fell $14 behind in his rent, and one day Mills served him with a notice to vacate the property. McConnell was to say later that he was deliberately withholding the rent to force Mills to make overdue repairs to the property. On January 5, 1876, enraged by the eviction order, the tenant went to the Millses' home at the corner of King and Queen Streets with one of his butcher knives and pounded on the door. The landlord wasn't home. McConnell turned to leave but saw Mills approaching and attacked him. McConnell stabbed Mills eight times and fled. Mills fell to the ground bleeding. The first person to reach him was his father-in-law, Andrew Gage. He got Mills to the doctor, but four days later Mills suffered a case of the hiccups, blew out his stitches, encountered complications, and died. McConnell was convicted of murder and hanged at the Barton Street Jail.

"The attack … was so brazen, violent and senseless that the community was deeply disturbed," the *Hamilton Spectator* wrote at the time. "Nelson Mills was one of Hamilton's most prominent citizens."

Military Exhibit

Sometimes staff members use the adjoining room for schoolchildren's wool-making workshops, but mostly the space serves as an exhibition space for War of 1812 artifacts. A portrait of Billy Green the Scout, who supplied the British with the American password, hangs on the wall. A small statue shows Green as a Paul Revere–type figure incongruously racing on his brother's old workhorse, Tip, to deliver the password. Copies of old maps show the battlefield as sketched by an American aide-de-camp. In one corner, mannequins model British uniforms, those of a captain in the 8th Regiment, also called the King's Regiment, and of a foot soldier in the 49th Regiment. The British hero of the battle, Sergeant Alexander Fraser, was with the 49th Regiment when he bayonetted seven American soldiers and captured two enemy generals. Nearby can be seen the British musket, the Brown Bess, common at the time throughout the empire.

Battlefield Monument

It stands one hundred feet tall to commemorate the one hundredth anniversary of the Battle of Stoney Creek, and it opened on June 6, 1913, exactly one hundred years after the battle. An estimated eight thousand people attended the dedication ceremony, historian Peter Hanlon writes in the *Dictionary of Canadian Biography*. Hamilton author James Elliott, in *Strange Fatality*, puts the number at fifteen thousand. The number, he says, included "1,800 schoolchildren and several hundred boy scouts and girl guides, detachments from four battalions of militia, four regimental bands, a large contingent of Six Nation[s] Indians, dozens of politicians and army brass and the granddaughter of the celebrated Stoney Creek veteran James FitzGibbon."

James and Mary Gage's granddaughter Sara Calder presided. "Probably the happiest lady on the grounds," the *Hamilton Evening Times* called her. The highlight of the day came at 1:25 p.m. when Queen Mary, consort to the reigning British monarch King George V and grandmother to the future Queen Elizabeth II, pressed an ivory telegraph key. Her action closed an

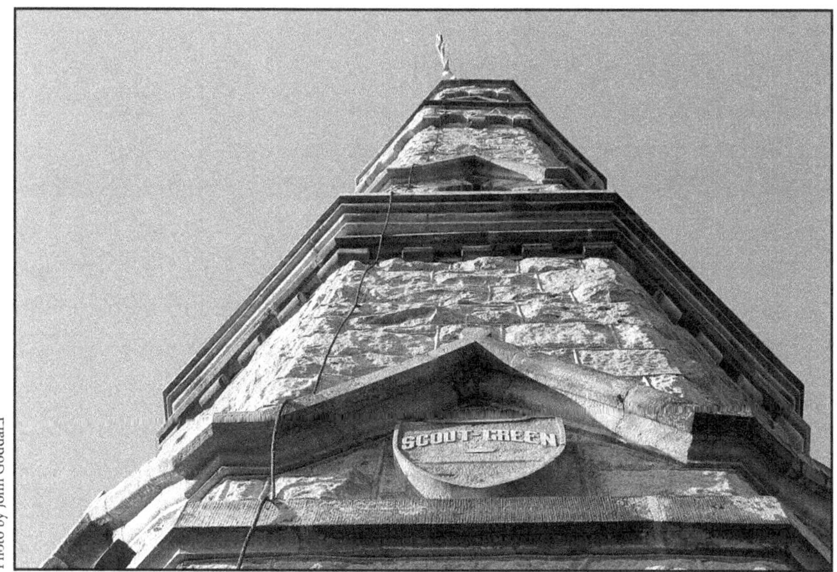

Photo by John Goddard

One of eight ceremonial shields gracing the Battlefield Monument exterior honours Billy Green, sometimes remembered as "Billy Green the Scout." When the tower was built, Alexander Fraser's heroics had not yet been fully recognized.

electric circuit connected by transatlantic cable to the Battlefield Monument. A tiny fuse burned, a bell rang, and white fabric fell away to unveil the tower.

The monument commands a hill above the Gage House. An internal spiral stairwell leads visitors to a lookout at the top of the monument's square base, although the stairs up the tapering octagonal tower to the top are closed. On the ground floor, explanatory panels highlight some of the personalities connected to the site. One panel calls Calder a "Victorian Dynamo" and says "this park, its grounds, residences and monuments, would not exist today were it not for [her] efforts." Another panel shows Queen Mary in a tiara and elaborate pearl necklace along-side a photo of something called a "marine galvanometer." The instrument informed the Queen that she had successfully sent her electronic transatlantic signal to unveil the monument. Around the outside of the monument can be seen eight ceremonial shields, each with the name of a participant in the battle on the British side. Most are officers, but Billy Green is included, as is Calder's grandfather, James Gage. Notably absent is Alexander Fraser, whose derring-do in the 1813 battle had not yet been recognized when the monument was built.

Battlefield Cemetery at Smith's Knoll

Opposite Battlefield Park and a bit east, at 70 King Street West, lies the knoll where the desperate British raiding party frontally attacked the American artillery position and reversed the course of the battle. Major Charles Plenderleath commanded the assault. Sergeant Alexander Fraser bayonetted seven men. His brother Peter bayonetted four. The party took two enemy generals prisoner, and the Americans, who outnumbered the British five to one, fled. In 1899, a farmer named Allan Smith unearthed human remains and bits of cloth from British and American uniforms with his plough, giving the site its name.

The knoll today features a stone cairn presided over by a carved stone lion to memorialize the British soldiers killed in the battle. Several historic cannons appear to guard the cairn. Markers commemorate the American soldiers killed defending their artillery, and a stone crypt honouring both sides in the battle contains seven hundred bone fragments found on the site by archaeologists.

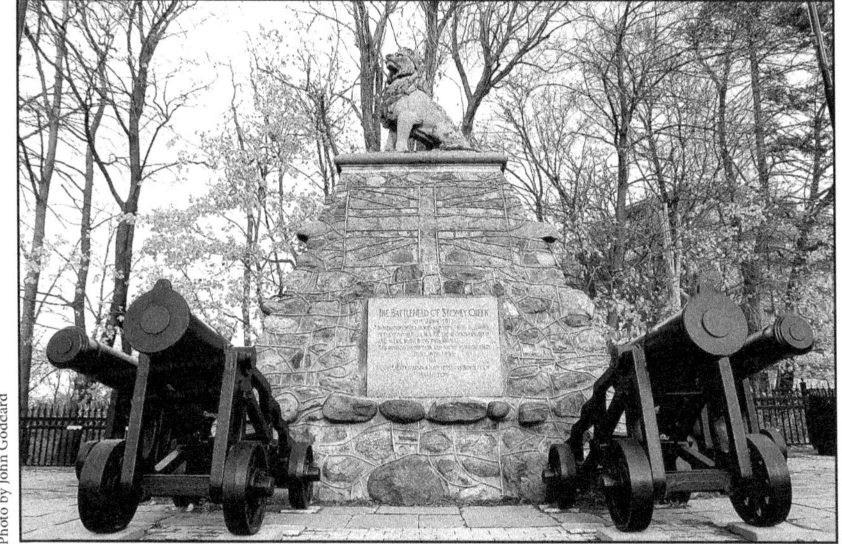

Photo by John Goddard

A stone lion and period cannons guard a cairn at Battlefield Cemetery on Smith's Knoll across from the Battlefield House Museum and Park. The cemetery honours the war dead from both sides.

GRIFFIN HOUSE

Why Go?

Griffin House honours one of Ancaster's earliest black settlers, Enerals Griffin, and pays tribute to the black slaves from the United States who fled to freedom in Upper Canada. In 1834, Griffin bought the modest clapboard farmhouse and moved in with his wife, Priscilla, and their infant son, James. Their descendants continued to occupy the home for more than 150 years.

Address

733 Mineral Springs Road, Ancaster.

FIELDCOTE MEMORIAL PARK AND MUSEUM

Why Go?

Fieldcote, built as a private home in 1948, functions as a gallery space for rotating exhibitions and as a museum administrative centre. It operates Griffin House, maintains the village historical archive, and on its lawn stages a popular Sunday night summer concert series. Fieldcote also administers Ancaster's Old Township Hall at 310 Wilson Street East, a short walk from the Fieldcote Museum. The 1871 heritage building is open for weddings, school programming, and other special events.

Address

64 Sulphur Springs Road, Ancaster.

Getting There by Public Transit

I have twice taken the GO bus to Hamilton from Toronto with my bicycle mounted on the front rack and disembarked at the first stop, Main Street West and Paisley Avenue South. Both times I rode south to the Hamilton-Brantford Rail Trail, followed it to Main Street West, and continued south to Ancaster, mostly up a long, gradual hill. Main Street West becomes Wilson Street, Ancaster's main thoroughfare. At Sulphur Springs Road I turned right and one block or so farther along found Fieldcote Memorial Park and Museum. Alternately, from the same GO bus stop in Hamilton, I have walked west a few blocks to Emerson Street and taken the No. 5 city bus to Ancaster. At Rousseaux Street, where the bus turns off, I disembarked and walked the few blocks up Wilson Street to Sulphur Springs Road and the Fieldcote Museum.

Getting from the Fieldcote Museum to Griffin House involves an extra step. On Emancipation Day, celebrated every year on or about August 1, the museum operates a frequent shuttle bus between the two venues. Otherwise there is no public transit. I have twice ridden my bicycle, a five-kilometre round trip involving an exhilarating ride down the escarpment to Griffin House and a steep climb back into town.

GRIFFIN HOUSE (WITH FIELDCOTE MEMORIAL PARK AND MUSEUM)

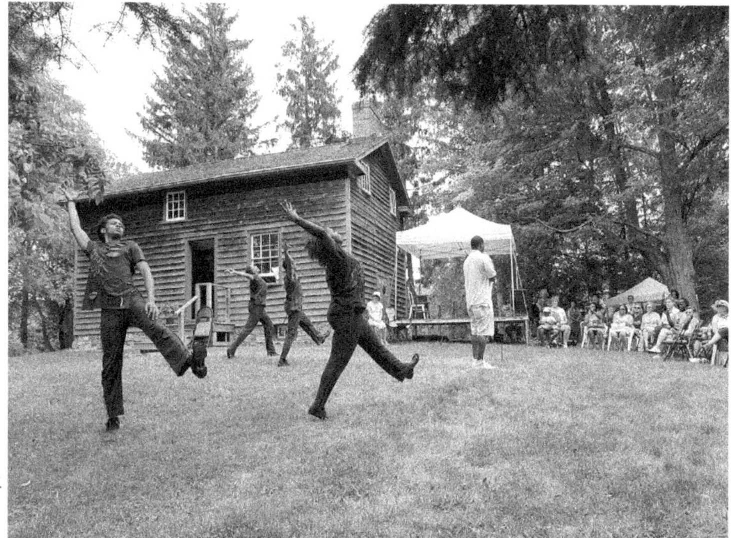

Photo by John Goddard

Members of Toronto's KasheDance perform at Griffin House as part of the 2015 Emancipation Day celebrations. Dancers left to right: Dezjuan Thomas, Aisha Nicholson, Shakeil Rollock, and Tereka Tyler Davis. Spoken-word artist Dwayne Morgan appears in light-coloured shorts and T-shirt.

GRIFFIN HOUSE: THE SURPRISE ANCESTOR

Hazel Costello's children inherited a hilltop farm that had been in their family for generations. In 1988, they decided to sell it. The farm adjoined the Dundas Valley Conservation Area, an expanse of Carolinian forest and open meadow crisscrossed by cold-water streams and hiking trails on the Niagara Escarpment. To extend the preserve, the conservation authority bought the Costello estate.

An old house stood on the hill. The authority intended to knock it down, but when conservationists took a closer look they changed their plan. Within a closet they found a lithograph print of a famous painting, *Negro Life at the South*, by Eastman Johnson, an American artist and co-founder of New York's Metropolitan Museum of Art. The lithograph, from Johnson's original oil painting of 1859, shows a domestic scene behind a dilapidated house. Most of the people are black but of varying shades. A man plays a banjo. A woman dances with a child. On the left, a young couple appears to be flirting, the woman much lighter-skinned than the man. Elsewhere on the closet wall conservationists found pages from magazines dated 1890 and 1891, and concluded that the lithograph was pasted there at the same time. The question arose: what significance did a lithograph of black domestic life have for the Costellos?

Research revealed that Hazel Costello, before she married, had been Hazel Griffin, and that her great-grandfather was Enerals Griffin, a former black slave from Virginia. Griffin bought the house and twenty-hectare plot in 1834. He had married a white woman and all his descendants married white people so that with each succeeding generation the Griffins changed from black to white, passing through almost every shade of skin tone illustrated in the painting.

Archivists dug up everything they could on Enerals Griffin. It wasn't much. From census records they deduced he was born a slave in Virginia in 1794. Whether he left Virginia as an escaped slave or moved from there as a freeman, nobody knows. He lived for a time in Ohio, and in 1829 fled racial troubles there for Upper Canada. Exactly what route he took is unknown. One account has him crossing the border at Detroit. Another has him landing at Port Stanley on Lake Erie. Evidence suggests he was married and arrived with his wife, Priscilla. Where did they live after that? All that can be said for certain is that in 1834 Enerals purchased twenty hectares, a four-room house, and some simple outbuildings on a hill outside Ancaster for himself, his wife, and their newborn son, James.

Three years later, in 1837, a column appeared in an abolitionist paper called *The Emancipator* under the title "Letter from Mr. Wilson." "Visited Ancaster," the correspondent wrote, "called on Mr. Griffin … an enterprising farmer who was driven from Ohio in 1829 by oppression. He cultivates one of the best farms in the country."

Assessment records from 1851 show that Enerals, seventeen years after his arrival, had twelve hectares under cultivation, including six hectares for crops, five hectares for pasture, and one hectare devoted to a vegetable garden and fruit orchard. Another six hectares served as a woodlot. That year, in the measurements of the time, his ledgers show he produced two hundred and fifty bushels of wheat, two hundred bushels of oats, twenty-five bushels of corn, twenty bushels of potatoes, and one bushel of beans. His ledgers also show fourteen tons of hay, one hundred and fifty pounds of butter, and forty pounds of wool. His livestock totalled fifteen sheep, nine pigs, three horses, two cows, and one calf.

By then Enerals and his only child, James, were working the land themselves. Priscilla had died the year before on December 1, 1850, at the age of fifty-five. In 1854, at twenty, James married a young Scottish immigrant, Euphemia Purvis. They settled into the house with Enerals, and over the course of their marriage had eight children. Enerals continued to live with them until his death in 1878 at eighty-four. Afterward the entire estate went to James. Eventually, his son George acquired it, as did George's daughter Hazel, who bequeathed it to her children, who offered it for sale.

Knowing the history, the Hamilton Conservation Authority decided to restore the house. Evidence suggested that it had been built in 1827. Enerals bought it in 1834. By 1988 white stucco covered the exterior walls, but restoration architects stripped them to the original weathered clapboard to reveal what they called the home's "elegant simplicity." In 2008, Parks Canada designated the house a National Historic Site, calling it "a fine example of vernacular domestic architecture of the early period in this province's settlement." Griffin House now functions as a summertime museum and Canadian Black History site, open Sundays in July, August, and September.

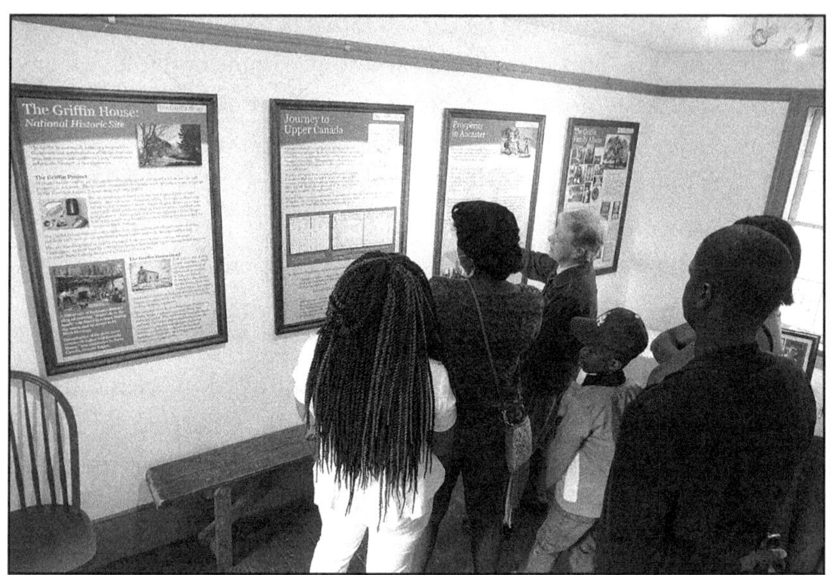

Photo by John Goddard

Historical interpreter Anne Jarvis steers visitors through four panels about the Griffin family, including one detailing the journey that former slave Enerals Griffin took to Upper Canada from Virginia and Ohio. He was born a slave in 1794.

The high point of the museum's calendar falls on a weekend day close to August 1 — Emancipation Day. On August 1, 1834, a British law abolished slavery in all British colonies, including Upper Canada. In 2015, the anniversary festivities fell on Sunday, August 2. Two outdoor stages were erected, one on the side of Griffin House, the other on the banked lawns of the Fieldcote Memorial Park and Museum. The blues duo and mixed-race couple Chris Whiteley and Diana Braithwaite headlined the show. Other acts included: the Akwaaba Drummers, originally from Ghana and now based in New Hampshire; Steve Frise, a white blues guitarist and banjo player living in Toronto; and Toronto's Afro-contemporary dance company, KasheDance.

Anybody entering the Griffin House Museum that day would have heard a running commentary in the kitchen by program coordinator Daryl MacTavish. He spoke of the *Negro Life at the South* lithograph, the home's restoration, the Griffin family, and — in his entertaining way — various details of early-nineteenth-century Upper Canada life. What follows is a transcript, only slightly edited and with added subheadings, of MacTavish's 2015 Emancipation Day commentary.

The Griffin Family

Enerals Griffin was a slave from Virginia who made his way to freedom in the 1820s from Virginia to Ohio. He went from a slave state to a free state, but in 1829 race riots broke out in Ohio and he decided to come to Canada with his wife, Priscilla. She is one of the biggest mysteries of our story. We don't know where he met her. Did she come with him from Virginia, or did he meet her in Ohio? We know that they arrived together in Canada in 1829 and that in 1834 Enerals and Priscilla bought this house. It was already built, and they moved in with their son James, who had just been born.

The year 1834 happened to be a census year, and the census taker wrote beside Enerals's name that he was black. The official wrote nothing next to Priscilla's name, but for their only child, a little baby named James, he wrote "mulatto," which in those days meant one black parent, one white parent. This means that Priscilla was either white, or she was so light-skinned that the census taker assumed she was white.

They had only one child. Their little boy, James, grew up, and when he was sixteen his mother died. When he was twenty, he married a young woman from Scotland named Euphemia. They became the parents of eight children, who grew up and married in the local area, and every generation in the family changed in appearance.

We take it that James was half white, half black. His children had a Scottish mother, making them one-quarter black, three-quarters white. Their children were one-eighth black, seven-eighths white. They weren't trying to hide who they were — you married who you fell in love with and who

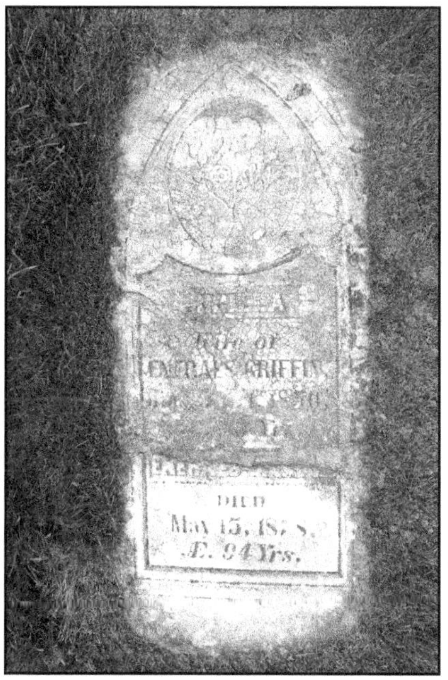

Photo by John Goddard

A flat stone covers Priscilla Griffin's grave at St. Andrew's Presbyterian Church, across from the Fieldcote Museum. She died at fifty-five in 1850. Enerals Griffin was buried with her in 1878 at the age of eighty-four, not "94."

lived nearby. So the family over the generations changed in appearance, and by the 1980s most descendants of Enerals and Priscilla Griffin had no idea they had black ancestry. They were redheads with freckles and blonds with blue eyes, and it was a big discovery that their ancestor had been a slave from Virginia. But they are proud of their ancestor and they still come to all our special events. If Enerals Griffin hadn't made his way to Canada and to freedom, they wouldn't be the family they are today. Have a look in the room next door. A row of four panels tells the story of the Griffin family. In the fourth panel, you see photographs of the Griffins in 1988 and in 2012, and you see a lot of redheads and blonds.

Layout of the House

Originally, the Griffins were a family of three — mother, father, one child. The next generation, James and Euphemia, had eight children, but it was still a four-room house. Four rooms with three people is a lot of space. Four rooms with eleven people is not quite as spacious. We think James and Euphemia had the bedroom upstairs. The small bedroom across the hall would have been for the three girls. Out in the hallway would have been a bed for two boys. Downstairs in what was their parlour, Enerals would have had his own bed and the other three boys would have shared a bed there.

Everyone shared. We don't miss flying cars because cars don't fly yet, and they didn't miss privacy because they never had it. Back then any family, black or white, if you were a farm family, there was no privacy and you shared. They wouldn't have thought anything of it.

White Sugar Versus Maple Syrup, Macaroni Versus Beef

If a recipe said, "add a cup of sugar," it meant brown sugar. If it said, "add a cup of fine sugar," it meant white sugar. If a recipe called for "flour," it meant "whole-wheat flour," and if it asked for "fine" flour, it meant "white" flour. Try this yourself: make two batches of cookies, one with brown sugar and whole-wheat flour, the other with white sugar and white flour, then taste the difference. The brown sugar with whole-wheat flour cookies will always taste better because they have more flavour, and they will be healthier for you. Ironically, poor people ate the better-tasting healthier ones and rich people ate the others.

That was one difference between rich and poor. White sugar was really expensive. If you couldn't afford it, you bought the brown, if you couldn't afford the brown, you bought molasses, and if you couldn't afford molasses, you could tap maple trees in spring and get maple syrup for free, or find a beehive and take out the honeycomb. People without a lot of money used maple syrup and honey a lot more than they used any kind of sugar, which is also ironic because today you can buy a great big bag of white sugar for a little bit of money and a small amount of maple syrup for a whole lot of money.

I'll tell you something else about rich people's food. In the 1750s, a group of Englishmen decided to take a Grand Tour of Europe, and for the first time they tasted all these — for them — exotic foods. For us, eating food from everywhere is common, but back then it was rare to eat foods from another country unless you were rich. When they reached Italy, these Englishmen were so amazed at the flavour and taste of Italian food that they decided to find some way of continuing to eat it after they returned to England. They formed a club where they could eat Italian food whenever they wished. Only rich people could afford to join the club, and their monthly membership fees paid for the cost of hiring a chef trained in Italian cooking and for importing the ingredients from Italy. They called it the Macaroni Club. Poor people ate roast beef and roast chicken, but the rich ate macaroni.

The word *macaroni* became a high compliment. It meant "stylish and elegant" because only stylish and elegant people could afford to eat macaroni. So if you were going to church in a brand-new dress, your friends would say, "Your gown is absolutely macaroni." And if you were walking along wearing a new jacket, they would say, "He's turning macaroni," because you were so stylish-looking. It was an Englishman who wrote the lyrics "Yankee Doodle went to town, riding on a pony, stuck a feather in his hat and called it 'macaroni.'"

Fire as Energy, Fire as Killer

If you were a woman back then, you spent ninety percent of your day stuck in the kitchen next to a roaring fire. Fire is your energy source. You need fire to cook food, heat water for washing, and heat irons for ironing. To make pickles, vinegars and jams, soap and candles, you need fire. Except for spinning wool on a wheel, everything a woman does she does using the fireplace. Some houses had a separate building called a summer kitchen where you could cook and make things using fire without overheating the house in summer, but for the woman it doesn't matter. Whether she is in a regular kitchen or a summer kitchen, she is stuck there all day long beside a burning fire. You can imagine in January how wonderful that is, and in July and August how awful that is.

The fire was also dangerous. Today, if a spark lands on us at a campfire, we can just stomp the spark out and not worry about it. Back then, if you were a woman at a cooking fire all day turning and moving, a spark could land on the back of your dress and burst into flame because your clothing was so dry. For women and their daughters, the number one cause of accidental death was having their clothes catch fire. The burn didn't kill them, the infection did. Somebody would rub cold butter onto the burn because it felt soothing to the skin, but unpasteurized butter rubbed onto a burn could cause an infection, and there were no antibiotics.

Overall, the primary cause of death for women was childbirth. Childbearing was dangerous. It was common for a man to have two or three wives during the course of his life, because every day that a widower wasn't married was a day that his children needed looking after. So his first marriage was for love, and his second, third, or even fourth marriages were for necessity, for looking after the children.

The Griffin family did not follow the pattern of mothers dying young. Enerals's wife, Priscilla, died when James was sixteen years old. He was grown and Enerals did not remarry. James and Euphemia had eight children. She survived giving birth to all eight and lived to be a great-grandmother.

Upstairs Bedrooms

You will notice a fireplace here and a fireplace directly above upstairs, but there are no fireplaces on the other side of the house. Heat doesn't travel sideways particularly well. Seventy percent of the heat goes up the chimney, so this room would be warm but not the room across the hall. Similarly, the bedroom above us would have been warm but not the bedroom across the hall.

When you went to bed in the wintertime, you tried to bank your fire so that the coals were still hot in the morning. If you didn't bank your fire properly, and your fire went out, you could wake up in the morning with your house the same temperature as the outdoors. A lot of settlers and pioneers — in their journals and in letters back to families living in warmer areas — wrote that it was so cold in Canada you could wake up in the morning with your fire out, and not only could you see your breath in your bedroom but your top blankets were also covered in frost.

Go upstairs and look at the bedrooms. If you were rich and eating macaroni, you were also probably sleeping on a feather bed, but if you were a farm family, you were sleeping on a mattress stuffed with straw. When you first put it on your bed, the straw was thick, but after two or three months it got really dry and brittle. Every time you climbed into bed the straw would break a bit, and gradually your mattress would condense down into something much smaller, and the smaller it got the harder it got, which meant that every spring and every fall you

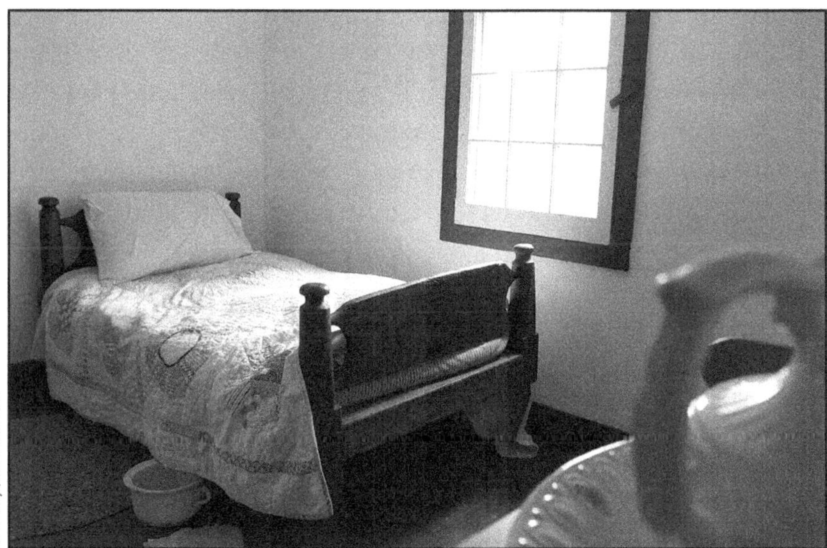

Photo by John Goddard

The "elegant simplicity" of Griffin House extends to the upstairs bedroom where the three daughters of James and Euphemia Griffin once slept. Under the bed lie squares of cloth of the type that program coordinator Daryl MacTavish describes in his commentary.

would take all your mattresses off your beds and carry them out to the barn. You would cut open the tops, tear out the old, dried straw, and put in new straw. Then you would resew the mattresses and put them back on the beds.

Now the mattresses would be big and plump again, but the straw in the barn had bugs in it, so the straw in your mattresses would have bugs, too. When you climbed into that big, soft bed, you were going to get bitten. You would wake up in the morning and feel incredibly itchy, so at bedtime that evening you would tell your children, "It's time to hit the sack." The children would stand around the bed they shared — there were usually two or three kids to a bed — and they would start pounding on the bed as hard as they could, trying to crush the bugs. If they were really good at hitting the hay, or hitting the sack, the bugs would all die and they would get a good night's sleep.

The second problem with the beds was that ropes supported the mattress. When the ropes were tight, the mattress was straight, but after a few nights a person's weight would stretch the ropes a bit and the bed would sink in the middle. If your children were sleeping three to a bed, the child in the middle was soon sleeping in a gully, and the others were rolling on top of their brother or sister. That meant that every two or three days you would have to twist the ropes to make them tight again, which was why parents would say, "Good night, sleep tight, don't let the bedbugs bite." "Sleep tight" means tighten the ropes so that nobody rolls onto you, and "don't let the bedbugs bite" means "remember to hit the sack."

Doing the Necessary

Outside and down the hill there was a little building called "the necessary" because you went out there when it was necessary. Whether it was summer or winter, sunny or raining, hot or cold, you went outside to the necessary. At nighttime, though, you used the chamber pot, the little pot under your bed. Two or three kids shared the bed, which meant two or three kids shared the pot, and in the morning you took the pots out to the necessary. You dumped out the contents, scrubbed the pots clean, and put them back under the bed. That was a pretty awful job, but it wasn't the

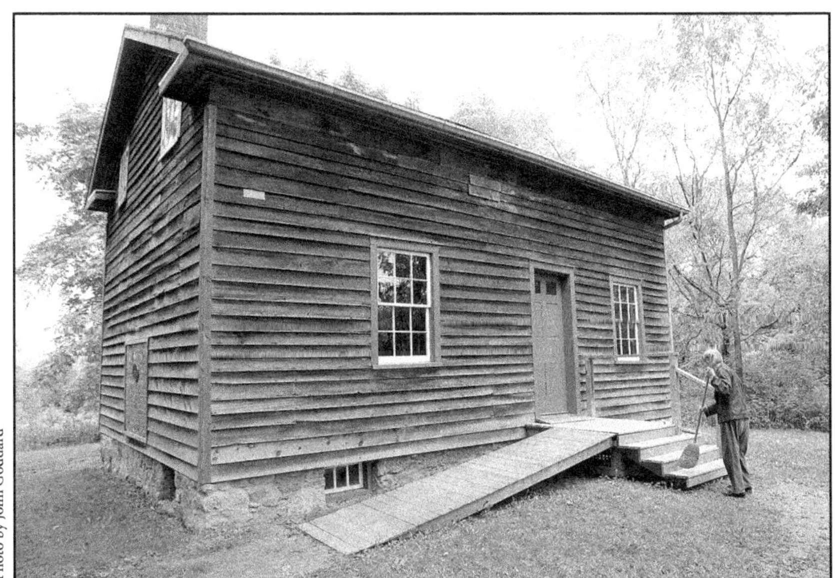

Photo by John Goddard

Historical interpreter Anne Jarvis sweeps the back steps of Griffin House in late summer. The museum keeps seasonal hours — open every Sunday in July, August, and September.

worst job. The worst job was there was no such thing as toilet paper, so you used little pieces of cloth cut into squares, and all those cloths when they got dirty somebody had to wash and clean. In the laundry area, there was a pot of water and some lye. You handed your daughter a long stick. She stood holding her nose and stirred the cloths around and around until all the cloths were boiled clean.

FIELDCOTE MEMORIAL PARK AND MUSEUM: HISTORY AND VISUAL ART

The first permanent settlers arrived in the 1790s, making Ancaster one of the earliest communities in Southern Ontario. The Fieldcote house itself counts as a relative newcomer. The building dates to 1948, when Tom and Doris Farmer constructed it on three hectares of scenic property near the village centre. Tom Farmer was a newspaperman who from 1966 to 1969 served as editor-in-chief of the *Hamilton Spectator*.

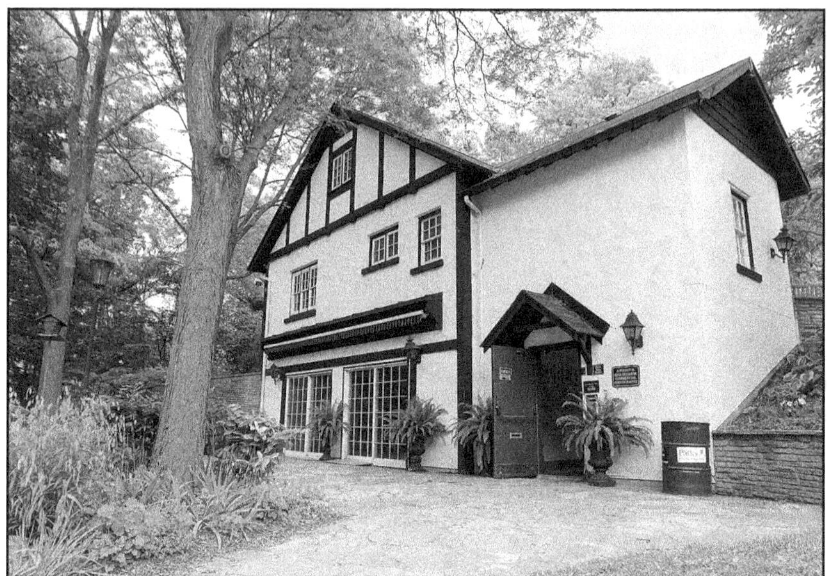

Photo by John Goddard

Tom and Doris Farmer built their dream home in 1948 on three hectares near the centre of historic Ancaster. Now known as Fieldcote Museum, the building functions as a gallery for exhibitions alternating between local history and the visual arts.

Doris Farmer volunteered for the Ancaster Township Historical Society. Both were amateur historians and community boosters. Tom died in 1976, Doris in 1983. She bequeathed the estate to Ancaster — the grounds for use as a park and botanical garden, the house as a museum and art gallery. Fieldcote houses no permanent displays. Curators devote its modest space to exhibitions alternating between village history and the visual arts. The museum is open five afternoons a week year-round.

In 2014, a special exhibition marked the two hundredth anniversary of one of the village's most traumatic historical events, the Bloody Assize. In the spring of 1814, during the War of 1812 between Britain and the United States, nineteen settlers from the southeastern part of the colony went on trial in Ancaster for high treason. The judges convened the court at the Union Hotel on Wilson Street where the Coach & Lantern Pub now stands. A temporary or travelling court was called a Court of Assize. The prisoners stood accused of actively siding with

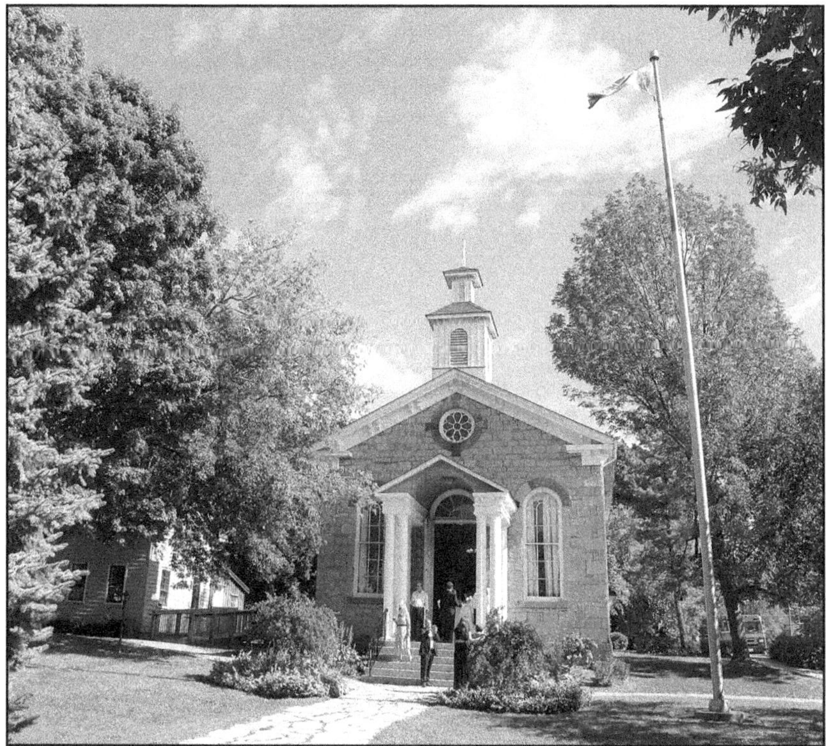

Photo by John Goddard

The Old Township Hall, built in 1871, stands just off Ancaster's main street at 310 Wilson Street East. It is walking distance from Fieldcote Museum, which operates the historic building for weddings and other special events.

the United States by providing information and supplies. Fifteen of the men were convicted as traitors and sentenced to hang. On July 20, 1814, eight were hanged at Burlington Heights, the remainder sent into exile. At a parkette near the Coach & Lantern, a plaque erected by the Archaeological and Historic Sites Board of Ontario commemorates the event.

Why Go?

The Joseph Brant Museum commemorates Burlington's most famous historical figure and one of the most famous Native leaders of his time, Thayendanegea, or Joseph Brant (1743–1807). The Mohawk leader built his final home at what was then called Head-of-the-Lake on a site bordering modern-day Hamilton in Burlington. A small permanent exhibition includes two national treasures. One is a gold ring engraved "Thayendanegea 1776" that the Mohawk chief wore to identify his body should he be killed. The other is a piece of ornamental throat armour, or gorget, that he received in 1776 as a gift from King George III.

Address

1240 North Shore Boulevard East, Burlington.

Getting There by Public Transit

I have taken the GO train to Burlington Station with my bicycle and cycled down Brant Street, which has a bike lane most of the way and at the bottom joins the Waterfront Trail for the short remaining ride west to the museum. From the GO station, buses 5, 10, and 50 also take you there.

JOSEPH BRANT MUSEUM

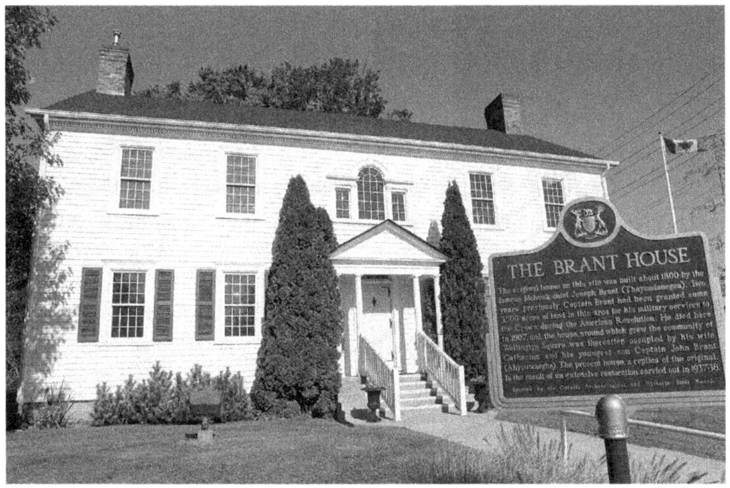

Photo by John Goddard

A replica of Joseph Brant's final home stands near the opening to what is now Hamilton Harbour. It honours Burlington's most famous historical figure and one of the most significant Native leaders of his time.

JOSEPH BRANT, CHIEF OF CHIEFS

Mohawk Chief Joseph Brant led the refugees of the Six Nations Confederacy north from the United States to settle along the Grand River in what is now Southwestern Ontario. One of the most famous Native leaders of his time, he learned as a young man to read and write English, fought on the British side in the American War of Independence, won the admiration of King George III, and spent his mature years working out a place for Aboriginal peoples within British colonial society.

Brant was born Thayendanegea in what is now Ohio, probably in 1743. He grew up in what is now Upstate New York. Early on he took the name "Joseph Brant," an English-sounding name, as though foreshadowing his remarkable life as an intermediary between First Nations and British colonial authorities. As a teenager, he enrolled in a missionary school under the Reverend Eleazar Wheelock, who praised him as possessing "a Sprightly Genius, a manly and genteel Deportment, and … a Modest courteous and benevolent Temper." Under Wheelock, Brant became literate in English and studied European agricultural methods. Later he assisted another missionary, John Stuart, in translating into the Mohawk language the Gospel of St. Mark, a history of the Bible, and an exposition of the catechism. "Perhaps … the only Person in America equal to such an undertaking," Stuart said of his protégé.

When war broke out between Britain and the American Thirteen Colonies in 1775, Brant sided with the British. As a Mohawk war chief and British captain in horrifically bloody battles, he distinguished himself for his bravery and compassion. "He emerges in the official dispatches as the perfect soldier," writes historian Barbara Graymont, "possessed of remarkable physical stamina, courage under fire, and dedication to the cause, as an able and inspiring leader, and as a complete gentleman."

Britain and its allies lost the war. The Americans won. In 1782, the British surrendered to the Americans all the lands it claimed west to the Mississippi River, including those occupied exclusively by Native peoples. In response, Brant began his career as a statesman. At the age of forty he became Grand Chief of the Six Nations, chief of the national chiefs. He played a major role in an effort to forge a pan-national confederacy to oppose settler expansion into the western American territories. He also secured an enormous tract of land for the Six Nations in British territory along the Grand River north of Lake Erie, along with £1,500 for other war losses. At Brant's insistence, the British granted a tract extending ten kilometres on either side of the river from source to mouth for the Mohawk, Cayuga, Onondaga, Oneida, Seneca, and Tuscarora Nations.

The British respected Brant. Twice he voyaged to England to lobby the government, and twice he was welcomed and celebrated by the highest levels of British society, including King George III. Brant made his first trip in 1776 to negotiate the role of the Mohawk and other Iroquois Nations in the American War of Independence. He made his second visit in 1785, after the war's conclusion. With his English manners and mixed English/Native dress, he projected the popular ideal of "the noble savage," the primitive man uncorrupted by civilization. On the first trip, George III met Brant twice and presented him with a silver-gilt gorget, a decorative piece of throat armour. It can be seen in a portrait, now owned by

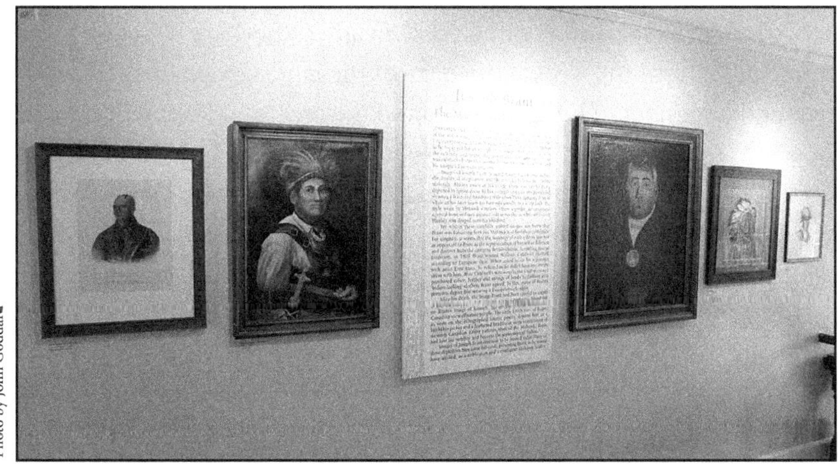

Photo by John Goddard

Portraits depicting Joseph Brant's many personas hang in the museum's upstairs hallway as part of a permanent exhibition. Some paintings reveal more about the artists' misconceptions than about the subject's true character.

the National Gallery of Canada, by one of eighteenth-century England's leading artists, George Romney.

What the British failed to make clear to Brant was that the Six Nations did not own their land grant the way other United Empire Loyalists owned theirs. Brant saw that the Grand River tract was too small for hunting and traditional farming, and began to sell and lease some of the property. He wanted both to raise capital for community projects and attract white settlers to teach European agricultural methods. (Among his buyers was Richard Beasley, who also owned Burlington Heights where Dundurn Castle now stands.) Colonial officials stopped Brant, however, saying that the Crown held underlying title to the Grand River reserve.

Traditionalists on the Grand River also opposed Brant's land sales and white settlement. One of his most dangerous critics proved to be his first-born son, Isaac. Brant had married three times; his first two wives had died of tuberculosis. Isaac was the elder of two children by Brant's first wife, Peggie. He had grown up unhappy and discontented. "Isaac gave plenty of trouble," writes Brant's most thorough biographer, Isabel Kelsay, in *Joseph Brant 1743–1807: Man of Two Worlds*. "At far too young an age, for he was only thirteen … [h]e learned to drink."

In 1795, Isaac's disaffection came to a head. The Mohawks and members of other First Nations gathered at Head-of-the-Lake to collect their annual gifts from the Crown, a legacy of the land agreements. Two taverns and a number of liquor huts dotted the area, and Joseph Brant and Isaac were visiting one. As Kelsay tells the story, Isaac became drunk and unruly. Joseph told him to be quiet. Isaac started raving and cursing, and came at his father with a knife. Brant fended off the attack, badly injuring one hand, and with his own dagger grazed his son's head. At first Isaac's wound did not appear serious, but once home on the Grand River the son quickly deteriorated. Three times he asked for his father, but Brant still had not returned. After two days Isaac died. His son's death was to haunt Brant for the rest of his life, but nobody held him responsible. When he surrendered to police, no charges were laid. Under Isaac's pillow, Kelsay writes, a pistol was discovered, apparently part of a plot to kill the Mohawk leader.

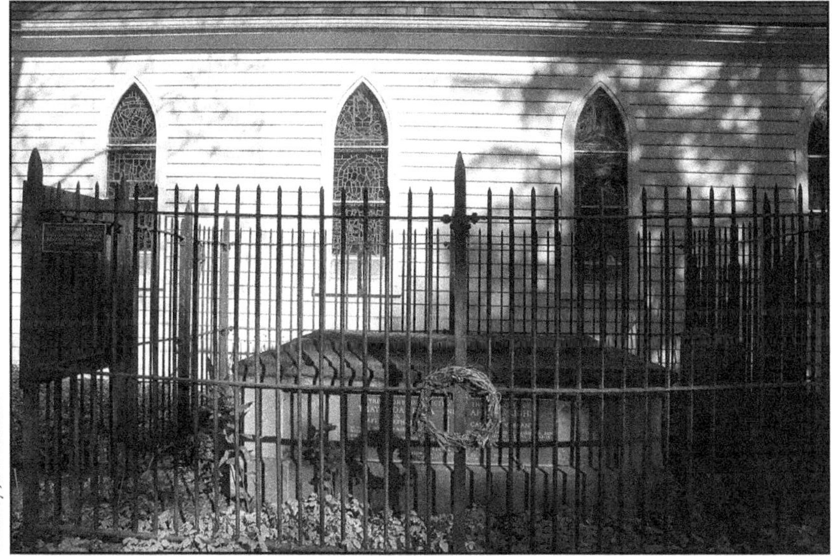

Photo by John Goddard

Joseph Brant rests in a gated tomb outside Her Majesty's Royal Chapel of the Mohawks, built in 1785 on the Six Nations Reserve at Brantford. Interred with him are the remains of his son Chief John Brant, or Tekarihogen.

On the Grand River, political tensions continued to mount. To escape another possible assassination attempt, Brant withdrew to a piece of land he had bought on Burlington Bay from the Mississauga people. In 1798, he began to build a house on a rise near the shore. It went up slowly, as Brant continued to travel and attend to other matters, but by mid-1802 he had settled in. Five years later, on November 24, 1807, he died in the house at the age of sixty-four. Kelsay says he died "in an English bed in an English room," but his last words to his friend, John Norton, were of his people. "Have pity on the poor Indians," he said, "if you can get any influence with the great, endeavor to do them all the good you can."

Brant's remains are interred on the Six Nations Reserve at Brantford, the city that takes his name, in a tomb at Her Majesty's Royal Chapel of the Mohawks. It is Ontario's oldest Protestant church, built in 1785. Among Mohawks, Brant's legacy is mixed. Some praise him for his progressive leadership. Others disparage him for compromising with the British and failing to create a sovereign Aboriginal nation.

THE ENSLAVEMENT OF SOPHIA POOLEY

Joseph Brant owned more than thirty black slaves. Archives of Ontario researchers established the number for their perennial travelling exhibition *Enslaved Africans in Upper Canada*. One was Sophia Pooley, who was kidnapped and sold to Brant as a child, and who late in life told her story. Brant biographers, however, barely mention slavery. Some ignore the subject altogether. In her sweeping 775-page tome on Brant's life, biographer Isabel Kelsay entirely disregards Pooley's testimony but makes passing reference to Brant as a slaver.

"Joseph already had the beginnings of a retinue of Negro slaves whom he had captured or who had run away to join him," Kelsay writes of Brant in 1779, when he was thirty-six years old and living in Lewiston on the American side of the Niagara River. "If any of these [slaves] expected an end to their labor, they were mistaken. Their duties may have been somewhat different, but they still had duties; and it was always said of Joseph that he tolerated no nonsense from his slaves."

Two domestic slaves served Scottish traveller Patrick Campbell during his two-day visit to Brant's home at Brant's Town, Upper Canada, in 1792, Kelsay also says. "Dinner the next day was another lavish meal," she writes, "with handsomely attired Negro slaves waiting on table."

Brant left the United States in 1784. He moved across the Niagara River to what was still called the Province of Quebec, or sometimes British North America. In 1791, the British government divided the colony to create Upper Canada, now Ontario, and one year later John Graves Simcoe arrived as Upper Canada's first lieutenant governor. Simcoe detested slavery. He moved to abolish it but faced tough opposition. Some members of the colonial elite owned slaves, and United Empire Loyalists who were helping to settle the colony were bringing slaves with them from the United States. Simcoe compromised. In his Anti-Slavery Act of 1793, he allowed existing slaves to remain enslaved until death. He also stipulated, however, that any child born of a slave mother must be freed at the age of twenty-five and that no new slaves could be brought into Upper Canada. In 1834, the Emancipation Act abolished slavery in British colonies outright.

Of all Brant's slaves, history best remembers Sophia Pooley. In old age — "more than ninety years old," she says — she spoke to Benjamin

Drew, an American abolitionist from Boston who travelled through Upper Canada in the mid-1850s to interview former U.S. slaves. In 1856, he published their testimony as *The Refugee: or the Narratives of Fugitive Slaves in Canada*. The book includes Pooley's story, possibly the only first-person narrative of somebody living as a slave in what is now Canada. Her account runs to a mere 1,100 words.

"I was born in Fishkill, New York State, twelve miles from North River," she begins. Her parents, Oliver and Dinah, were slaves. When she was seven years old, she and her sister were stolen from them. "My master's sons-in-law, Daniel Outwaters and Simon Knox, came into the garden where my sister and I were playing among the currant bushes, tied their handkerchiefs over our mouths, carried us to a vessel, put us in the hold, and sailed up the river," she says.

At Niagara, on the American side, Pooley was sold to Joseph Brant, whom she refers to as "old Indian Brant, the king." What happened to her sister she does not say. When Pooley relocated with Brant north of the border, she saw few other white or black people.

"I guess I was the first colored girl brought into Canada," she says at one point. "There were hardly any white people in Canada then," she says at another, "nothing here but Indians and wild beasts. Many a deer I have helped catch on the lakes in a canoe: one year we took ninety."

Over the years, Pooley witnessed substantial change.

"Canada was filling up with white people," she tells Drew. "And after Brant went to England, and kissed the queen's hand, he was made a colonel. Then there began to be laws in Canada."

Brant met the king not the queen and was made a captain not a colonel, but Pooley was right about new governmental regulation. Colonial authorities were opening the territory to white settlement, and Brant led the move to stake out a rightful place for the Mohawk, Oneida, Onondaga, Cayuga, Seneca, and Tuscarora refugees from the American Revolutionary War, distinguishing himself as the foremost leader of the Six Nations, their chief of chiefs.

Pooley describes Brant with a hint of affection. "A good-looking man," she calls him. "When Brant went among the English, he wore the English dress," she also says. "When he was among the Indians, he wore the Indian dress — broadcloth leggings, blanket, moccasins, fur cap. He had his ears slit with a long loop at the edge, and in these he hung long silver ornaments. He wore a silver half-moon on his breast with the king's name on it [the gorget from George III], and broad silver bracelets on his arms. He never would paint, but his people painted a great deal. Brant was always for making peace among his people; that was the reason of his going about so much."

Of Brant's wife Catherine, on the other hand, Pooley has nothing good to say. "Brant's third wife, my mistress, was a barbarous creature," the former slave tells Drew. "She could talk English, but she would not. She would tell me in Indian to do things, and then hit me with any thing that came to hand, because I did not understand her. I have a scar on my head from a wound she gave me with a hatchet; and this long scar over my eye, is where she cut me with a knife. The skin dropped over my eye; a white woman bound it up. Brant was very angry, when he came home, at what she had done, and punished her as if she had been a child. Said he, 'you know I adopted her as one of the family, and now you are trying to put all the work on her.'"

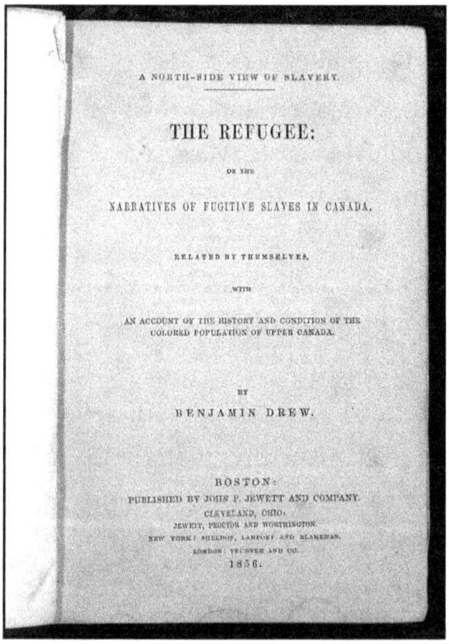

Photo by John Goddard

In 1856, Boston abolitionist Benjamin Drew published a book taken from his travels in Upper Canada. The text includes possibly the only first-person narrative of somebody living as a slave in what is now Canada.

While the Archives of Ontario researchers put the number of Brant's slaves at "over thirty," Pooley writes of knowing only two others. "Brant had two colored men for slaves: one of them was the father of John Patten, who lives over yonder, the other called himself Simon Ganseville. There was but one other Indian that I knew, who owned a slave." Perhaps the two slaves she names were the two "handsomely attired Negro slaves waiting on table" who so impressed the traveller Campbell. Perhaps she knew only the two domestic servants, like herself, and not others.

A few other discrepancies arise from Pooley's account. Her dates and numbers do not add up. Pooley says she was kidnapped and sold to Brant at the age of seven, that she served him for twelve or thirteen years, and that Brant sold her when she was twelve, none of which makes sense. Historians have had to construct an alternate timeline through conjecture.

One such researcher is Jane Mulkewich, a lawyer and human-rights advocate living in Dundas, now part of Hamilton. She often tells Pooley's story at Black History Month events. She takes the phrase "more than ninety years old" loosely. Like other researchers, as a starting point, she puts Pooley at ninety years old in 1856, the year Drew's book came out. By that calculation, Pooley would have been born in 1766 and kidnapped at the age of seven in 1773.

"Sophia Pooley says Brant sold her when she was twelve, but I think she's mixed up," Mulkewich says. "I think she was sold to Brant at twelve."

Such a chronology would mean that Brant bought the girl five years after she was kidnapped, leaving five years unaccounted for, but the timeline makes sense. Pooley said that Brant bought her at Niagara. He moved there in 1778 when Pooley was twelve.

"I was a woman grown when the first governor of Canada came from England: that was Gov. Simcoe," Pooley also says. Simcoe arrived in 1792. In Mulkewich's chronology, Pooley would have been twenty-six, which also makes sense.

Brant did eventually sell Pooley.

"I was sold by Brant to an Englishman in Ancaster, for one hundred dollars," she says. "His name was Samuel Hatt, and I lived with him seven years."

Mulkewich puts the year of the Hatt transaction at 1807. Hatt got married on October 21 that year, a good reason to acquire a domestic servant. As it turned out, Brant also was to die that year on November 27. By the Mulkewich timeline, Pooley would by then have served Brant for twenty-nine years and left his service when she was forty-one.

During the War of 1812, Hatt fought heroically. As the head of a militia known as "Hatt's Volunteers," he marched with British General Isaac Brock to help capture Detroit. Hatt also fought in the 1812 Battle of Queenston Heights, where Brock was killed, and in the 1813 Battle of Lundy's Lane, where Hatt was wounded.

Pooley mentions the war. In the early morning of June 6, 1813, apparently from Hatt's home in Ancaster, she said she heard the American cannons firing in the Battle of Stoney Creek. "I was seven miles from Stoney Creek at the time of the battle — the cannonade made every thing shake well," she recalls.

After the war she escaped.

"I lived with him seven years," Pooley says of Hatt, meaning that — according to the timeline — she left at the war's end in 1814. "The white people said I was free, and put me up to running away," she says. "[Hatt] did not stop me."

She moved to Waterloo, she says, and married a black man, Robert Pooley, who later ran off with a white woman. Brant died in 1807 at sixty-four. Hatt died in 1842 also at sixty-four. By the Mulkewich timeline, Pooley died in 1856 at the age of ninety.

WALK-THROUGH: NATIONAL TREASURES

Mohawk statesman Joseph Brant began building his final home at Head-of-the-Lake in the late 1790s. After his death, the building functioned as a summer resort, then as a staff house for a military hospital. In 1923 it was abandoned and in 1937 demolished. At the prodding of the historically minded Thomas McQuesten of Whitehern, when he was a cabinet minister, the Ontario government built a replica of the home, which opened in 1942 as the Joseph Brant Museum. Ambitious future plans call for an addition that would nearly triple the square footage. Next door stands the Joseph Brant Hospital.

On the main floor, in what would have been Brant's parlour and dining room, curators stage temporary local-history exhibitions. The museum takes special pride in its Eileen Collard Collection of Historic Costumes and Textiles, amassed by local fashion historian and author Eileen Collard and one of the largest collections of nineteenth-century clothing in Ontario. The upstairs hallway houses the permanent showcase. On the walls hang a series of portraits depicting Brant's many personas, and behind glass rest a number of rare objects of special personal significance to the famed Mohawk leader. Four artifacts are detailed here.

1. Gorget:

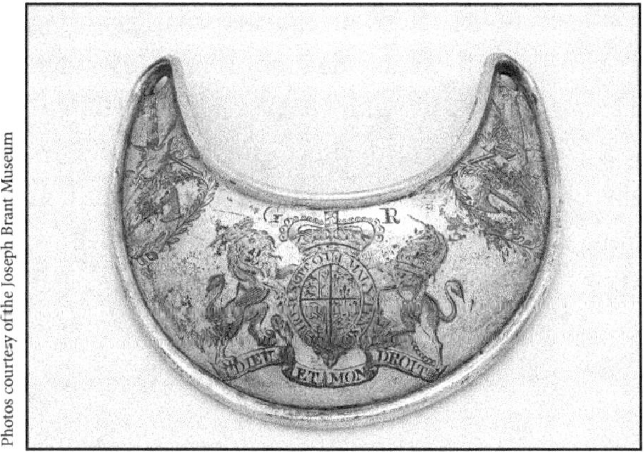

Photos courtesy of the Joseph Brant Museum

King George III presented Joseph Brant with this silver-gilt gorget as a gift during Brant's first visit to England in 1776. Considered a national treasure, it is an ornamental piece of throat armour named from the French word *la gorge*, meaning "throat." At the centre can be seen George III's royal monogram "GR," along with an English coat of arms flanked by English and Native war implements. An inscription on the back reads, "The gift of a Friend to Captn. Brant." On Brant's death, the gorget passed to his daughter, Elizabeth Kerr, who bequeathed it to the Sero family, also direct descendants. In 1968, the Joseph Brant Museum bought it at auction for $13,000, outbidding a Florida museum and the Smithsonian Institution in Washington, D.C.

2. Gold Ring:

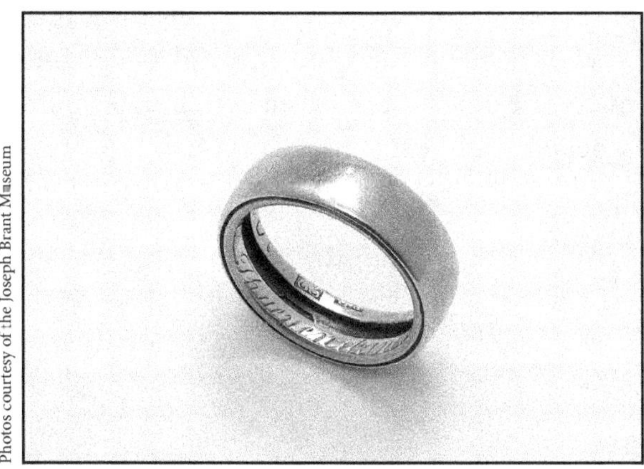

Photos courtesy of the Joseph Brant Museum

While in England in 1776 to negotiate terms of his involvement in the American War of Independence, Brant bought an eighteen-carat gold ring and had it inscribed on the inside with "Thayendanegea 1776." He wanted his body to be positively identified if he were killed. When he died of natural causes in 1807, the ring went to his third wife, Catherine. Four years later she lost it. Twenty-five years after that, in 1836, she found it again in a field near Wellington Square, now downtown Burlington, while visiting her daughter, Elizabeth Kerr. In 1966, the museum bought the ring from the widow of a Brant descendant.

3. Powder Horn:

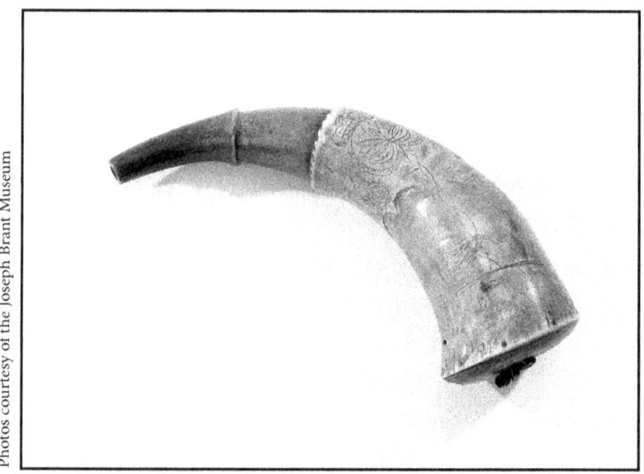

Photos courtesy of the Joseph Brant Museum

The powder horn is believed to have been Joseph Brant's, passed through the family of Brant's adoptive daughter, Margaret Clive. It is made of wood, with a metal toggle at the wide end and a remnant piece of leather, likely once part of a strap. Carved sketches decorate the piece, showing birds, people, and such animals as a turtle, a beaver, and a porcupine.

4. Miniature:

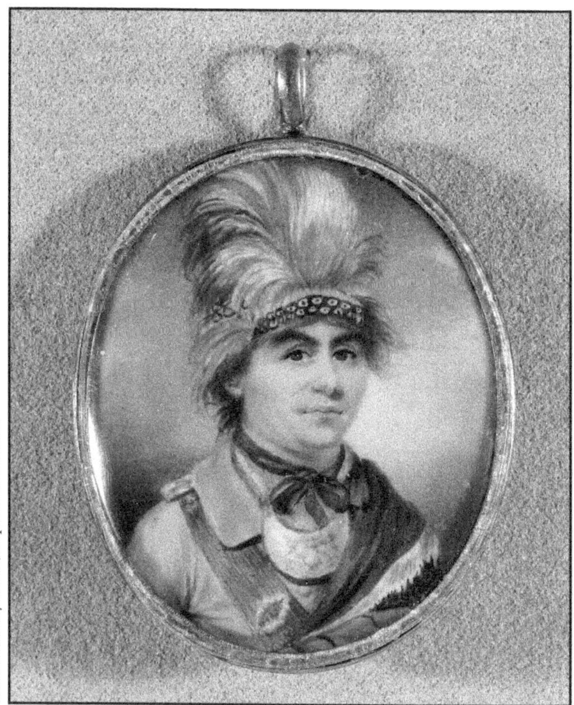

Photos courtesy of the Joseph Brant Museum

Renowned English artist Henry Bone painted this enamel miniature of Joseph Brant during his second visit to London in 1786. It was commissioned by Francis Rawdon-Hastings, 1st Marquess of Hastings, also known as Lord Rawdon, who made his name as a British military officer in the American Revolution. On the reverse are inscribed the words "Katerine, Rone 1786." A museum panel explains that *rone* is believed to be the Anglicized Mohawk word for "wife."

Why Go?

On the walnut dining room table in 1897, Janet Lee, advised by her husband, Erland, and two other men, composed the constitution and bylaws for an organization to improve the lives of rural women. The group spread internationally, turning Erland Lee House into a pilgrimage destination, the "birthplace of the Women's Institutes." For 164 years, from 1808 until 1972, the home also evolved through six generations from pioneer cabin to handsome estate for the enterprising Lees, who helped shape Stoney Creek and Saltfleet Township.

Address

552 Ridge Road, Stoney Creek.

Getting There by Public Transit

On weekdays, from Main Street downtown, board the No. 10 B-Line Express to Eastgate Square, then take either a 55A Stoney Creek or 58 Stoney Creek and get off at Highway 8 and DeWitt Road. Some No. 10 B-Line buses automatically become either a 55A or 58, which means not having to transfer. Ride all the way to DeWitt Road. From there walk for about twenty minutes uphill — up the escarpment — to the museum, located just after DeWitt Road turns onto Ridge Road. On Saturday or Sunday, take the No. 1 King bus from the Hamilton GO Centre to Eastgate Square, proceed on the 55A or 58 bus to DeWitt Road, then walk.

ERLAND LEE MUSEUM

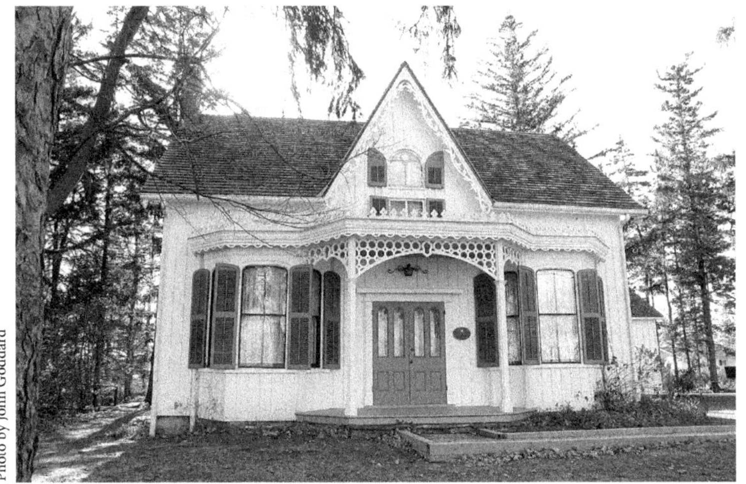

Photo by John Goddard

Erland Lee House stands as an excellent example of Ontario Gothic Revival architecture. A fourteen-year-old carpenter's apprentice carved the decorative maple-leaf motif on the gable's bargeboard.

ADELAIDE HOODLESS: HOMEMAKER'S CHAMPION

Adelaide Hoodless never forgave herself. Her youngest child died one summer of meningitis, apparently after drinking contaminated milk. Such contamination was not uncommon. Farmers often stored milk in open containers, attracting bacteria from flies and unwashed hands. Hot weather compounded the dangers. Dairies mixed milk from several farms, delivery men left milk bottles uncovered on the doorstep, and mothers sometimes inadvertently tainted their baby bottles through improper sterilization. Hoodless considered herself a skilled mother knowledgeable in childcare, but she somehow blamed herself for her infant son's death. Almost from the moment of the tragedy she embarked on a campaign to teach women and girls across the country how to properly cook, sew, raise a family, and especially how to practise the highest standards of cleanliness and sanitation.

"Rinse in cold water, then in scalding water," she writes of baby-bottle preparation in her pioneering home-economics textbook, as though aching to undo that fateful summer day. "If particles of milk adhere to the bottle use coarse salt or raw potato cut in small pieces. If the glass looks cloudy, add a little ammonia to the water. Turn the rubber tops inside out and scrub with a stiff brush; boil them every alternate day for 10 minutes." With italics and lingering self-admonition, she adds: "*Absolute cleanliness is a necessity* in the care of baby's food, bottles and rubber tops."

Adelaide Hoodless is mostly remembered now as the inspiration behind the Women's Institutes, an international organization for rural women, but she was also a tireless campaigner for urban women. She grew up a poor farm girl and married a wealthy urban manufacturer. She was born in 1857, the youngest of twelve children in a clapboard farmhouse in the rolling hills outside the village of St. George, a few kilometres north of Brantford. A few months later her father died, and her mother raised the children alone. Adelaide attended the nearby schoolhouse, worshipped at the Presbyterian church, and from her mother and elder sisters learned how to cook, sew, preserve, garden, keep house, and tend bees — all the skills essential to becoming a competent farm wife.

She met her husband through a family connection, says biographer Cheryl MacDonald in *Adelaide Hoodless: Domestic Crusader*. While attending Ladies' College in Cainsville, now part of Brantford, Adelaide boarded with her sister Lizzie, whose husband had a brother, a former mayor of Hamilton, who knew John Hoodless. He worked for his father, Joseph, who owned the successful Hoodless Furniture Company of Hamilton. In 1881, John and Adelaide married. They moved into comfortable rental quarters in the city and in six years had four children: Edna, Joseph, Muriel, and John. On August 10, 1889, at the age of fourteen months, little John died and Adelaide's life took an urgent new direction.

Photographs invariably show Adelaide Hoodless as a big-bosomed, matronly woman with a self-confident air. Early in her career, mostly as an unpaid organizer, she discovered a talent for management and public speaking, and for the kinds of executive skills that might have made her a good business leader. She might easily have run a furniture company. To her, however, running a business would have meant working for a living, and to her working for a living was strictly for men.

Throughout her life, Hoodless articulated an essentially contradictory philosophy. On the one hand, she devoted herself to elevating women's work to the level of men's. She called homemaking "domestic science" and emphasized the skills of time and money management. She debunked the attitude that girls naturally learned from their mothers how to be housewives and campaigned in favour of advanced instruction. "Why should a daughter go on making bad bread and the indigestible mixtures her mother and grandmother inflicted upon their families?" she would say. She also championed the home as the foundation of society. "A Nation," she would say, "cannot rise above the level of its homes."

On the other hand, Hoodless remained stuck to the idea that homemaking was a woman's destiny. She recognized that some women had to take jobs out of necessity, but said the workplace was really no place for a woman. Similarly, she saw no need for women to demand the vote because her sons could vote on her behalf. "A woman who has not succeeded in training her sons to vote so that they will guard their mother's best interests and the best interests of the nation is not herself worthy to vote," she said.

Hoodless lived a paradox. She enjoyed organizing, travelling, making speeches, and attending conferences — enjoyed working outside her own home — but restricted herself to mostly volunteer positions in the service of women as wives and mothers. She raised the value of homemaking, but hurt women's career ambitions and dragged down the women's suffrage movement. In 1876, Emily Howard Stowe, Canada's first female doctor, began campaigning in Ontario with her daughter, Augusta Stowe-Gullen, also a doctor, for a woman's right to vote. Partly because of the entrenched view that women must be homemakers, the effort was to take forty years.

Hoodless entered public life in 1889, when a gathering of Hamilton women voted to establish a Young Women's Christian Association (YWCA) branch, as other Canadian cities were doing. Within months she became president. In 1893, she travelled to Chicago, one of sixty Canadian women to attend an international women's congress as part of the Chicago World's Fair. There she encountered the International Council of Women, founded six years earlier in Washington, D.C. The council elected Hoodless president of a new Canadian section. Later that year she helped establish a full branch of the organization, to be called the Canadian National Council of Women. Hoodless became treasurer. Lady Aberdeen, wife of the soon-to-be-appointed governor general, John Hamilton-Gordon, 7th Earl of Aberdeen, was elected president. In a speech to the founding meeting, vice-president Mary McDonnell made clear that the council would not help women obtain the vote but would work instead to "conserve the highest good of the family and the state."

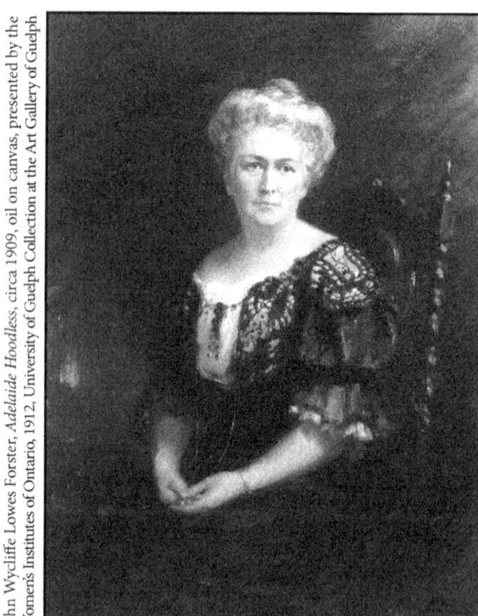

John Wycliffe Lowes Forster, *Adelaide Hoodless*, circa 1909, oil on canvas, presented by the Women's Institutes of Ontario, 1912, University of Guelph Collection at the Art Gallery of Guelph

Adelaide Hoodless projects the ideal image of the matronly homemaker in an oil painting by J.W.L. Forster. She occasionally spoke at Women's Institute meetings, but otherwise left the organization to rural women.

Seven local women's councils were also founded that year. Hoodless helped form the Hamilton one. At the same time she worked to expand the YWCA into a national organization and to redirect its mission, which to that point had been to support working women by housing them. In Hamilton, Hoodless founded a YWCA cooking school, the first of its kind in the country. The public education system, she said disapprovingly, was taking girls and young women out of the home. "[It was] offering everything to enable them to fill commercial occupations," she said, "[and] not doing one thing to develop the domestic side."

By then John and Adelaide Hoodless were well established. John had taken over from his father as head of the Hoodless Furniture Company, which was thriving. He also served as chairman of the Hamilton Board of Education, and was later elected president of both the Hamilton Board of Trade and the Canadian Retail Furniture Dealers Association. In 1894, the family moved into "Eastcourt," a sumptuous mansion, since demolished, near present-day Main Street East and Sherman Avenue South. Only its dilapidated coach house survives. The family was to live stylishly at Eastcourt for the next sixteen years.

As she settled into the new home, Adelaide began her push to make domestic science part of the regular Ontario school curriculum. She went from strength to strength. In 1897, the provincial government introduced legislation to include such courses in its elementary schools. In 1898, at the government's request, Hoodless wrote the first textbook on the subject, *Public School Domestic Science*. In 1900, in Hamilton, she opened the country's first school for domestic science teachers, the Ontario Normal School of Domestic Science and Art, with herself as president and manager. And in 1903, she co-founded, with Montreal tobacco magnate Sir William Macdonald, a college for women called the Macdonald Institute, now part of the University of Guelph. The college offered three programs: a three-month course for domestic science teachers wishing to upgrade their qualifications, a two-year course for women wishing to become domestic science teachers, and a one-year program nicknamed "the diamond-ring course" for women intending to marry.

Through Hoodless, domestic science — later renamed home economics — became part of the standard school curriculum across the country. Tirelessly, she organized, raised money, travelled, spoke in support of her cause, and at one point sailed to England where, with other delegates to the fourth International Council of Women conference, she took tea with Queen Victoria.

The day before her fifty-third birthday, Hoodless gave her final speech. On Saturday, February 26, 1910, she took the train to Toronto from Hamilton to speak to a gathering of the Toronto Women's Canadian Club. Ten minutes into her talk, "Women and Industrial Life," she stopped and put her hand to her head. The emcee, sitting behind her, rose and handed her a glass of water. Hoodless took a sip. She spoke four more words, "The interest in domestic —" and dropped dead of a cerebral hemorrhage.

By then her views on women were already out of date. That same year the National Council of Women, which Hoodless helped to found, announced its support of women's suffrage. In 1916, women won the right to vote in Manitoba, Saskatchewan, and Alberta. In 1917, they won the vote in British Columbia and Ontario. In 1918, with some conditions, women also won the right to vote federally. One of the women leading the campaign was Nellie McClung, a bestselling author and member of the Canadian Women's Press Club, who also championed women's economic independence.

Ironically, Hoodless's legacy endures mostly through an organization she inspired but in which she took little active participation — the Women's Institutes. Erland Lee and his wife, Janet, a farming couple from Stoney Creek, attended a lecture that Hoodless gave in early 1897 at the Ontario Agricultural College in Guelph. She spoke of scientific advances in farming. Today's farmer, she said, understands the earth's chemistry and climatic conditions better than his father and grandfather, and benefits from labour-saving devices on his fields and in his barns. Similarly, science must come to the farmhouse, she said. Is it right that the farmer's wife, she asked rhetorically, "toils and drudges on the same old treadmill instituted by her grandmother, perhaps even to carrying water from a spring, a quarter of a mile from the house, which I know has been done, and providing the pies, hot cakes, etc., which cause so much of the unrest and discontent in country homes?" To bring scientific advancement to the farmhouse, Hoodless called for an organization of rural women.

Erland was secretary of a rural men's organization in Wentworth, County called the Farmer's Institute. He was also in charge of recruiting speakers for the group's meetings. After the Guelph talk, he invited Hoodless to address the institute's next "ladies' night" in mid-February 1897. He asked that she elaborate on her idea for a rural women's organization.

One hundred women turned out and, inspired by the talk, formed what was to be called the Women's Institute of Saltfleet Township. Hoodless was named honorary president. On the Lee family dining room table, Janet wrote the institute's constitution and bylaws, advised by Erland and two other men, jam manufacturer E.D. Smith, who was to become the local Member of Parliament in the next election and later a senator, and F.M. Carpenter, the local Member of Provincial Parliament. The document perfectly reflected Hoodless's values.

"The object of this Institute," Janet wrote, "shall be to promote that knowledge of household science which shall lead to the improvement in household architecture with special attention to home sanitation, to a better understanding of economics and hygiene value of foods and fuels, and to a more scientific care of children with a view to raising the general standards of our people."

The group would meet regularly to hear trained instructors — not just academics but women who, in Hoodless's words, "can show how to do a thing," such as cooking, butter making, and walking into a garden to destroy pests. Soon the rural women of Whitby, east of Toronto, formed a sister Women's Institute. By 1913 such groups had formed in all ten Canadian provinces. In 1915, Canadian-born Madge Watt founded the first one in Britain in the Welsh town of Llanfair and went on to form groups throughout Wales, England, and Scotland. "The greatest idea that has come out of the colonies to the Motherland," British Prime Minister Stanley Baldwin said of the organization. In 1919, representatives from across Canada founded a national body, the Federated Women's Institute of Canada. The institutes also spread to Australia, New Zealand, and Sri Lanka.

Hoodless occasionally spoke at a meeting, but otherwise left the organization to rural women. At the same time she gave the Women's

Institutes the perfect figurehead. She was the girl from the rural homestead, youngest of twelve fatherless children, who as a young mother lost her infant son, John, to a tragedy that might have been prevented. She also valued their work. She raised farm women in the kitchen to the level of farmers in the field and gave importance to the rural woman's social contribution.

In gratitude, the Women's Institutes keep memories of Adelaide Hoodless alive. In 1907, they paid to have celebrated Toronto artist J.W.L. Forster paint her portrait. In 1959, they bought and furnished her childhood home as a museum, the Adelaide Hoodless Homestead. In 1972, they also bought and restored Erland and Janet Lee's home as a museum marking the birthplace of the organization. Both museums attract busloads of women from Women's Institutes and their affiliated organizations internationally. Both are designated National Historic Sites.

WALK-THROUGH: THE DINING ROOM TABLE

Six generations of Lees inhabited the farmhouse on the lip of the Niagara Escarpment, with a panoramic view of Stoney Creek and Burlington Bay. As a museum, the house is especially celebrated for a single event that took place on February 25, 1897. On the walnut table in the dining room, Janet Lee, guided by her husband, Erland, and two other men, wrote the charter for an organization to improve the education and skills of rural women, making the house "the birthplace of the Women's Institute."

The Lee family story begins with James Lee and his wife, Hannah. They arrived in the area as United Empire Loyalists from Maryland in 1792 and started a farm. Their eldest son, John, married a local woman, Mary, who inherited her father's farm and turned it over to John. By 1808 they had built a log cabin. A single main-floor room served as their kitchen, dining room, and living room, and a half-storey above functioned as sleeping quarters. At some point, Hannah moved in with them. In 1804, James was hewing wood with another man, whose axe head flew off its handle and struck James in the leg, severing an artery and killing him.

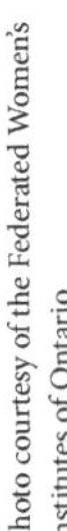

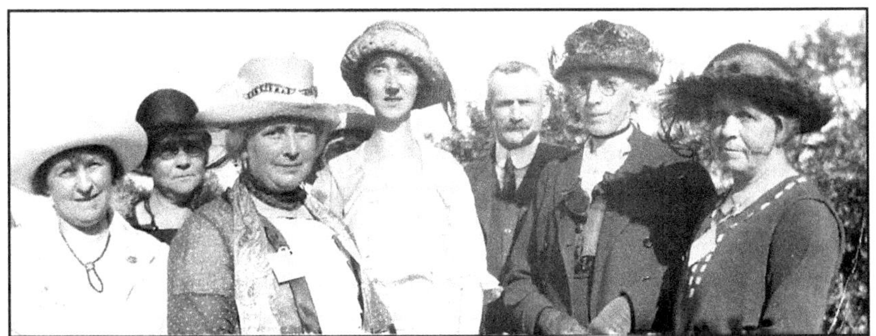

Founding members of the Women's Institute gather in 1922 to celebrate the twenty-fifth anniversary of the organization. Pictured from far right: Janet Lee; E.D. Smith's wife, Christina Smith; and Erland Lee.

John Lee farmed and served in the militia. In the War of 1812, he volunteered with the 5th Regiment of the Lincoln Militia and fought with the British at Queenston Heights under General Isaac Brock. When Brock fell mortally wounded from a musket ball to the chest, John helped carry him off the battlefield, and when Brock succumbed to his wound, John served as one of his pallbearers.

John and Mary had eleven children. The births were spread out, meaning that some of the eldest children grew up and moved out before the youngest were born. Still, the cabin proved a tight fit. When the youngest son, Abram, inherited the property, he decided to expand.

Abram represents the third and transformational generation of the Lee family. He was the son and grandson of pioneering farmers who went into farming, business, and politics, raising the family to a new level of affluence and social standing. He became the first commercial grower of Concord grapes on the Niagara Escarpment and went into partnership with his neighbour, Ernest D'Israeli Smith, who in 1882 started a cannery that was to grow into the E.D. Smith jam and pie-filling food company. Abram also served as reeve of Saltfleet Township, set aside land from his farm for a school called the Lee School, and worked at the Saltfleet and Binbrook Mutual Fire Insurance Company, serving his last eighteen years there as president.

He and his wife, Jemima, had four children. In 1873, when he was forty-four, Abram built a new house onto the original pioneer cabin. He chose a Gothic Revival style popular in Ontario at the time, characterized by steep roofs, high ceilings, and ornate decorations on the gables and other trimmings. The house later went to the third child, Erland, and is known today as the Erland Lee House.

In 1890, Erland married Janet Chisholm, sister of prominent Hamilton lawyer James Chisholm. He appears in the Whitehern chapter of this book as Isaac McQuesten's law partner and mentor to Isaac's son, Thomas McQuesten. Janet had been a schoolteacher and one of the county's first kindergarten teachers. Schoolteachers had to be single, however, and when she married Erland she resigned.

Erland trained as a teacher but, like his father, took up farming and other activities. He carried on his father's close friendship with E.D. Smith, selling produce to Smith's canning operations and running a dairy with Smith on the Lee farm called the Vinemount Creamery. Erland also served as treasurer-clerk of Saltfleet Township and helped form the South Wentworth Farmers' Institute to help promote the latest developments in agricultural science. In 1897, while in his early thirties, Erland took the initiative for which he is best remembered. He invited Adelaide Hoodless to address a "ladies' night" of the farmers' group, leading to the formation of the Women's Institute.

Erland and Janet left the house to their son Frank. He and his wife, Katherine, had four daughters, the sixth generation to live at the Lee homestead. When Frank died in 1966, his sister Marjorie inherited the home. She was the last Lee to live in it. In 1972, she sold the property to the Federated Women's Institutes of Ontario.

Kitchen

Visitors enter the house through a back section added in 1860 but start the tour in the room that began as the original log cabin, built by John and Mary from primary pine forest on the property. The floorboards are John and Mary's original pine floorboards. The latch on the door to the former upstairs sleeping loft is the one that John and Mary used. The pine cabinet at one end of the room was also theirs, built in 1808 possibly by John himself, again from the property's great pine trees. In the cupboard portion for the dishes, notice the bubbles in the original

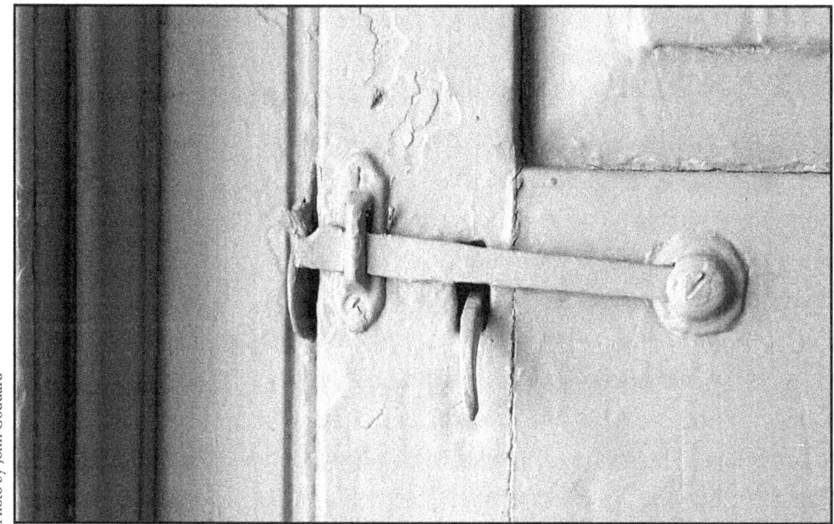

Photo by John Goddard

The latch on what was once the door to the upstairs sleeping loft is the one John and Mary Lee used after building their one-room log cabin in 1808. The wood came from primary pine forest on the property.

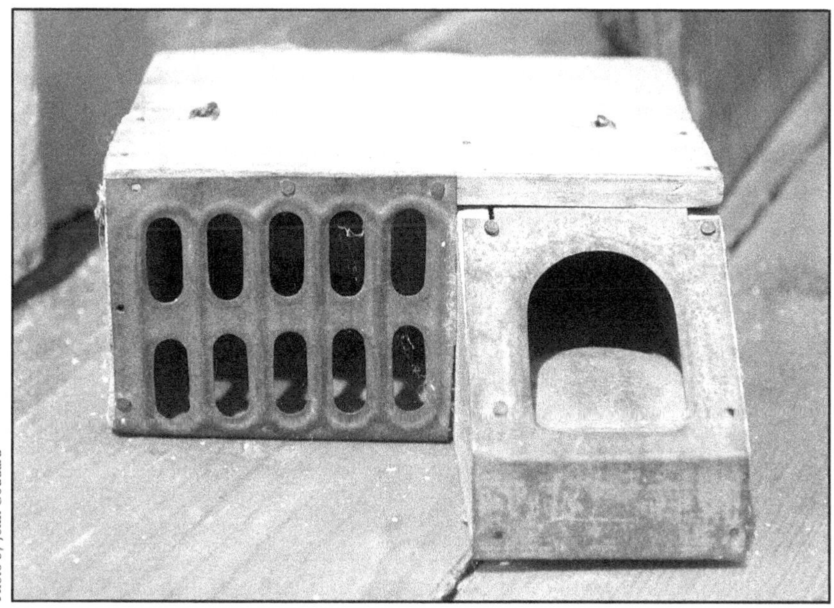

Photo by John Goddard

Children enjoy the handmade catch-and-release mousetrap in one corner of the kitchen. A mouse seeking bait would be trapped live inside for later release.

handmade glass. The eight-day clock on the wall is also believed to have belonged to the couple.

In 1873, their son Abram installed a stone cistern beneath the floor with a hand pump to replace an outdoor well, and most of the room is displayed as it might have looked between 1870 and 1890. Women's Institute members have donated kitchen tools and other artifacts true to about the 1860s. *Anne of Green Gables* author Lucy Maud Montgomery, an active Women's Institute member, donated the 1850s dinner plates along the kitchen cabinet's bottom shelf. A yoke for carrying water lies in one corner, along with heavy irons for ironing clothes and a bread pan for mixing dough. An early washing machine used a crank and roller to scrub clothes against a scrub board. The coal-burning stove comes with special pans for making pancakes and cornbread. On the kitchen table can be seen a seagull's wing, which visiting children are allowed to pick up and use to clean the stovetop as Mary and her daughters would have done. Children also enjoy the catch-and-release mousetrap in one corner. A mouse seeking the bait would enter a door and be trapped live inside what looks like a miniature jail until somebody — usually a child in the family — released the prisoner in a field.

Parlour

In 1873, attached to the front of the original log cabin and facing the escarpment edge, Abram built a symmetrical two-storey house. He set the front door at the centre, and the main-floor parlour and dining room on either side. The old cabin became the kitchen.

In Abram's time, the parlour would have been for adults only. The door to a porch is Abram's original door, as are the pine floorboards, taken from the property. On one wall hangs a framed copy of Abram's formal retirement certificate of 1902 as insurance company president. The 1850s wall clock belonged to Marjorie, a fifth-generation Lee who lived from 1891 to 1974 and was the home's last resident.

Front Vestibule

As a tribute to Erland and Janet Lee's joint initiative to establish the Women's Institute, a sketch of the couple hangs on the front vestibule wall. Erland appears a generation older than his wife, like father and daughter. In reality

Janet was a year and a half older than Erland. She was born in 1862, he in 1864. The artist took Janet's image from her 1890 wedding photograph, and Erland's from a much later photograph.

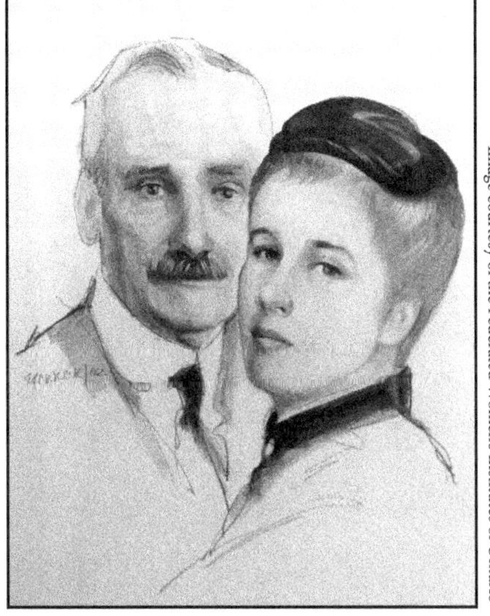

Image courtesy of the Federated Women's Institutes of Ontario

A sketch in the front vestibule presents Erland and Janet Lee as a May-December couple. In reality Janet was a year and a half older than Erland. She was born in 1862, he in 1864.

Upstairs Boys' Bedroom

Erland and Janet had five children, including two boys — Frank, born in 1896, and Gordon, born in 1894. The desk in the room was theirs, as were some of the books in the book cabinet, which also belonged to the Lee family. The beds originally used rope supports for the mattress but were later converted to take steel frames. On one wall hangs a photograph of Gordon with his 1916 graduating class at the Ontario Agricultural College. He was killed in France not long after incrementally leading his company one thousand metres up Vimy Ridge in the First World War and being promoted to major. Frank, who contracted polio as a child, served overseas as an ambulance driver and survived.

Upstairs Girls' Bedroom

Two beds are shown here for Erland and Janet's three daughters, Marjorie, Hilda, and Alice. Between the beds on a side table sits a particularly beautiful china set from the 1850s, including a wash basin and pitcher. In one corner can be seen a rare surviving Wanzer sewing machine manufactured by Richard Wanzer's Hamilton sewing machine factory, which operated from 1870 to 1890. The curling irons on the dresser would have been heated on the stove or on top of an oil lamp for curling hair. The loom-woven bedspreads are late nineteenth century from the United States, one showing the U.S. Capitol, the other a large American eagle.

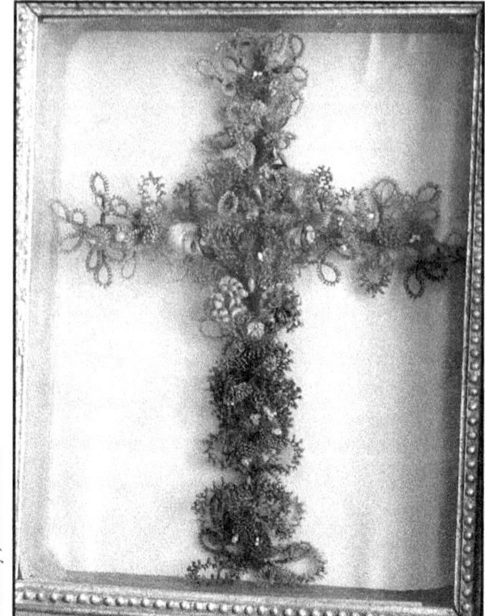

Photo by John Goddard

The cross was made using a process called "tatting," developed in the early nineteenth century to imitate point lace. Sometimes the craftsperson used the hair of elders who had died, but in this example no grey hairs can be seen.

Upstairs Hallway

On the wall hangs a cross made from human hair. When women brushed their hair, they sometimes saved strands caught in the brush and used them for artworks and religious icons. This small masterpiece of knots and loops by unknown hands would have taken months to make through a process called tatting.

Upstairs Master Bedroom

Janet brought the bedroom set with her in 1890 when she married Erland. Family photos on display include one of Janet at the time of her engagement surrounded by five of her sisters. All six siblings look deadly serious.

Nursery

Off the master bedroom lies the nursery, now displaying an array of children's toys — including antique dolls — and furniture dating from the mid-1800s to the 1920s. One is a finely crafted cane chair. Another is a child's 1905 metal rocking chair rigged like a Jolly Jumper.

Main-Floor Dining Room

For Women's Institute members, the tour climaxes with the dining room. "When they come here, they just can't wait to see this room and this table," museum volunteer Barbara Stones says. She is speaking of the celebrated walnut table where Janet composed the original Women's Institute constitution and bylaws. Coaching her were her husband, Erland; their close friend, E.D. Smith, later their Member of Parliament and a senator; and F.M. Carpenter, their local Member of Provincial Parliament.

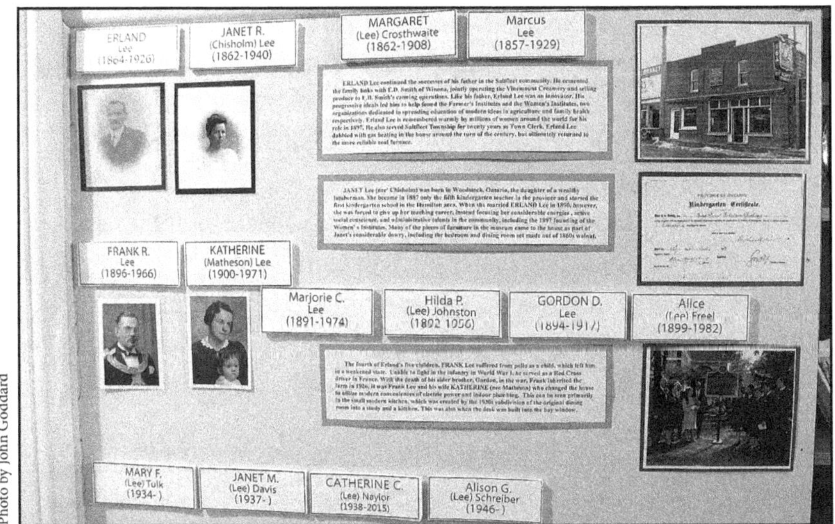

Photo by John Goddard

Erland and Janet Lee appear at the top left, as part of a family tree mounted on a wall off the dining room. They had five children: Frank, Marjorie, Hilda, Gordon, and Alice.

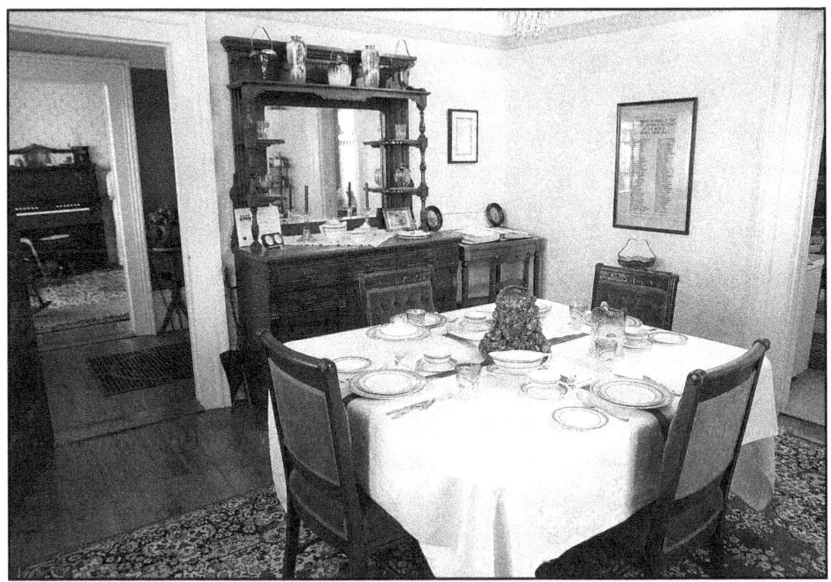

Photo by John Goddard

The famous dining room table anticipates an intimate dinner party. Janet penned the founding charter of the Women's Institute at this table, guided by Erland, E.D. Smith, and F.M. Carpenter.

Three leaves can expand the table surface to seat a dozen people, but the museum usually shows it at its smallest size. On one wall hangs a framed list of the institute's charter members. Along with "Mrs. E.D. Smith" and "Mrs. Erland Lee" can be seen the names "Miss McFarlane" and "Miss M.F. McFarlane." A small inaccuracy might have crept into the list. Mary Fraser McFarlane was the first wife of Hamilton Waterworks chief engineer James McFarlane, who appears in the third chapter of this book. She died in the late 1860s, or perhaps in 1870, but one of her daughters, Christy Ann, was a Women's Institute charter member. So was Jennie McFarlane, the daughter of James McFarlane and his second wife, the former Sarah Lottridge.

Adelaide Hoodless, the inspiration for the Women's Institute and recognized as co-founder in 1897, likely never set foot in this room, but it already had a Hoodless connection. In 1888, Erland and Janet Lee bought the handsome dining room cabinet from the Hoodless Furniture Company. Adelaide's father-in-law, Joseph Hoodless, founded the company, and on his retirement in the early 1890s her husband, John, took it over.

BIBLIOGRAPHY

Anderson, Mary. *The Life Writings of Mary Baker McQuesten: Victorian Matriarch*. Waterloo, ON: Wilfrid Laurier University Press, 2004.

____. *Tragedy & Triumph: Ruby & Thomas B. McQuesten*. Dundas, ON: Tierceron Press, 2011.

Bailey, T. Melville. *Hamilton: Chronicle of a City*. Burlington, ON: Windsor Publications, 1983.

Beer, Donald R. *Sir Allan Napier MacNab*. Hamilton: Dictionary of Hamilton Biography Inc., 1984.

Berton, Pierre. *Pierre Berton's War of 1812*. Toronto: Anchor Canada, 2011.

Best, John C. *Thomas Baker McQuesten: Public Works, Politics and Imagination*. Hamilton: Corinth Press, 1991.

Cameron, Elspeth. *And Beauty Answers: The Life of Frances Loring and Florence Wyle*. Toronto: Cormorant Books, 2007.

Crowley, Terry. "Adelaide Sophia Hunter." In *Dictionary of Canadian Biography*, vol. 13. University of Toronto/Université Laval, 2003–.

Drew, Benjamin. *The Refugee: Narratives of Fugitive Slaves in Canada*. Toronto: Dundurn, 2008.

Elliott, James. *Billy Green and the Battle of Stoney Creek, June 6, 1813*. Stoney Creek, ON: Stoney Creek Historical Society, 1994.

____. *Strange Fatality: The Battle of Stoney Creek, 1813*. Montreal: Robin Brass Studio, 2009.

Fraser, Robert L. "Richard Beasley." In *Dictionary of Canadian Biography*, vol. 7. University of Toronto/Université Laval, 2003–.

Goddard, John. *Inside the Museums: Toronto's Heritage Sites and Their Most Prized Objects*. Toronto: Dundurn, 2014.

Graymont, Barbara. "Thayendanegea." In *Dictionary of Canadian Biography*, vol. 5. University of Toronto/Université Laval, 2003–.

Greenfield, Katharine. "James Gage." In *Dictionary of Canadian Biography*, vol. 8. University of Toronto/Université Laval, 2003–.

Hanlon, Peter. "Sara Galbraith Beemer [Calder]." In *Dictionary of Canadian Biography*, vol. 14. University of Toronto/Université Laval, 2003–.

James, William, and Evelyn M. James, *"A Sufficient Quantity of Pure and Wholesome Water": The Story of Hamilton's Old Pumphouse*. London, ON: Phelps Publishing Company, 1978.

Keefer, Thomas C. *The Canals of Canada: Their Prospects and Influence.* Toronto: Andrew H. Armour & Co., 1850.

____. *Philosophy of Railroads*. Toronto: Andrew H. Armour & Co., 1850.

Kelsay, Isabel Thompson. *Joseph Brant 1743–1807: Man of Two Worlds.* Syracuse, NY: Syracuse University Press, 1984.

Laking, Leslie. *Love, Sweat and Soil: A History of Royal Botanical Gardens from 1930 to 1981*. Hamilton: Royal Botanical Gardens Auxiliary, 2006.

MacDonald, Cheryl. *Adelaide Hoodless: Domestic Crusader*. Toronto: Dundurn, 1986.

MacNab, Sophia. *The Diary of Sophia MacNab*. Hamilton: Watermark Communications, 7th ed., 2014; 1st ed., 1968.

MacRae, Marion. *MacNab of Dundurn*. Toronto: Clarke, Irwin, 1971.

McKay, Alexander. *Victorian Architecture in Hamilton*. Hamilton-Niagara: Architectural Conservancy of Ontario, 1967.

Mulkewich, Jane. "Sophia." In *Brought to Light: More Stories of Forgotten Women*. Niagara Falls, ON: Seraphim Editions, 2015.

Paxton, James W. *Joseph Brant and His World: 18th Century Mohawk Warrior and Statesman*. Toronto: James Lorimer & Company Ltd., 2008.

Simcoe, Elizabeth. *The Diary of Mrs. John Graves Simcoe*. Toronto: William Briggs, 1911.

Smith, Edward. *Dundurn Castle: Sir Allan MacNab and his Hamilton Home*. Toronto: James Lorimer & Company Ltd., 2007.

Wilson, J. Donald. "William Tassie." In *Dictionary of Canadian Biography*, vol. 11. University of Toronto/Université Laval, 2003–.

INDEX

ALSO BY JOHN GODDARD

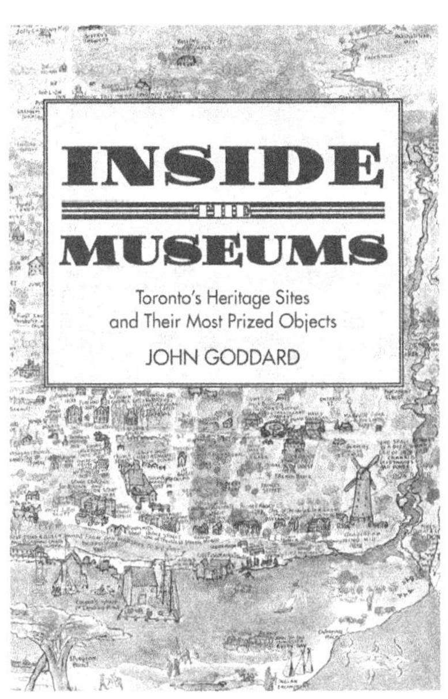

Inside the Museums:
Toronto's Heritage Sites and Their Most Prized Objects

Shortlisted for the Heritage Toronto Book Award, Non-Fiction
Illuminates Toronto's early history through its small heritage museums.

A portrait of William Lyon Mackenzie stares from a mural at Queen subway station, his face as round and orange as a wheel of cheese. He served as Toronto's first mayor, led the Upper Canada Rebellion of 1837, and was grandfather to William Lyon Mackenzie King, Canada's tenth prime minister, whose own orange-pink visage graces the Canadian fifty-dollar bill. Three blocks from the station, Mackenzie died in the upstairs bedroom of a house now open as a heritage museum, part of a network of such homes and sites from early Toronto. *Inside the Museums* tells their stories. It explains why Eliza Gibson risked her life to save a clock, reveals the appalling instructions that Robert Baldwin left in his will, and examines how the career of postmaster James Scott Howard shattered on the most baseless of innuendos at one of the most highly charged moments in the city's history.

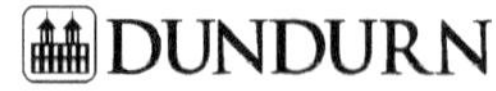

VISIT US AT

Dundurn.com
@dundurnpress
Facebook.com/dundurnpress
Pinterest.com/dundurnpress

www.ingramcontent.com/pod-product-compliance
Lightning Source LLC
LaVergne TN
LVHW050632100826
845148LV00011B/1838

* 9 7 8 1 4 5 9 7 3 3 5 4 1 *